# The True History of
# Sun Sign Astrology

# The True History of Sun Sign Astrology

Kim Farnell

The Wessex Astrologer

Published in 2022 by
The Wessex Astrologer Ltd
PO Box 9307
Swanage
BH19 9BF
For a full list of our titles go to www.wessexastrologer.com


© Kim Farnell 2022
Kim Farnell asserts her moral right to be recognised as
the author of this work


ISBN 9781910531709
Originally published as *Flirting with the Zodiac* in 2007 ISBN 1902405234


Cover art by Kim Farnell

Typesetting and cover design by KMDigital


A catalogue record for this book is available at The British Library


No part of this book may be reproduced or used in any form or by any means without the written permission of the publisher.

# Table of Contents

| | | |
|---|---|---|
| Foreword by Nicholas Campion | | vii |
| Foreword by Shelley von Strunckel | | x |
| Introduction | | xv |
| 1: | The Ancient World | 1 |
| 2: | The Dark Ages | 10 |
| 3: | The Middle Ages | 18 |
| 4: | The Shepherd's Calendar | 26 |
| 5: | Sixteenth Century | 32 |
| 6: | Almanacs | 39 |
| 7: | Astrology's Golden Age | 45 |
| 8: | Eighteenth and Early Nineteenth Centuries | 54 |
| 9: | Nineteenth Century Revival | 62 |
| 10: | Theosophy | 72 |
| 11: | Solar Biology | 78 |
| 12: | Alan Leo | 87 |
| 13: | Evangeline Adams | 93 |
| 14: | Astrology and the Law | 99 |
| 15: | Popular Astrology in the 1920s | 114 |
| 16: | Cheiro | 133 |

| | | |
|---|---|---|
| 17: | Popular Astrology in the 1930s | 139 |
| 18: | The Legal Challenge | 151 |
| 19: | Astrology and the Press in the 1930s | 159 |
| 20: | The War and After | 182 |
| 21: | 1960s and 70s | 187 |
| 22: | Linda Goodman | 196 |
| 23: | Attacks on Popular Astrology | 200 |
| 24: | Thirteen Signs | 209 |
| 25: | 1980s and 1990s | 220 |
| 26: | Astrology Online | 228 |
| Bibliography | | 232 |
| Index | | 241 |

# Foreword

## Nicholas Campion

Popular astrology is a phenomenon of our time, and an established mainstream part of modern mass culture. With its pre-Christian, pre-scientific roots, it enrages many fundamentalist or evangelical Christians and horrifies devout believers in the universal power of modern science. Yet it fascinates millions. Recent research indicates that most people read horoscope columns at least occasionally (if not regularly) and that a majority either agree that their astrological personalities fit them, or use astrology when it suits them; in the modern West, astrology is a majority belief. Yet popular astrology makes virtually no appearance either in histories of astrology or of academic studies of contemporary culture. For anthropologists and sociologists it is, inexplicably for something so popular, either invisible or misunderstood. If we are to understand the world we live in, it's therefore necessary to understand and appreciate astrology's history, role and function.

The Western system of astrology, with its familiar twelve zodiac signs, originated in Mesopotamia, modern Iraq, or what historians call the 'Fertile Crescent', probably between three and four thousand years ago. Originally, it was used only by kings for matters of state and military strategy. However, shortly after 500 BCE it appears that some great cultural change took place. Today we would call it the discovery of the Self, with a capital 'S'. Somebody, probably a priestess or priest in one of the great temples of ancient Babylon, had the bright idea of using the positions of the zodiac signs and planets at a baby's birth in order to work out the child's destiny. The system devised in the temples also revealed insights into character and personality, and so what we know today as the notion of the individual was born, or at least reached a new level of importance.

Every one of the twelve zodiac signs was endowed with a set of personality characteristics, as were the seven known planets (including the Sun and the Moon). The basic typology, the first ever system of psychology, was therefore simple to learn yet contained infinite variety, as the constantly moving planets assumed different relationships in the various signs. Ever since then, astrology has adapted to different conditions and adopted new technologies.

The astrology we find today in women's magazines, on the internet and social media, is the direct descendent of the system worked out in the Babylonian temples. This does not mean it is a fossil. Rather it is a living, vibrant and, for its practitioners and users, a powerful means of relating one's life to a wider cosmic environment, one full of meaning and purpose. The twelve-paragraph horoscope column, sometimes known a Sun-sign or star sign column, is the most familiar interface between astrology and the public. It was standard wisdom in the heyday of women's magazines, until the recent rise of the internet led to the decline of print media, that when a new publication was launched, the astrologer was the second person to be hired, after the agony aunt.

Every column relates the character of each zodiac sign to celestial patterns for the day, week or month, providing advice or making predictions, sometimes directly, often hedged by qualifications, or occasionally couched in riddles, recognizing that nothing is certain. The popularity of such columns is testimony to a widespread desire for self-understanding and connection with a great reality. Their appeal is enhanced by the fact that all one needs to know in order to read one's sign for the day, week or month, is one's date of birth.

Kim's erudite examination of the past and present of Sun-sign astrology and the invention of the horoscope column explores this remarkable story. She has brought together material which has been scattered in different archives, has challenged a few myths, set the record straight in a number of areas, and provided a sound foundation for anyone who wishes to take this exploration further. It opens new historical ground and enhances our understanding of a major feature of the modern world view. It is an accessible, scholarly and authoritative account of the development of a vital part of the modern mass media.

**Dr Nicholas Campion,**
University of Wales Trinity Saint David


From 1986 to 1992 Nick wrote the daily horoscopes for the *Daily Mail*. In 1997 he returned to academia to write his PhD on 'The Extent and Nature of Contemporary Belief in Astrology'. He's now Associate Professor in Cosmology and Culture and Principal Lecturer in the Institute of Education and Humanities at the University of Wales Trinity Saint David, and Programme Director of the University's MAs in Cultural Astronomy and Astrology and Ecology and Spirituality.

# Foreword

## Shelley von Strunckel

How can you make sure everyone reads what you have to say? Offer a newspaper horoscope.

I write them. And I've witnessed many who, shown my column, state with conviction "I don't believe in that rubbish". They then grab the newspaper from my hand, read their stars – out loud and usually theatrically. And they announce that they're "amazingly correct".

For most people, everyday life doesn't offer much space for reflection. And the media doesn't exactly focus on meditative topics. In fact, today most struggle with their heads so full of mental clutter that can't – and don't know how to silence the chatter. What's more, while many long to quiet that mayhem, they find the idea of 'stillness' distressing and panic at the mention of meditation.

Reading the daily stars is one of the best ways to pause, to get away from the clatter of everyday life - even if only for a few minutes. Yet those same individuals are longing for something to draw them within, that links them to their feelings. They're also hoping to benefit from their nagging inner chatter, and be more aware of the here and now. Of what's likely to be next and, better yet, how to benefit from it. With persistence it can be done.

This is what horoscopes are about – a different kind of focus, sometimes about the future, but often about the present. This shift of perception deals with everything from mundane dramas to minor joys and (on good days) contributes towards a narrative that helps develop the skill of celebrating life's joys.

Shelley von Strunckel

While the columns we see today are late-comers, for most of history astrology has been part of life. In this book Kim takes us back into the distant past to observe the evolution and increasing influence of horoscopes. Over the years, paper was really the only medium used – in pamphlets and books, and of course, more recently, newspapers and magazines. However, today's familiar newspaper horoscopes aren't yet a hundred years old. And this is changing – with readers' focus shifting to the screen - the daily, weekly and monthly stars are often read online. What's more, nowadays, fans can order their stars delivered to their own, personal, electronic device.

However the information is delivered, the need to know what's next and to get a grip on the future is as compelling as it ever was. This is what horoscopes have offered since humanity began paying attention to what was going on in the heavens, and began linking their observations to events here on Earth.

## THE DAWN OF ASTROLOGY

The earliest forms of astrology (and astronomy, because in those days the observation of the heavenly bodies and the interpretation of their influence were one and the same) appeared when humanity settled, mostly in the river valleys, in Africa and Eurasia. Being in one place, they were able to track events in their world and in the heavens. Initially, they focused on the seasons and the Moon's monthly shifts, from narrow crescent, to luminous orb, then back to a sliver, then to disappear and reappear on the other side of the heavens in a few days. This wasn't just fascinating, it was also useful information as the lunar cycle is linked to the tides or flow of rivers.

Gradually, their eyes turned upwards, observing the heavens. Settlers noticed that while most stars were in fixed positions, others moved across a particular and unchanging path. Those were the planets. In fact the word 'planet' comes from the ancient Greek word for wanderer (*planetes*). What's more, they moved across a series of constellations (arrangements of stars) following the same path each year. These became the zodiac signs and remain the same today.

From observing the dance of the heavenly bodies across those constellations, astrology was born. The movements ranged from Mercury's moving forward, then three times a year suddenly going backward. Meanwhile, luminous Venus remained close to the Sun while red Mars crossed the heavens at its own pace. And the slower but brilliant Jupiter and Saturn followed an entirely different rhythm. What's more, each was linked to (and often thought to be) the actual physical presence of the gods and goddesses who were already central to the ancients' world. While the names of those deities varied from one area, culture and language to another, the main characters (in the heavens and in their role in our dramas here on Earth) were consistent from one place and culture to another.

These days, we continue to view the heavenly bodies' movements, but online. We observe the Sun and planets in modern terms as physical objects in their orbits. We're aware the Moon is our satellite and that the planets Jupiter and Saturn have their own satellites as well. This observation is precise, it's scientific, and in the process the essence of humanity's mystical link to those heavenly bodies has been lost. In scientific circles, it's been dismissed as 'astrological rubbish', yet that 'rubbish' persists, and those who write about it now are as enchanted by its mystery and magic as many were in ancient times. This is the art of living in, and honouring, our modern and science-based world with the ancient mysticism that formed the basis for planetary observation and the lore that has become today's astrology.

This applies as much to this book's focus (published horoscopes for the general public) as to those forms of astrology that focus on individuals and their lives and relationships – which involve individual horoscopes being calculated and interpreted and compared.

Today, the public is most familiar with the subject of this book, popular horoscopes, based on an individual's zodiac sign. In reality, these brief, thumbnail sketches for the day are perfect for most of a public who's happy with exactly that amount of information. They don't have the inclination to go deeper. In fact, some have complained that they're puzzled by the stars I write for some days. They just want to know if it will be a good day or not. If not, they'll swiftly change the subject.

The range of the character and expectations of readers is wide. While some truly want to know what the stars hold for them and no more, others want options. They want to hear about possibilities. Obviously, the fixed interpretations of one astrologer suit some while others can't stand anything so rigid and want to know about potential – times for growth and to take chances. Then there's style. While some contemporary media astrologers take on the role of protective mother, encouraging their readers to pursue their dreams, they also go into hyper-protective mode, especially with astrological phenomena such as unsettling eclipses or the period when the communication planet, Mercury, is retrograde. While the heavens that different astrologers deal with are the same, the interpretation and the description of 'what the planets hold for you' varies, with the individual and from one part of the world and culture to another.

There are two other components to understanding both the history of astrology in general and in its published form – the period of history and the culture in question. In the distant past, humanity was constrained by the setting they lived in and what was permitted for their gender, class and knowledge. Astrological predictions focused on the wellbeing of the collective. As relatively few people knew precisely when they were born, there was little focus on the individual and more on trends influencing the leaders and the populace.

## PAST AND FUTURE

Media astrology has taken a range of forms and is reshaping itself as I write, and this process will continue. In ancient times, it was believed the heavenly bodies actually caused events. However, by Shakespeare's time, the perspective had shifted and, in the words of Shakespeare, who in his play, had his main character, Julius Caesar, state: "The fault, dear Brutus, is not in our stars, but in ourselves". Increasingly, we will begin to choose how we shape our destiny. It's just the beginning.

For now, be aware that if the world says you 'can't' do something but your instincts say you can, then you are, yourself, ushering in an era of seizing your own power and breakthroughs.

You will no longer be talking about the change. You will BE it.

**Shelley von Strunckel**

Shelley von Strunckel was discovered in 1991 by the late Patric Walker, with whom she shared a byline in London's *Evening Standard*. A year later she created her astrological column in the London *Sunday Times* - the first in a quality broadsheet newspaper. Her current columns can be accessed on her website: shelleyvonstrunckel.com.

# Introduction

This is the story of Sun sign astrology - the sort of astrology that makes up horoscope columns. The sort of astrology that leads people to believe that there are twelve types of people and that those types are described by their zodiac signs. In fact, this is often cited as a reason for its invalidity - how can there be only twelve types of people in the world? Oddly, this statement is often made by people who have no problem in classifying people as either extrovert or introvert.

There are plenty of histories of astrology. They detail thousands of years of astrological practice and theory, highlighting famous practitioners, placing them in their historical context and describing their techniques. Along the way, they mention Sun sign astrology, often as an aside. This book takes a different approach. Here our main concern is popular and mass market astrology, which in the West *is* Sun sign astrology.

Many people's awareness of astrology begins and ends with Sun sign astrology. Almost everyone in the West today can tell you the sign they're born under, and most of them can tell you something about what that sign means. The majority of newspapers and women's magazines in most areas of the world carry horoscope columns. There are thousands of websites based on Sun signs and thousands of books published each year on the subject. It features in films, on television programmes, in popular songs, in novels and in games. It's hard to avoid it.

To understand why Sun sign astrology is so popular and accessible, we need to be aware of how astrology works. In an individual's horoscope the positions of all the planets, including the Sun and Moon (planets in astrological terms) are calculated according to their zodiacal position. The degree of the zodiac sign rising on the east at the time and location of a person's birth is calculated and placed on the left-hand side of the chart wheel. The wheel is then divided into twelve sectors, representing the houses, or areas of life, in which the influences of the planets are active. The relationships between the planets are calculated and the combination of all of these factors is analysed by an astrologer. A variety of techniques can then be employed to make forecasts. As an individual's horoscope depends on their time and place of birth, it's impossible to make generalised forecasts applying to large groups of people from this information.

However, the Sun takes one year to travel through the twelve signs of the zodiac, spending about one month in each sign. The precise date when it enters each sign varies from year to year, hence the discrepancy of dates in different sources, and the concept of being born 'on the cusp'. The zodiac sign that the Sun falls in when you're born may be referred to as your 'zodiac sign' or 'star sign'. One twelfth of the population falls under each sign, making it practicable to offer character descriptions for that group of people. By using only the Sun's position, it is possible to simplify astrology to such an extent that large numbers of people can partake of the same predictions.

Sun sign astrology takes two basic forms – the first is simply an analysis of character according to the zodiac sign that the Sun occupies on the date of birth. Most people will be familiar with passages such as the one below:

> Aries is the first Sign of the zodiac, and that's pretty much how those born under this Sign see themselves: first. Aries are the leaders of the pack, first in line to get things going. Whether or not everything gets done is another question altogether, for an Aries prefers to initiate rather than to complete. Do you have a project needing a kick-start?

Introduction

> Call an Aries, by all means. The leadership displayed by Aries is most impressive, so don't be surprised if they can rally the troops against seemingly insurmountable odds – they have that kind of personal magnetism. An Aries won't shy away from new ground, either. Those born under this Sign are often called the pioneers of the zodiac, and it's their fearless trek into the unknown that often wins the day. Aries is a bundle of energy and dynamism, kind of like a Pied Piper, leading people along with its charm and charisma. The dawning of a new day – and all of its possibilities – is pure bliss to an Aries.
>
> (I-Village)

The second form of Sun sign astrology comprises forecasts derived by comparing actual planetary placements with the Sun's zodiacal position when you were born. Horoscope columns as published in newspapers and magazines take the latter form, and consist of brief readings, generally of fifty to seventy words for each sign, offering generalised advice and predictions. Depending on the publication, predictions can be made on a daily, weekly, or monthly basis.

> YOU'RE in demand now Jupiter has taken the brakes off the Sun in Gemini. Despite these calls on your time, you manage brilliantly. If you want something done, ask a busy person - and spending less time on certain tasks frees you up for what really matters.
>
> (Frank)

In addition to these columns, numerous titles are published at the start of each year giving predictions for the year ahead. These often include more astrological detail than the shorter columns cited above, including notes about the other planets' movements and how they relate to your Sun sign.

> If you are typically Gemini, I'm sure your relationships have been changed beyond recognition over the last few years. With Pluto still moving slowly through your opposite number Sagittarius, this trend is set to continue. This may be alarming news for you, as variety is the

xvii

> spice of life where love is concerned, but Pluto insists that you take relationships more seriously. Perhaps you've realized that playing the field is not as satisfying as it used to be and you are looking for more stability. Freedom is something you demand within relationships but your emotions have been more engaged than usual. This state of affairs caries on and when Pluto turns retrograde on 26 March, you may realize that one particular relationship is much more complicated that you realize. By the time Pluto resumes direct motion on 2 September, you understand how much this person means to your life.
>
> (King)

The validity of Sun sign astrology has caused as much argument between astrologers as elsewhere. Some serious astrologers claim that Sun sign astrology isn't 'real' astrology and it brings the whole field into disrepute. Others quietly write such columns themselves. A few become renowned for this work. Many people use the fact that Sun sign predictions are, by their very nature, broad and generalised, and apply to huge numbers of people simultaneously, to decry the whole of astrology.

> I would never write a Sun-sign column. For one thing it must be mind-numbingly boring, having to churn out such drivel day after day. More important, I would fear for my immortal soul. I think a special place in hell is being warmed over for those who cynically trivialise a great truth. All the arguments for and against Sun-sign astrology apply equally to prostitution. Of course, the highest paid call-girls are good at what they do!
>
> If the odious Sun-sign columns have a value, it is to persuade everybody that astrology is just a bit of fun. They serve as a smoke screen. In fact astrology is dangerous knowledge, which could be devastating in the wrong hands. Perhaps it is better for people to be kept in ignorance.
>
> (Philipson)

Introduction

There's no doubt as to the popularity of Sun sign astrology, whatever its shortcomings. But because of its ephemeral nature - and that it's classed as a 'low' form of astrology - Sun sign astrology has received scant attention by astrological historians. What is the true story of Sun sign astrology? Where did it come from? Is it really a modern phenomenon, designed to suit the needs of mass media?

Most histories of astrology rely on using texts that are purely astrological in nature, but Sun sign astrology in its early stages was commonly found in fortune-telling books and compendiums, and birthday books, many of which no longer exist as they were produced in a cheap, disposable format. Sun sign astrology has always been disposable astrology. It's not easy to find representative copies of early publications as they rarely appear in libraries. Many of the sources I've used for this book come from private collections, including my own.

The accepted account of the birth and rise of Sun sign astrology is that it emerged on 24 August 1930 when the astrologer R.H. Naylor wrote a column for the *Sunday Express* newspaper. The full story is detailed in a later chapter. You couldn't be blamed for assuming that Sun sign astrology didn't exist before this date and that Naylor simply had a bright idea one day that was to change the face of popular astrology. He certainly believed so:

> I claim entirely to have altered the public attitude towards astrology. Since my *Sunday Express* articles first appeared in 1930, the attitude of the man in the street in regard to astrology has changed. Before then it was either a contemptuous or amused skepticism.
>
> (Naylor, *Year Book*, p.8)

This version of events is popular enough for Derek and Julia Parker to state in their *History of Astrology*:

> The incursion of astrology into the popular press was pioneered in London as recently as 1930 by R.H. Naylor... it was Naylor who

xix

invented the Sun sign column. He had to find a way of writing so that each reader could feel involved, and chose to divide his essays into twelve paragraphs, one for each person born when the Sun was passing through a particular zodiac sign.

Clever Mr. Naylor. Although neither the Parkers, nor Ellic Howe, in his authoritative astrological history book *Urania's Children,* state that Naylor actually invented Sun sign astrology, the implication is that he did so, and this view is repeated again and again. The Parkers' and Howe's version of events are used as the main references in most sources that discuss the history of Sun sign astrology, and this leads to statements such as:

> Before Naylor, there were not sun sign horoscopes. He invented them for commercial reasons.
>
> (James, Jonathan)

> Naylor is the father of sun-sign astrology, as he was the one who invented the Sun sign newspaper column.
>
> *(History of Astrology told as timelines)*

> Naylor and the *Sunday Express* gave birth to Sun-sign astrology.
>
> (Geary)

If Sun sign astrology were Naylor's idea, it was certainly a bright one. After his column appeared, popular astrology exploded in the press. Naylor's career was made and dozens of other astrologers jumped on the bandwagon as newspapers sought to emulate the success of Naylor's column.

The problem is that it simply isn't true. Naylor was no more the inventor of Sun sign astrology than he was the first astrological columnist in the popular press. He wasn't even called Naylor – his real name was Harold Thropp. Granted, Naylor's work ensured that this would be the main form of astrology known to the general population, but not through his waking up to a bright idea one day. At least half a century before, astrological columns had appeared in newspapers, and a form of Sun sign astrology was commonly used to delineate character.

Even then, it wasn't a totally new concept as Sun sign writings appear in the mid nineteenth century. So, perhaps it was a nineteenth century technique that Naylor revived? That would be a nice theory if it weren't for the fact that Raphael discusses it as an ancient form of astrology in 1831.

### Ancient Superstitions
### Of which one of the most curious is
### The Knowledge of Fate by the
### Solar Horoscope

> In the dark ages of Popery, almost every science was engrossed by the priesthood, and even the self evident theories thereof linked with superstitious formulas, and therefore it could not be expected that a science like Astrology should escape the follies of the period... Amongst the various Astrological authors, Arabian, Persian and Italian, who have written upon the effects of the Solar Horoscope, the most conspicuous are Taisnier, Junctinus, Indagine and Agrippa.
>
> (Raphael, *Familiar,* p.248)

Of course, 'ancient' could mean anything. Raphael was fond of employing a little hyperbole. He could have simply meant astrology from the seventeenth century when it experienced its last golden age. There are certainly references to a type of Sun sign astrology being used then.

But he didn't.

It appears that Sun sign astrology may date back to at least the sixteenth century when authors such as John Indagine were writing. But that's hardly 'ancient', especially to Raphael writing at the beginning of the nineteenth century. How old *is* Sun sign astrology? The answer appears to be that it's as old as astrology itself.

# 1

# The Ancient World

Just as from this distance in time it's impossible to know precisely when astrology began, we can't tell exactly when Sun sign astrology started. But to me at least, it has always seemed a little unlikely that after millennia of astrology it took a twentieth century

> little man who looked like a schoolmaster...
>
> (Russell, p.112)

To come up with the idea that people could be divided into groups according to the Sun's position in the zodiac when they were born, and that predictions could be made from this. Surely the ancient Babylonians were smart enough to have grasped this concept with their extensive astronomical knowledge? Of course they were.

Astrology originated in ancient Babylon. During the seventeenth and eighteenth centuries BCE, Babylonia was a hotbed of omens and prophecies. Observing astronomical phenomena was only one aspect of humanity's attempt to predict the future. Forms of astrology are found in several early civilisations, where the planets that could be seen by the naked eye – Mercury, Venus, Mars, Jupiter, and Saturn – were identified as gods with names and personalities.

Gradually, astronomers acquired more knowledge and began to observe the ways in which the planets moved. As they did so, they developed predictions based on these movements. From the second millennium BCE, a vast amount of omen literature developed in Mesopotamia and was collected and organised into the work known as the *Enuma Anu Enlil* in about 1000 BCE.

The astrology contained in these tablets was about the nation as a whole, or about kings and princes. None of it was to do with the fate of individuals. However, they made it clear that to the ancient Babylonians at least, there was a relationship between what happened in the sky and what happened on Earth.

The Hittites, who invaded Babylon, produced the earliest reference to the use of Sun sign astrology known today in the thirteenth century BCE. These texts describe how the fate of a child is dependent on the month of its birth.

From about the seventh century BCE, exact observation began to grow in importance. Although the names of the constellations were frequently used, at that stage there were no signs of the zodiac as such. The first divisions of the paths of the Sun and Moon were used as a way of measuring time. The Babylonians evolved a calendar, and by 500 BCE were moving towards the invention of the zodiac. The Sun's path in the year was originally divided into four – the four seasons. The twelve zodiac signs as we know them first appear on a Babylonian tablet from 419 BCE.

It isn't clear when this time-measuring zodiac was first linked with astrology. But by the beginning of the fourth century BCE, Babylonian astrology had reached the stage of plotting the movements of the Sun, Moon, and planets through the zodiac.

The zodiac is a circle around which twelve constellations are set, each marking a segment of the imaginary path the Sun seems to follow on its journey round the Earth, called the ecliptic. As that journey takes about 365 days, astronomers arrived at the idea of dividing the ecliptic into 360 degrees, easily divisible into twelve sections.

Obviously, the circle had to start somewhere. In ancient times, it started in a variety of different places. In modern astrology it starts from the vernal equinox, or the point at which the Sun seems to cross the equator from south to north at the spring equinox, which takes place in the northern hemisphere around 20 March each year.

Some of the constellations got their names because of their appearance – Gemini has bright twin stars in its constellation and Scorpio has a tail like that of a scorpion. We can't be sure how many of the constellations' names arose, although there are a number of theories.

The earliest Babylonian zodiac had eighteen constellations, ten of the twelve we still use, and also the Pleiades, Hyades, Orion, Perseus, Auriga, Praesepe and the southern and northern Fish. The eighteen-sign zodiac was still in use between the sixth and third centuries BCE. The earliest record of a twelve-sign zodiac being used for prediction dates from the fifth century BCE in Babylon, and the third century BCE in Egypt. Before the sixth century BCE the eighth month was known to the Babylonians as 'the month of the star of Scorpio', the tenth belonged to the 'star of the goat' and the twelfth to the 'star of the Fish of Ea'. There's an allusion to Gemini in a Babylonian tablet recording an observation made in about 273 BCE.

As Babylonian ideas spread to other countries, they were adapted by native beliefs. In the zodiac used by the Egyptians, the hippopotamus, jackal and ox's leg were substituted for the Babylonian Draco, the Little Bear and the Great Bear. In some Egyptian inscriptions, the crocodile replaces the hippopotamus. In all the ancient zodiacs, the year begins with Taurus.

Astrology could also be found in ancient Persia. The Persians originated the idea of the four elements (fire, earth, air and water) that would be later brought into the astrological scheme by Ptolemy. The religion of Mithraism arose and flourished in Persia between 100 BCE and 400 CE and was responsible for the spread of astrology throughout the Roman Empire. The signs of the zodiac were found in every Mithraic temple.

We don't know how the signs of the zodiac acquired their characteristics, but these characteristics appeared very early, from at least the third century BCE. It seems unlikely that their names arose from the patterns of the constellations. One possibility is that the symbols of the zodiac signs reflect an aspect of the seasons or weather. Once the signs and planets began to assume their characteristics, the zodiac was formed and a reliable calendar devised. The simple omens of early times gave way to more elaborate predictions.

The earliest astrologers we know of lived in the seventh century BCE. They were established in workshops attached to the temple of Ea, the god of oracles and inventor of writing.

The common people of Babylon would have known something of astrology (even if they were unaware of its intricacies as practised by astrologer-priests) through *The Epic of Gilgamesh*, which survives in fragments. Each of Gilgamesh's twelve adventures correspond to a zodiac sign. He meets a Scorpion Man in the sign of Scorpio, reaches the waters of death in Capricorn, consults a half-man, half-bull in Taurus, and receives a proposal of marriage in Virgo. These stories were a tale of a quest for immortality, and of the Sun god as he travelled through the constellations.

By the third century BCE, astrologers were able to plot the positions of the Moon and planets at regular intervals over a number of years. The influence of the planets was all-pervading. From Babylonia the Chaldeans, recognised throughout history as astrologers, carried astrology into Egypt and Greece.

A problem in searching for early references to Sun sign astrology is that the term itself is relatively new. In the past we may have considered 'solar horoscopes', 'solar biology', 'astrological periods', 'zodiology', 'zodologia', and other such terms. All these refer to what we know as Sun sign astrology.

Sun sign astrology is disposable and ephemeral astrology. It isn't the learned version of astrology, which in earlier times was so entwined with astronomy that the two couldn't be separated. Nor is it the sort of astrology that survives today in long and learned Latin texts. Rather, it's the astrology of ordinary people, those who were either not skilled enough to perform the calculations necessary for more complex astrology, or those who weren't interested in doing so. Sun sign astrology often falls into the same basket as fortune-telling - creating a marriage that serious astrologers have sought to divorce themselves from for centuries. However, it is possible to find occasional ancient references to the use of Sun signs.

For example, an extract of the *Dead Sea Scrolls* (dating from the third century BCE to 68 CE) refers to someone being born under the sign of Taurus.

> And his thighs are long and slender, and the toes of his feet are slender and long. He is from the second column. He has a spirit with six parts in the house of light and three parts in the house of darkness. This is the sign in which he is born: the period of Taurus. He will be poor. This is his animal: a bull.
>
> (Wright, p.142. 4Q186(1) II)

Some Babylonian texts exist, known as *zodiologia*, which address the fate of people born under a particular sign of the zodiac. They describe people's appearance, as well as their character and destiny, according to the sign they were born under. In classical times, zodiologia became very popular. Having a horoscope cast by an expert was complicated and expensive, and too complex for most people. Predictions based on Sun signs alone were available to everyone who could use a calendar.

The Greeks began to study astrology soon after the sixth century BCE. After the Persian invasion of Babylon in 538 BCE, astrology made numerous developments including the first use of zodiac signs. Divination was a major part of Greek life and it was even known to resolve legal cases through drawing lots. Astrology entered Greece both from Babylon and Alexandria. (Egypt's system of divination mainly centred on dream interpretation).

There were two bodies of works in particular that had a huge influence on astrology. The first of these were the texts attributed to the Pharaoh Nechepso and his priest Petosiris. They contained the secrets revealed by Petosiris after he had studied the stars.

At about the same time the works of Hermes Trismegistus appeared. Trismegistus means 'thrice great', and the Hermetical writings were a compendium built from the library at Alexandria. They contained the zodiacal man, a diagram of bodily correspondences to the zodiac that was to feature heavily in almanacs in later centuries. In the second century CE, Claudius

Ptolemy drew together astrological theories that had been circulating for centuries and created the system that is recognised as astrology today in his book the *Tetrabiblos*.

When astrology entered ancient Rome, it was destined to flourish under the Caesars. However, during the second century BCE, it was little more than a Greek novelty. But by the first century BCE, ancient Romans had become firm believers in 'Babylonian Numbers' – a commonly used euphemism for astrology. The demand for horoscopes came before the names of the twelve signs were standardised. The first clearly identified astrologer in Rome was Publius Nigidius Figulus in the first century BCE.

According to the biographer Suetonius in his *Lives of the Caesars,* Augustus temporarily banned horoscopy in 33 BCE to restore the faith of the fathers and bolster tradition. After becoming Emperor, Augustus began to seek astrological advice and by 19 BCE, he had silver coins struck with the profile of Capricorn clutching the world's rudder.

Augustus completely identified himself and his empire with the sign of Capricorn. After his triumph over Antony at Actium in 29 BCE, he minted dozens of coins and commissioned artworks that permanently enshrined his name with Capricorn among the traditional symbols of Rome. Augustus was actually a Libran. Capricorn may have been his Moon sign, but it was also the birth sign of the Sun at the winter solstice, a sign for an emperor.

It seems likely that Augustus' reasons for banning astrology were political. To cement his control over the power of astrology, he issued the first decree proscribing its use in 11 CE, prohibiting private consultations without witnesses and astrological discussions relating to death, especially his own. The prohibition continued under the reign of his successor Tiberius. Astrologers and their clients could be tortured and executed if discovered. Tiberius believed in astrology and had horoscopes cast for all his potential rivals. Subsequent emperors studied their own Sun signs and Roman legions carried zodiacal standards. Often, zodiac signs were used to show the dates the legions were recruited. At the races, chariots were started from stalls, each bearing a sign of the zodiac, and then raced around a course where each circuit represented one of the seven planets.

By the end of the first century CE, astrology dominated Rome and in 52 CE, Claudius expelled astrologers from the city. However, astrology was now so widespread that Petronius could refer to it in his *Satyricon*. In a banquet given by Trimalchio, a rich ex-slave, the dishes were chosen to represent the signs of the zodiac.

> Our applause was followed by a dish hardly as ample as we had expected. But its strangeness drew every eye upon it. It was a round plate with the twelve signs of the zodiac spaced around the edge, and on each the chef had put a morsel of food suited by nature to its symbol. Over the Ram, ram's head chick-peas; over the Bull, a bit of sirloin; on the Twins, pairs of kidneys and testicles; a crown on the Crab; on the Lion, an African fig; on the Virgin, the womb of a sow that had no litter; on the Balance, a pair of scales with a tart on one side and a honeycake on the other; over the Scorpion, a small salt-water fish; a hare on the Archer; a langouste over the Goat; a goose on the Water-carrier; and two mullets over the Fishes. In the centre was a fresh-cut sod of turf bearing a honeycomb.
>
> (Petronius)

Trimalchio gave an impromptu lecture on their meaning, saying that he was born under the sign of the Crab and so well able to defend himself.

> These heavens up there – they are inhabited by twelve gods and turn into as many figures. Then they become a Ram. And whoever is born under that sign has many flocks, many fleeces, a hard head besides, a brazen front and a sharp horn. The greater part of pedants and cavillers is born beneath this sign.
>
> Then the whole heavens become a miniature Bull. Under it are born those who kick against the pricks, cattlemen and those that find their

> own food. Under the Twins are born team-horses, randy men and such as have it both ways. Myself, I was born under the Crab. Therefore I stand on many feet and possess much in the sea and much on land, for your crab's at home both here and there. That's why I've placed nothing over it for some time, for fear of jeopardising my constellation.
>
> (Petronius)

In Hippolytus' treatise *Against Heresies* (third century CE) appears a description of those born under the sign of Taurus.

> Those who belong to the sign of Taurus are recognized by their round head, abundant hair, their square-shaped, dark eyes and bushy, black eyebrows, and their broad face. The whites of their eyes are covered with red veins, the eyelid is thick ...
>
> (Bock)

The Sun was at the centre of ancient Roman life. In the second century CE, the cults of Mithras and Sol Invictus flourished. Aurelian (270-5 CE) proclaimed Sol Invictus the supreme god of the state, and built a temple to the Sun at Rome, declaring himself the Sun's divine representative on Earth. The Sun cult persisted under Diocletian (emperor from 284-305 CE) and culminated under Constantine.

Constantine is now primarily remembered for bringing Christianity to dominance. However, he also indulged in the Mithraic cults popular with his soldiers. During his reign, Constantine united the Sun god of the official state cult and popular Mithraism, with the Judeo-Christian god. He established a state religion with the Sun at its core. Amongst many other changes to the calendar, he proclaimed Sunday, the Sun's day, to be a holy day and the first day of the week.

Christ's birthday became fixed at the winter solstice, the birth of the Sun, and he was increasingly arrayed in solar imagery. Christmas wasn't the only Christian festival tied to the solar year; the feast of Saint John the Baptist was celebrated at the summer solstice, Saint Patrick's Day, the Annunciation, and Easter were tied to the spring equinox, and the conception of Saint John and the feast of Saint Michael followed the autumn equinox.

Sun signs, at least as descriptions of character, were well known in the ancient world. Whether or not predictions were made based on Sun signs is arguable, as there is no conclusive evidence the signs were used in such a way. But it doesn't take a great leap of faith to think that at least some people attempted it.

# 2

# The Dark Ages

After Rome fell, and the Dark Ages began in Europe, astrology in Western Europe disappeared off the map. Certainly, there's little evidence that Sun sign astrology was used in a way we'd recognise today in the following centuries. Does this mean that astrology died out? It's only possible to make a case for the death of astrology during this period if by astrology you mean the calculation of full horoscopes, astrological theorising, and astrology being studied by great thinkers. Even then, it's arguable. Natural and folk astrology, including the observation and use of lunar cycles, didn't stop to draw breath.

Astrology as an intellectual discipline re-emerged during the eighth and ninth centuries, and was revitalised by the introduction of Arabic and Greeks texts into Europe. Although people in general lacked the mathematical skills necessary to produce a full horoscope, there was still widespread interest in celestial motion and its meaning.

Before then, astrology had existed in a variety of forms in Britain for many centuries. Early Christian literature provides examples of Druids predicting a child's future from the date of its birth and the Druids operated a system of lucky and unlucky days.

> They compute the divisions of every season, not by the number of days, but of nights; they keep birthdays and the beginnings of months and years in such an order that the day follows the night.
>
> (Pliny's *Caesar*, Chapter 18 of *De Bello Gallico V.*)

Unfortunately, our knowledge of the Druids is limited, as they guarded their knowledge jealously and refused to entrust it to written record. What we do know is gleaned from the accounts of outside observers. This means that we don't know exactly *how* they used astrology or cast horoscopes, we can only be certain that they did.

There was no debate over whether the heavenly bodies exercised any influence. Arguments that did take place were based around how they did it, and what should be done with that knowledge. Natural astrology was rarely the cause of contention, although a number of early Christians ranted against those who had the temerity to forecast the future. Despite learned arguments against astrology, most people carried on exactly as they had been doing for hundreds of years.

That popular astrology survived is clear from the volume of complaints made against its practice by the common people. The Church complained frequently, particularly about the Moon cults, but also about what was seen as Sun worship. However, even those opposed to astrology would often give the Moon significance, particularly in relation to agriculture and medicine, and comets and eclipses were agreed to be harbingers of disaster.

We know that throughout the period people were alert to what sign the Sun was in. Gregory of Tours, writing in the 570s, gave detailed instructions for the timing of Nocturns. The calculation was partially dependent on where the Sun was in the zodiac.

Few written records survive from this period. One of these, *The Anglo-Saxon Chronicles* was originally compiled on the orders of King Alfred the Great at the end of the ninth century and maintained and added to until the middle of the twelfth century. Records of eclipses and other planetary phenomena were included, showing that astronomical observation continued throughout the Dark Ages.

> A.D. 538. This year the sun was eclipsed, fourteen days before the calends of March, from before morning until nine.

A.D. 540. This year the sun was eclipsed on the twelfth day before the calends of July; and the stars showed themselves full nigh half an hour over nine.

A.D. 678. This year appeared the comet-star in August, and shone every morning, during three months, like a sunbeam.

A.D. 734. This year was the moon as if covered with blood; and Archbishop Tatwine and Bede departed this life; and Egbert was consecrated bishop.

(www.britannia.com)

It wasn't only the Anglo-Saxons who wrote on astronomy and astrology. The earliest surviving Irish zodiacal chart dates back to the eighth century CE. Texts in Irish and Hiberno-Latin date back to the seventh century. (Gaulish Celts, who wrote in Latin, were writing about astrology far earlier). Zodiac signs were carved on some of the Irish High Crosses, such as the tenth-century cross of Muiredach at Monasterboice. That astrology was an important part of life in Ireland can be seen from the fact that there are at least seven words that mean astrologer in old Irish. The earliest surviving text in Old Welsh, from the tenth century, is an astronomical text in which the zodiac is discussed.

Most astronomical reports contain records of exceptional incidents, including the most famous comet of all, Halley's, which appeared in 1066 and is featured in the Bayeaux Tapestry.

Much of the art and architecture of Britain before the eleventh century contains astrological references. For example, the old Abbey of Glastonbury had a zodiac in its floor. There is zodiacal ornamentation in a number of pre-Conquest churches in Kent, and Canterbury Cathedral contained zodiac figures.

We know that astrology survived, but can we assume that knowledge of Sun sign astrology still existed? The fact that the Sun spent about a month in each sign, and that this in itself had meaning, was regarded as ancient knowledge, sometimes superstition, by the eleventh century.

> After June comes July: it has thirty-one days according to the course of the sun, and thirty according to the course of the moon. And on the 18th July the sun enters the sign which is called Leo... Our forefathers imagined that they got spirit from the sun, and body from the moon, and intelligence from Mercury, and sensual pleasure from Venus, and blood from Mars, and temperance from Jupiter, and humour from Saturn. Such was at one time the folly of the wise men of old: praise be to God that young people disdain the error.
>
> (Crawford, p.87)

This appeared in *Byrhtferth's Manual* of about 1011, which is the only pre-Conquest English work with any mathematical content. We know little about Byrhtferth (active c.988- c.1016). He spent most of his life as a monk and teacher in Ramsey Abbey (East Anglia), one of the main Benedictine establishments of the time. His *Manual* (or *Enchiridion*) was written in both Latin and Old English, and it is basically a teaching book that explains the calendar and basic arithmetic. Byrhtferth sprinkles exotic asides throughout the text (for example, he gives the names of the months in Latin, Old English, 'Egyptian', Greek and Hebrew). His diagrams show various quaternities of time, space and matter: the four seasons, with their related months and parts of the zodiac; the four cardinal directions and winds; the four elements and their properties; and the four humours and ages of man.

Though it might seem that Byrhtferth disdained astrology, it was too deeply embedded in the culture of his time for him to ignore it. As well as pointing out the dates on which the Sun entered each sign, he acknowledged that his readers sought information about Sun signs.

> The circle which the twelve signs traverse is called the zodiac; it is called the horoscope because of the course of the hours during which

the sun traverses the circle...We will next draw this circle, in order that the rustic priest may know its name and those of the twelve signs. His heart may be the gladder because he understands something about this.

(Crawford, p.115)

Whatever the Church's view on astrology, rustic priests seem to have fallen into a different category. It's not clear whether Byrhtferth was bothered about the level of education of the rustic priests, or whether they were simply the type of people to be more interested in zodiac signs. We'll never know, but it's tempting to imagine them glad-heartedly explaining the meanings of the signs to their parishioners. Failing that, as we know certain herbs were meant to be gathered when the Sun was in an appropriate sign, our rustic priests may have needed to develop their skills in herbalism.

As the twelfth century wore on, many astrological texts were translated into Latin. By 1150, most major astrological texts were available in that language. They weren't all learned works, circulated only amongst the intelligentsia. One of the reasons that 'Arabic' (Islamic or Jewish) astrology was taught in this period was to reduce the influence of pagan folk-astrologers. The Church sought to make the process of reading omens from the stars 'scientific,' placing it more firmly under their control. To predict an eclipse is much more impressive than making it go away once it has happened, and compiling a horoscope laboriously from a book of tables is a more convincing process than the more traditional method of adding up all the letters in the subject's name and subtracting the age of the Moon.

Some books became highly popular. Bernard Silvester (c.1085–c.1178) produced three books dealing with astrology. We know little about Silvester. It's likely he was born at Tours, and he studied and taught at Chartres, home of the most important school in Western Europe until the rise of the universities later in the twelfth century. The number of manuscripts that survive and are attributed to him make it clear his work was widely read.

Silvester's *Experimentarius* was a verse translation of a work on astrological geomancy (a form of involving patterns of dots or lines being read as lots). His *Mathematicus* was a poem based on an astrological prediction, and *De mundi universitate* (on the totality of the world, also known as *Cosmographia* – cosmography) was about the stars and their effect on the whole of creation. This book can safely be regarded as one of the first astrological best sellers.

According to Geoffrey of Monmouth, in the twelfth century there was:

> A college of two hundred philosophers, who, being learned in astronomy and the other arts, were diligent in observing the courses of the stars, and gave Arthur true predictions of the events that would happen at that time.
>
> (Giles, p.241)

Geoffrey of Monmouth (c.1100-c.1155) was one of the major figures in the development of British history. He wrote several works, the earliest to appear being *Prophetiae Merlini* (Prophecies of Merlin). It was the first work about this legendary prophet in a language other than Welsh, and so was widely read. *Historia Regum Britanniae* (History of the Kings of Britain) followed, relating the history of Britain to the seventh century. It includes numerous legends and is one of the first texts to mention King Arthur. (Geoffrey's work is often seen to be largely fiction containing little trustworthy historical fact.)

Along with most Europeans, the British were thrown into a panic by the conjunction of all the known planets in Libra announced for 16 September 1186. From 1179 onwards, astrologers predicted disaster - exacerbated by the solar eclipse five months previously.

Most astrologers predicted disastrous storms, leading many to dig underground shelters in which to pass the crisis, and services were held in many churches in an attempt to persuade God to overrule the planets. Predictions varied wildly: an astrologer called Corumphiza predicted that the Arabs would be destroyed by storms, gales, and a great stink.

> Almighty God knows, and the rule of number makes known, that the planets both superior and inferior are inevitably to converge in Libra in September... This conjunction will be preceded in the same year by a partial solar eclipse, of every colour, at the 1st hour of the 22nd day of the month of April, and by a total eclipse of the moon in the same month of April. . . . Therefore, in the aforementioned year the planets, by God's command, will come together in Libra, which is an airy and windy sign. Moreover, cauda draconis, the tail of the dragon, will also be in that very place. A terrible earthquake will affect the places most vulnerable to such things, and they will be destroyed, and their air and water made foul. In the Western regions, a violent wind will rise and will most strongly blacken the air and corrupt everything with a poisonous stench. Thereupon, much death and sickness will take place and crashes and voices will be heard in the air and will terrify the hearts of those listening. The wind will lift up the sand and dust from the surface of the earth and the cities of the plains will be buried, especially in sandy regions. In the 5th climatic zone, Mecca, Barsara, Baldac and Babylon will be destroyed. They will be buried in the earth, brought down by sand and dust, and the regions of Egypt and Ethiopia will be left almost uninhabitable...
>
> (Lawrence-Mathers and Escobar-Vargas, p.92)

Someone called William, clerk to the constable of Chester, predicted the victory of the Christians over the pagan threat. A letter from a monk called Anselm in Winchester tells of a lay brother who fell into a trance, recited a dreadful Latin verse concerning the dreadful things to happen at the conjunction, and promptly expired.

The widespread panic died out when the weather proved to be unremarkable, although some astrologers would point out that there was a small earthquake in England in 1185, and there were floods in 1187, which was also the year that Jerusalem fell.

One area in which astrology was of paramount importance was that of medicine. The astrological man (a figure with body parts associated with each sign of the zodiac) often appears in manuscripts of the period. Astrology was so integral a part of medicine that it wouldn't be possible to untangle the two for hundreds of years.

# 3

# The Middle Ages

By the early Middle Ages, from the sixth to the eleventh century, doubt was arising in educated circles about astrology's use on a personal level, but most people admitted it to be useful in meteorology and agriculture. Most scholars took the view that astrology was an important element of general knowledge. One attraction of astrological theory was that it could be applied to absolutely every facet of human life - or death. An estimated twenty-five million, or up to half of the population of Europe, died of the Great Plague in the mid fourteenth century.

The Black Death, believed to be bubonic plague, and now thought to be associated with anthrax, killed millions in 1348 and 1349. It shook the institutions of medieval life to their core.

Conditions in Europe were prosperous in the twelfth and thirteenth centuries. There was little infectious disease and the climate of Europe had warmed. Summers were longer and harvests were good. But the good times weren't to last.

Originating in China, the plague began in Italy in late 1346 and reached England in early 1347. By 1349, almost every town and village in Britain had been affected. England lost forty percent of its population. Some European cities lost almost all their inhabitants: in Venice, at least three-quarters died. In Pisa, seventy percent of the inhabitants died.

The plague accomplished its work in three to six months and then faded from view. Its appearance and movement were completely unpredictable - in northern cities, the plague lay dormant in winter and reappeared the following spring. In 1349, plague reappeared at Paris and spread to Holland, Scotland and Ireland. By the end of 1349, Sweden, Denmark, Prussia, Iceland, and Greenland had felt its full effects. By mid-1350, the plague was almost finished in Europe.

The plague forced people to run from each other. Lawyers refused to witness wills, doctors refused to help the sick, priests wouldn't hear confessions, parents deserted children, and husbands deserted their wives. People flew from infected areas but it was just as bad in the countryside, where animals also fell victim to the plague.

The most famous treatise on the causes of the plague, the *Paris Consilium*, was written by forty-nine physicians at the University of Paris in October 1348 at the request of King Philip VI. It stated that the ultimate cause of the plague would never be known but one possibility it gave as to its cause was astrological.

That cause was the result of the conjunction of Saturn, Jupiter, and Mars, in Aquarius, that took place in 1345, following both solar and lunar eclipses. The Paris Consilium cited Aristotle's notion that the conjunction of Saturn and Jupiter would bring disaster. According to Albertus Magnus (Albert the Great) in his book Concerning the causes of the properties of the elements, the conjunction of Jupiter and Mars would bring plague. Jupiter was hot and wet – two qualities that led to rotting or putrefaction, leading in turn to plague.

The force of the triple conjunction was increased by its coinciding with the revolution of the year, and the vernal equinox of 12 March. The comet Negra had been noticed passing through Taurus in 1347, another harbinger of death. In a lunar eclipse which took place on 18 March, lasting for almost three and a half hours, the Sun, Moon and Earth were in one straight line. The time of the conjunction was given precisely by many commentators – at 1:17 pm with Saturn at 17 degrees and 45 minutes of Aquarius.

Plague treatises abounded, offering advice and hope to physicians. Thousands of works were circulated in Latin and the vernacular, in manuscript and print, throughout the Middle Ages and the Renaissance. England especially, produced a huge number, of which many survive. The Church couldn't provide answers to the pestilence, and its numbers were so depleted in many areas, that priests couldn't even be found for burials. Astrology appeared to at least offer an explanation for what had occurred, and the relationship between medicine and astrology became more firmly cemented.

Victims were treated by blood-letting, purging and lancing of boils. Physicians burned herbs to purify the air. The times at which to begin treatment were worked out through astrological means, primarily by the zodiacal sign of the Moon. Astrological medicine was at least as effective as non-astrological medicine. Although faith in the Church was shaken, faith in astrology became strengthened.

The reliance on astrology continued throughout the next centuries. Planetary influence was a subject of popular interest. Numerous manuscripts discussed astrology, and it made its mark in early printing through the appearance of block books. A block book is made up from pages printed from woodcut blocks. A sheet of paper was laid over an inked block and the back of the paper rubbed with a burnisher to transfer the ink. As only one side of the paper could be printed with this method, a common way of binding books involved stacking the sheets so that alternate openings of the book would reveal a pair of printed pages, then a pair of blank backs. The blank openings were frequently glued closed. Most block books date from the 1450s to 70s. Block books consisted mainly of pictures with only a small amount of text and appealed to the large number of people who were totally, or nearly, illiterate. They were also cheaply produced.

Planetary block books contained pictures of each planet, with an illustration of the past times, professions, and conditions of its children - people who were influenced at birth by the planet. For example, if you were born under the sign of Leo, you were a child of its ruling planet, the Sun. Each of the planets was associated with many different types of activity, in the same way as popular astrology today attributes certain powers to the Sun sign you're born under. The images of the occupations of the planets' children constitute a panorama of secular life in the late Middle Ages.

Texts that described the powers and associations of the seven planets texts were often combined with medical texts. People believed that the Earth was at the centre of the planetary system and that each planet affected human life. Each day of the week is ruled by a planet and so being born on a particular day of the week had a meaning in itself. The approach was similar to how we use Sun signs today. The planets were sometimes seen as the souls of the zodiac signs, only able to act within the body represented by the sign.

Medieval England was an astrological backwater. For most people, astrology meant Moon lore. Lunaries were popular containing predictions based on the day of the month, the zodiacal position of the Moon, or the lunar mansions. Other manuscripts dealt with the relationship of birth to month. In these, each month was associated with a zodiac sign and predictions made according to the Sun sign you were born under. Destinaries relied on Sun sign positions for character analysis and to make predictions. Sometimes they were combined with lunaries, at other times they were solely concerned with Sun sign analysis.

> Mensis Januarij. Aquarius. Who þat hath the fortune of Aquarij schall be honowyrd in on tyme seke, another tyme hole. Many contrary thyngis schall com to hym and Gode schall deliver hym of all. There he louythe he schall not be honowyrt. He schall be hurte with ire or wyþe stone. He schall have a marcke of a worme or of another beste. He schall be bytte in the cheke.
>
> (Taavitsainen, p.53)

Month January. Aquarius. He who has the fortune of Aquarius shall be sometimes sick, sometimes whole. Many contrary things shall come to him and God shall deliver him of all. If he loves them he shall not be honoured. He shall be hurt by anger or with stone. He shall have the mark of a worm or of another beast. He shall be bitten in the cheek.

Lunaries tended to focus on the Moon's position in the zodiac and were used to help choose the appropriate times for various actions. Readers could calculate the position of the Moon from tables included in the book, or by using a volvelle. (Usually made of paper, a volvelle had one or more moveable circles attached to a backboard, often the inside cover of a book, and was used to calculate Moon phases. They could also be used for other purposes, including as fortune-telling devices.) Lunaries were primarily used for medical purposes, enabling the reader to check the best time for bloodletting, for example.

A number of medieval lunaries are still in existence. They tend to be translations from Latin, either directly or through Anglo-Norman versions. Versions can also be found in German and Swedish. However, not all were scholarly texts intended for medical practitioners. The zodiacal lunary in the *Guild-Book of the Barber Surgeons of York*, for example, has a light and jocular tone and seems to be mainly a fortune-telling manual.

> Nowe yt ys to wytte what gude or herm maye betyde whene the mone ys in ony of the signes. When the Mone is in Aries, yt ys gude to speke wythe grete lordis or myghty men... and for to gange to fyght in batell aganys thy foys, and for to take vyages into the estward, for this is an esterne signe and in the est he standis. Also, yt ys gude for to make marchandysse and to deyll wyth golde, and to wyrke all maner of werkes that ys wroght wyth ffyer, for this [ys] a signe that mekyll hath of the ffyer, and for to do all maner of werkes that thowe walde haue hastely done, for this is a hasty signe. Bot yt ys yll and perilus to do oght tyll a manys hede, as to wesche or to keme yt or to schaue, or to do ony medicyne therto...
>
> (Matheson, p.294)

Now it is to wit what guide or harm may betide when the Moon is in one of the signs. When the Moon is in Aries, it is good to speak with great lords or mighty men... and for to gang to fight in battle against you foes and for to take voyages to the eastward, for this is an eastern sign and in the east he stands. Also it is good for to make merchandise and to deal with gold, and to work all manner of works that are wrought with fire, for this (is) a sign that metal has of the fire, and for to do all manner of works that you would have hastily done, for this is a hasty sign. But it is ill and perilous to do ought to a man's head, as to wash or comb it, or to shave or do any medicine thereto...

The meanings of the zodiac signs themselves were frequently outlined, so that the Moon's passage through them could be interpreted, or to help interpret the other planets in the signs.

Aries is a signe meuable, hoot and drie, of þe kynde of fire, colre and masculine...And he hath of a man to kepe þe hede, þe eyen, þe eren, and þe face. And perfor loke þou do no medicine to þat partie þe while þe mone is pere and while þe mone is in þat signe. þe man þat is bore shal be of myddel stature. And he shal haue faire shuldres and streight longe hoghes, and a long nekke and a long face, grete feet, and a sutil witte... diuerse and chaungeable in wil...And in þe risinge of þis signe he yeueth weperinge hoot and dry.

Aries is a moveable sign, hot and dry, of the kind of fire, choler and masculine...and he has of a man to keep the head, eyes and ears and the face. And therefore, do no healing to that part while the Moon is there and while the Moon is in that sign. The man that is born (there) shall be of middle stature. And he shall have fair shoulders and straight long legs, and a long neck and a long face, great feet and a subtle wit... diverse and changeable in will... And in the rising of this sign he acts hot and dry.

The passage above seems to describe the character of someone born under the Sun sign of Aries. Being 'born under Aries' could mean that your birth chart had the sign of Aries rising, but not necessarily. In this case, separate references are made to interpreting the Moon in Aries and how to interpret

Aries rising. In any event, the interpretations given to the signs could easily be used as a basis for analysing Sun signs.

Astrological understanding was high amongst the population in general. One way that we know this is from the frequent references to astrology in the writings of Geoffrey Chaucer. Chaucer (1340-1400) is one of the most important figures in English literature. He is best known for his *Canterbury Tales,* written mostly after 1387. This introduces a group of pilgrims journeying from London to the shrine of St. Thomas à Becket at Canterbury. To pass the time they decide to tell stories.

In *The Franklin's Tale,* the Sun in December is described as being in Capricorn and calculations are made to fix the date of the next new and full Moon. In *The Squire's Tale,* Cambuscan is associated with the planet Mars. *The Wife of Bath* has an astrological theme running throughout the tale. The wife of Bath's temperament and character are explained by using her horoscope, yielding a possible three birth dates. *The Knight's Tale* contains characters represented by the planets.

But the astrological significance of *The Canterbury Tales* may go further than direct references such as these. Recent research shows that it's likely to be a solar pageant. There are twenty-four tales, which can be associated with the twelve signs of the zodiac. Many of the astrological components of the *Tales* are subtle, and take astrological knowledge to bring them to light. It was commonplace in medieval times for writers to compose their work with layers of significance. Writing was filled with allegory and allusion. Allegory was an integral part of culture as it drew together biblical and classical traditions. People in the Middle Ages saw continuity with themselves and the ancient world, using allegory as a synthesizing agent to bring together a whole image. Even animals and plants were interpreted as symbols of biblical figures and morals.

On balance, although there was a wide awareness of the zodiac signs, Sun sign astrology seemed to have almost disappeared from view. Of course, we don't know how many manuscripts haven't survived, and this type of material would be the most ephemeral. However, it would be easy to return to the idea that Sun sign astrology as we know it is a modern phenomenon, and that ancient references have been misinterpreted, forcing a meaning familiar to our present day way of thinking. Yet, Raphael named a number of prominent astrologers from the past saying that they used solar horoscopes.

Did they?

# 4

# The Shepherd's Calendar

What Sun sign astrology needed to ensure that the concept of it was planted firmly in the minds of the masses was a best seller - and that's precisely what it got with the *Shepherd's Calendar*.

The *Shepherd's Calendar* is well known as a hugely popular late medieval text that went through numerous reprintings in most European languages. Along with other content to appeal to the populace in general, it contained sections on astrology, with delineations of Sun signs.

The *Calendar* wasn't a book so much as a compilation of various older works. The idea of a runaway best seller arising from a text aimed at shepherds seems strangely surreal. Of course, it wasn't a book for shepherds. The shepherd of the title was both the ordinary man, a worker who was literate but not especially well educated, at the same time as being an allusion to the Chaldeans, that race thought to be responsible for astrological knowledge. (The image of a ploughman rather than a shepherd appears at the beginning of some English versions, although the title remains unchanged. The ploughman was a recognised and commonly used symbol of a working man in England.)

Calendars were commonly made for ecclesiastical use and usually written in service books. This led to the practice of compiling calendars for the use of the laity. It's difficult to draw a line between what can be described as a calendar and what as an almanac, but for our purposes, all we need to note is the level of astrological content in the differing versions of the *Shepherd's Calendar* and its focus on Sun sign astrology.

## The Shepherd's Calendar

Originating in the late fifteenth century, the *Calendar* soon spread from Paris to England and Germany. The astrological information within, enabling you to find out your lucky and unlucky days, good times for certain medical operations, particularly bleeding, and optimum times for agricultural pursuits, proved so popular that the book continued to be published in London until past the middle of the seventeenth century.

In addition to astrology, the *Calendar* contained moral instruction and useful information: analyses of the vices and virtues; expositions of the paternoster, the creed and the commandments; dissertations on astronomy, physiology, and anatomy, illustrated by woodcuts that are still to be seen today. The precise history and dating of the *Calendar* is a tangled one and open to dispute. The precise history and dating of the Calendar is a tangled one and open to dispute, and we need no more than a summary of the highlights.

Generally, the first example of the *Calendar* is the version published 2 May 1491 in the Latin Quarter of Paris by Guy Marchant. Only one copy is known to exist of the first impression, which now lies in the Bibliothèque Mazarine in Paris. However, *Le grant kalendrier and compost of the bergiers avecq their astrology and several aultres choses* by Nicolas le Rouge appeared in 1480.

A reprint of Marchant's version appeared in the same year as the original under the title *Le Compost et Kalendrier des Bergiers*. As well as the addition of the word 'compost' (manual of the calendar arts) to the title, the contents were also expanded from thirty to fifty-four pages. This version was to be reprinted unchanged about forty times in France alone.

English editions soon appeared as well, initially still published in Paris by Antoine Vérard in 1503, but in London starting in 1506. The first German edition was printed in Lübeck in 1519. The first Dutch version was printed in Brussels in 1511 by Thomas van der Noot. By 1560, nineteen French editions had been printed, and there had been eight different issues of the English translation.

The *Calendar* was only one of a number of French books to be translated and cross the Channel. A wide variety of subject matter was covered, the majority of it aimed at ordinary people.

Antoine Vérard was a prominent Parisian printer and bookseller who in 1503 issued three books in English, *The traytte of good living, Castle of Labour,* and *Kalendayr of shyppars* (Shepherd's Calendar). For reasons which remain incomprehensible, he decided to employ a Scot for the translation, a man who was competent in neither French or English. As Vérard was himself ignorant of English, he had no way of judging the translation.

Although the 'translation' detracted badly from the text, it seemed clear that there was enough of value for a new version to be made. Therefore, in 1506, Richard Pynson tried to rework the English, although he didn't trouble himself with looking at the original French. Pynson borrowed most of the blocks used by Vérard in 1503. Two years later, Robert Copland translated the French edition of 1497, for Wynkyn de Worde. Copland is said to have been an apprentice of William Caxton, although this is disputed. Wynkyn de Worde, born in Alsace, ran Caxton's press after his death. He has achieved immortality by being the historical basis for the character William de Worde in Terry Pratchett's *The Truth*.

Pynson's major change to the *Calendar* consisted of adding the astrological section on Sun signs. All the English editions contain delineations for births under the twelve Sun signs, giving the dates in which the Sun appears in each sign. These only appeared in France a few years later. The Sun sign section soon became a standard part of the *Calendar*, although there is debate regarding when the addition was first made and to which version. However, it was certainly an early addition.

The book opens with an address by the Master Shepherd comparing the stages of man's life to the months of the year. (The additional allusion here is to Jesus Christ). It's then divided into five sections:

There is a perpetual calendar and tables by which readers could find and remember the saints' days and feast days of the Church. The second and third parts are religious, containing the Creed, the Ten Commandments, the five commandments of the Church, and an account of Lazarus' visit to hell. The fourth section discusses when a man should be bled, and where. The fifth section comprises physiognomy and astrology, a brief account of the ten Christian nations, verses on an assault against a snail and so on. Like a modern magazine, the *Shepherd's Calendar* offers something for everyone.

As well as discussing the nature of the heavens, the signs of the zodiac, the houses and the associations of the signs and planets, the last section gave simple delineations for those born under each Sun sign and a case for the importance of knowing your Sun sign.

> Who that wyll knowe his propyetes ought fyrst to knowe ye monthe that he was born in and the synge that the sonne is in the same day. I wyll not say that such thynges shall be but ye sygnes have such propyetes and is the will of god...

> Who that will know his properties ought first to know the month that he was born in and the sign that the Sun is in the same day. I will not say such things shall be, but the signs have properties and is the will of God...

> (Sommer, p.157)

Each of the signs is delineated, the meanings being fundamentally what we read today, although often in a starker and more negative fashion than would appeal to modern readers.

> Aries is the fyrste syne that childe that is borne uncer this syne fro mydde marche to mydde aperell he shall be of grete wytte & he shall not be very ryche ne over pouer he shall be hurte by hid neyboures he shall be rych by dede pepels....

> Aries is the first sign, that child is born under this sign from mid March to mid April. He shall be of great wit and he shall not be very

rich nor over poor. He shall be hurt by his neighbours. He shall be rich by dead people...

Who so is borne from myd Iulii vnto mydd Auguste shall be fayer and hardy and shall be masterfull he wyll lyghtly wepe with them that wepys and shall be very hasty in wordys...

Who is so born from mid July to mid August shall be fair and hardy and shall be masterful. He will lightly weep with them that weep and shall be very hasty in words...

(Sommer, p.157)

The section on Sun signs came at the end of the *Calendar* and was preceded by other astrological material, including information on planetary hours and the properties of the planets.

Some versions only contained the illustration for January, but later versions commonly contained a woodcut for every month, showing the activities relating to that month and its zodiac sign. A number of the blocks of the *Compost des Bergères* had appeared in Joannes de Sacro Busto's *Sphaera Mundi*, printed by Marchant for Jean Petit, 1498/99, for example, the *Hund with a Sphere*, the large *Month of May* and the *Trumpeter of Death amid Flowers*. Others appear in Marchant's *Danse Macabre*.

The *Calendar* contained nothing new. The astrological interpretations were regarded as ancient even then, and often attributed to Ptolemy. However, as far as the history of Sun sign astrology goes, the *Calendar* is important as it spread the message of Sun signs, ensured greater familiarity with the signs of the zodiac, and people at the time regarded it as a good read. Like bestsellers up to this day, it was derided for its content. And like bestsellers today, it suffered no popularity problems owing to that. Astrology in general was gaining in popularity and there was always room for a simple form that appealed to the masses. We end this chapter with a delineation for Pisces. Should you be a

Piscean woman reading this book, you may want to treat yourself to a nice cup of tea before continuing.

> They that be borne under Pisces fro the myd Feveryere unto ye myd of Marche he shall be wyse and conynge / in many sciencs and shall go far and be a wedloke breker and a mocker and very covetous / he shall say one / & do another he shall fynde hyden money. He shall trust in his wysdome and shall defende wydowes and maydens / and motherlys chyldren / & shall passe very lyghtely all his troubles / & shall live lxxii yere / after nature. The woman that then is borne shall be delycyous / famulyer pleasaunt of corage and shall have grete sekenes in hir iyes and be sclanderyd and defamed. Hir husbande shall forsake hir / and with that she shall have great payne with strangeours and she shall nat have it that is hir owne / she shall have sekenes in hir stomake and in hir chyldebed / she shall leve lxxii yere after nature saterday & tuysday is to them evyll / as moche the man as the woman / and they shall lyve faythfully.
>
> Those that be born under Pisces, from mid February until mid March, shall be wise and cunning in many sciences and shall go far, and be a marriage breaker and very covetous. He shall say one thing and do another. He shall find hidden money. He shall trust in his wisdom, and defend widows and maidens and motherless children, and shall pass lightly all his troubles and shall live for seventy-two years. The woman that is born there shall be given to pleasure, have the courage to please with familiarity and shall have great sickness in her eyes and be slandered and defamed. Her husband shall forsake her and she shall have great pain with strangers and she shall not have it that it's her own fault. She shall have sickness in her stomach and in childbirth. She shall live for seventy-two years. Saturday and Tuesday are evil to them, as much to the man as the woman, and they shall live faithfully.
>
> (Parr, p.122)

# 5

## Sixteenth Century

In the late fifteenth and early sixteenth centuries, interest in astrology surged. A grand conjunction between Jupiter and Saturn was due to occur at the same time as a conjunction of the seven classical planets in Pisces. The availability of printing allowed for wide publication of the many and various views regarding the effects of this conjunction. As it was in a water sign, many of these predictions focused on the possibility of flooding. Some commentators asserted that there would be a worldwide deluge.

Over fifty astrologers published more than a hundred books and pamphlets on the subject. But the month of February 1524 contained only fair weather. Astrologers in Bologna were amongst those unpleasantly surprised at this outcome. However, on 19 March, there was heavy rain in the city, and from 12 May prayers were said continuously for three days in an attempt to stop the torrent. On 12 June, there was an hour-long storm of such ferocity that the citizens were terrified. The rain continued and, at the end of August, houses had to be abandoned because of the floods, which drowned much farm stock. It wasn't until December that the rains finally subsided.

Grand conjunctions had been known about since the eighth and ninth centuries. A grand conjunction is when Jupiter and Saturn, the two outermost and slowest planets, meet in the zodiac and occurs every twenty years. Astrologers such as Mashallah, Al Kindi, and Abu Ma'shar had developed the theory, interpreting grand conjunctions as indications of major historical, religious and social change, frequently accompanied by natural catastrophes and epidemics. This particular grand conjunction was evocative because of the involvement of the other planets.

Numerous popular texts appeared, as well as learned and complex astrological analyses. And it was against this background that John ab Indagine published his book on Sun sign prediction.

Born Johannes Rosenbach in 1467, Indagine (also known as John von Hagen or Jager/Jaeger) was a priest at Steinheim near Frankfurt. His chosen name of 'Indagine' was taken from the Latin and means 'sign' or 'investigation'. Little is known about his life other than he accompanied Archbishop Albrecht of Mainz to Rome in 1514 and he was the astrologer consulted for the election of Charles V in 1619. He became canon of Saint Leonhard in Frankfurt in 1515 and dean in 1521. After his death on 25 March 1537, a street was named after him in his parish in Steinheim (Indaginestrasse) which exists to this day.

Indagine's *Introductiones apotelematiscae* was published in Strasbourg in 1522 and appeared in German translation the following year. In English, his book was known as *A compendious description of Natural Astrology never so briefly handled before.* By the late seventeenth century, his book had appeared in numerous languages and cheap editions throughout Europe, despite his works being named on Pope Paul IV's Index of Prohibited Books in 1559.

Indagine advocated a natural astrology as opposed to an artificial astrology. Natural astrology, in Indagine's view, was more faithful and less superstitious. It was the consummation of natural philosophy, and Indagine couldn't see any reason to investigate the movements of the heavens if the stars had no effect by their motion. The main difference between natural and artificial astrology is that whereas the latter in drawing up horoscopes determines in detail all the positions of the planets, natural astrology observes only the Sun and Moon. However, although Indagine advocated focusing on both the Sun and Moon, a large part of his writing addressed the position of the Sun alone.

*In Part III of A compendious description of Natural Astrology,* Indagine describes how to set up a horoscope by placing the Sun sign of the individual on the ascendant, or cusp of the first house. The remaining planets are placed in the following signs in what is known as 'Chaldean order' – Saturn, Jupiter, Mars, Sun, Venus, Mercury, Moon.

This is the same order as that used for planetary hours, in which each planet rules an hour of the day. In modern Sun sign columns, the Sun is placed in the first house of a hypothetical chart, and the planets are then placed in the wheel in their actual positions. Although Indagine's method is more contrived, it takes only a small leap from his method to set up a chart in the way that Sun sign astrologers do today. It would appear more than likely that this was actually done in the sixteenth century.

> The same order of the signes is observed, herein that is in the artificial... if the Sun be in Cancer, thou shall place Cancer in the first house, Leo in the second, Virgo in the third, Libra in the fourth, Scorpio in the fifth, Sagittarius in the sixth, Capricorn in the seventh, which is opposite to Cancer and the others in their order as you well know.
>
> For what sign is ascendant, every planet according to the other is to be put in to every house. As if Aries be the ascendant of the birthplace, Aries is the first house, Taurus the second...
>
> (Indagine)

Indagine referred to the Sun sign as the ascendant, indicating that the Sun should be placed in the first house of the chart.

> I would not that any man should visit me herein, that when I speak of the ascendant... that I mean the ascendant of the houre of the horoscope, but of the sign that the Sun is in at that time.
>
> (Indagine)

He makes it clear that it's the *Sun sign* that he holds to be of greatest importance.

> We have described unto you, as well by the artificial horoscope, as also by the natural entering of the Sun into any of the twelve celestial

> signes, the whole effect and power that any of the Planets and erratical Stars may by any means work in US.
>
> (Indagine)

It's worth quoting Indagine at length, as this work appears to have escaped many commentators who believe Sun sign astrology to be a completely modern invention.

> If any man be born between the 10 or 11 day of March (when the Sun does commonly enter into Aries) and continueth there through three decanes or faces, unto the 10 or 11 day of April; Mars is found Lord in the day of nativity he being by nature fiery and Aries likewise both augment and increase the heat and fury and all other evil dispositions, more than if he had been in an earthy or watery figure ...
>
> (Indagine)

There is no doubt that Indagine directs his readers' attention towards the meaning of the Sun in the zodiac signs. Although he states that the Moon should also be considered, he writes at length only on the Sun, and includes the dates at which the Sun is in the signs, offering character delineations of the signs. The dates he offers may jar a little on the sensibilities of a modern reader, but we need to remember that Indagine is writing before the advent of the Gregorian calendar, which was not to appear in Europe until the end of the sixteenth century, and in England not until 1752.

> The Sun being in Aries, maketh them which are born, neither rich, neither very poor. Also angry, but born pleased, studious, eloquent, divers, proud, lying and luxurious, providing as they say mountaines of gold, and performing nothinge, evil reported amongst his kindred and that he broughte in danger by his enemies, which shall be men of power. He shall be hurte by foure footed beastes as being cast off a horse; he shall receive great woundes unto daunger of death. So much unfortunate and advers shall all kinde of hawking, hunting, fishing

and all thinges be done on horsebacke happen unto him; in other things he shall be more fortunate and happy, and also long lived. Also if it be a maid which is born, she shal be given to lying, angry, fair curious, delitinge in new and strange things, envious and fruitful in children, whose first child shall be slaine, she shall be in many perils and dangers whereby she shall get a marke or skar in the head, or els be naturally marked there, or in the feet. Thus we have also noted out of certain authors that the children of Aries, being born in the day, shal be fortunate and of great reputation and renowine amongst greate men and Princes; contrariwise they which are born in the night, to be unfortunate and of no reputation.

(Indagine)

Indagine's work was first translated into English in 1558 (by Fabian Withers) and became highly popular. In terms of character delineation, Indagine is one of the earliest documented Sun sign astrologers.

The sixteenth century was one of the highest points in astrology's modern history. Astrologers abounded and many scholars made an income from practising astrology to enable them to continue with what they regarded as more serious work. Some of the greatest mathematicians, astronomers and philosophers of the era, including John Dee, who was astrologer to Queen Elizabeth I, found employment at court. The founders of modern astronomy, Tycho Brahe, Johannes Kepler and Galileo Galilei worked as court astrologers. Many of them were also involved in magic and alchemy and so were at risk of attack for practising witchcraft or for being heretics. Astrologers were everywhere.

Indagine wasn't alone in proposing a simplified system of astrology during this period. In 1562 William Warde's translation of Richard Roussat's (written under the popular pseudonym of *Arcandam*) *The Most Excellent, Profitable, and Pleasaunt Boke of the Famous Doctor and Expert Astrologian Arcandam or*

*Aleandrin, to Find the Fatal Destiny, Complexion, and Natural Inclination of Every Man and Child, by His Birth* appeared.

The book opens with a discussion of conventional individually calculated horoscopes. We then move to the author's odd method of determining the sign under which a person is born based upon the numerology of the child's and mother's names. Detailed analyses follow of each of the signs, offering such comments as the below for those born under Cancer:

> This party shall be very irefull, and thereby a great lyar, a chider, and fighter even against his own friends...

This work, which ran into many editions, shows how there was a clear market for a simplified astrology.

Possibly the most well-known, and certainly the earliest figure of the names cited by Raphael, is Agrippa. Heinrich Cornelius Agrippa von Nettesheim was born in Cologne in 1486. In 1509, Agrippa became Professor of Theology at the University of Dôle in the Netherlands. It was at the end of this year that he sent the manuscript of *De Occulta Philosophia*, (On Occult Philosophy), to his friend and teacher Johannes Trithemius, the abbot of Spanheim. The first volume was published in Antwerp in 1531 but the second and third were delayed from publication by the Inquisitor of Cologne, Conrad Köllin, and finally appeared in 1533. Agrippa died in 1535.

Agrippa offered detailed delineations of the signs, which became highly popular and were cited by many authors who came after him. These delineations are what Raphael is thinking of when he writes about Agrippa's connection to the solar horoscope. He quotes Agrippa's delineations in his *Familiar Astrologer* of 1831.

> Of traditions relating to the Fate of Persons born from the 20th March to the 20th April.
>
> The Sun being in Aries, maketh them which are born, neither rich, neither poor. Also angry, but soon pleased, studious, eloquent, diverse,

> proud living and luxurious; promising (as they say) mountains of gold and performing nothing....
>
> (Raphael, *Familiar Astrologer*, p.249)

The mantle of Sun sign astrology in the sixteenth century was picked up next by Jean Taisnier. Taisnier wrote a number of books on chiromancy, physiognomy and astrology, drawing directly from Indagine in his work. Although he wrote in detail on natal astrology, Taisnier also advocated Indagine's natural astrology, a quarter of a century after Indagine's work first appeared. Both Taisnier's and Indagine's work of both was republished frequently in the following centuries.

Finally, we have the work of Francesco Giuntini, better known as Junctinus, who was born in Florence in 1523. A theologian, as well as astrologer, he is best remembered for his translation of Ptolemy's *Tetrabiblos*. The *Tetrabiblos* was only printed three times before the twentieth century. The two earlier editions by Joachim Camerarius contained numerous errors and alterations. Junctinus' edition of the text was the standard Greek reference for many years. He wrote a number of astrological works of a serious nature, and doesn't appear to have practised the sort of astrology Raphael credits him with. However, he does provide detailed descriptions of each of the zodiac signs, which are likely to have been used by Sun sign astrologers and he cites the dates that the Sun is in each sign.

The works of those such as Indagine and Junctinus were clearly influential, but their names weren't tripping off most people's tongues. The natural heir to the lunary was the almanac.

# 6

# Almanacs

In the Middle Ages, around the thirteenth to fifteenth centuries, almanacs were made of metal, wood or horn, with notches and symbols marking the lunar months and holy days. Clog almanacs, made of blocks of wood, were hung up in the home for common reference and sometimes carried as part of a walking-cane. They showed the Sundays and other fixed holidays of the year by means of notches along the angles of the block, each angle representing three months. The first day of each month was marked, as were the Golden Number (the year of the metonic cycle and used for calculating Easter) and the lunar cycles. Saints days were marked by symbols, for example a lover's knot for Valentine's day and a harp for St. David's day. Christmas was marked by a horn, the vessel used for drinking healths. The more important feast days had a point in the middle of them and in the preceding day if fasts or vigils were to be observed then.

Almanacs were also produced in manuscript form for the more literate. A typical list of contents appears in an almanac of 1386.

1. The Houses of the Planets and their Properties;
2. The Exposition of the Signs;
3. Chronicle of Events from the Birth of Cain;
4. To find the Prime Numbers;
5. Short Notes on Medicine;
6. On Blood-letting;

7. A Description of the Table of Signs and Movable Feasts;

8. Quantitates Diei Artificialis.

(Chambers)

Aquarius es a sync in the whilk the son es in Jan', and in that moneth are 7 plyos [pluviose] dayes, the 1, 2, 4, 5, 6, 15, 19, and if thoner is heard in that moneth, it betokens grete wynde, mykel fruite...

Aquarius is a sign while the Sun is in January and in that month are 7 rainy days, the 1, 2, 4, 5, 6, 15, 19, and if thunder is heard in that month, it shows great wind, much fruit...

(Chambers)

With the advent of print, additional information could be added and costs kept low. The first printed almanac was probably the *Astronomical Calendar* of 1448, printed by Johannes Gutenberg in Mainz - eight years before his famous Bible. Credit is usually given to Johann Muller, or Regiomontanus, for originating the almanac as we know it today. The earliest existing copy of his *Kalendarium Novocum* is from 1476, although it's believed to have originated in 1472. It contained a calendar, eclipses, and planetary positions, and was the first book to contain a title page. The first almanac printed in England was the *Shepherd's Calendar* as mentioned above. Manuscript almanacs circulated for a long time after the invention of printing, and some clog almanacs were still in use at the end of the sixteenth century.

Almanacs began as records of astronomical events during the coming year and contained notes of market days, holidays, saint's days, information about eclipses and Moon phases as well as more general information. They were cheaply produced, and bought in vast numbers. Printed almanacs were often imported from the Continent, containing weather forecasts, predictions of a good or bad harvest, notes of good or evil days, and suggestions of the future prices of cereals, fruit and other crops.

One of the most successful of all almanac makers was the astrologer William Lilly. He published his first almanac *Merlinus Anglicus Junior* in 1644 and continued to publish an almanac every year until his death in 1681.

An almanac was a calendar, but it wasn't only a calendar. It had always been obvious that almanacs were connected with astrology. A reliable calendar depended on the accurate prediction of planetary movements – just as essential to the practice of astrology. There was a tradition of almanacs being issued by astrologers. They often published within the almanac a list of predictions relating to the year. At first these predictions were separate, but by the seventeenth century the term almanac implied that some form of astrological prediction would be included.

There were two types of almanac, the book and the sheet. The book took on a standard appearance, beginning with an introductory page with list of cycles and eclipses in the coming year. Next, was the calendar, set out in twelve monthly pages. Each month had the phases of the Moon outlined at the top of the page. Extra astronomical information was also here, such as planetary aspects with the Sun or Moon. Below followed the days of the week alongside columns of information such as the times of sunrise and sunset, or the age of the Moon. After the calendar came other items of interest. There could be hints on health, interpretations of astrological charts, stories, and blank pages. The almanac was designed to be read and not just consulted. For some people, it was their only reading material.

A prominent feature of the vast majority of almanacs was a drawing of zodiac man – *homo signorum*. It originates from at least as early as 1300 in an almanac published by Petrus do Dacia. This was a drawing of a man with each zodiac sign marked nearest the body part that it ruled. A key explained the meaning of the diagram and its relation to the information on the calendar pages. It was used in a similar way to the earlier lunaries, to help interpret the medical meaning indicated by the sign that the Moon was travelling through at any particular time. Zodiac man was popular in American almanacs into the nineteenth century, but became rare in England during the second half of the eighteenth century. It appeared for the last time in an English almanac in 1828, *Poor Robin*.

Not all almanacs were astrological in nature, although the traditional layout was normally observed. In the nineteenth century, when lunar phases were removed from their position of prominence, the space left was filled with a morally uplifting or educational verse so that the page looked similar.

Early almanac readers were as interested in the activities of celebrities as readers of modern day gossip columns. The Laet family, in Antwerp, made a speciality of these, on one occasion predicting that Henry VIII of England would be inclined "to pass the time in honour among fair ladies," and later that he would experience matrimonial difficulties.

Almanacs sold at every social level. Lord Burghley, Queen Elizabeth's Treasurer, had a series in his library, some annotated in his own hand. Essex, the Parliamentary general, the Earl of Clarendon, and Bishop Wren of Norwich were also subscribers. Many university dons bought almanacs, and seamen were devoted to them.

Some almanacs offered educational supplements on religion, medicine, magic and sex. When the planets were in certain positions, love making was dangerous – the dog days of July and August especially so. Population studies suggest that their advice was followed.

In the seventeenth century the sale of most books was restricted by the Company of Stationers to about 1500 copies. But almanacs – like prayer books, grammars and catechisms – were exempt from the Company's restrictions, and some almanacs sold in tens of thousands. Although definite figures are only available from 1664, by this time average sales were about 400,000. Several million almanacs were sold during the seventeenth century.

Although astrological literature in general terms declined during the eighteenth century, almanacs continued to sell. The most popular almanac of the early nineteenth century was *Vox Stellarum,* which continued to print astrological beliefs about the weather and medicine. It appealed mainly to unskilled rural workers and women and was heavily criticised for perpetuating superstition – or producing precisely what its readers wanted.

Begun in 1699 by Francis Moore, in 1801 *Vox Stellarum* sold 362,449 copies, with a profit of over £2,595, by far the most successful almanac of the time. Its sales increased over the next decades, and the highest profit of the century was reached in 1838, when over 517,000 copies were sold with a profit of £6,414. *Vox Stellarum* was commonly known as Moore's, and it was the most copied almanac in England.

The story of the almanac is not that of Sun sign astrology. However, almanacs sustained popular astrology through to the mid nineteenth century, and were the main form of popular astrology in the seventeenth century. And some of them did include Sun sign delineations. One written under the popular pseudonym of 'Arcandam', for example, worked out the fate of women according to their Sun signs, saying that:

> Under Taurus they would be thieves, under Gemini liars, under Scorpio harlots and under Sagittarius witches – there seemed little prospect of safety anywhere in the zodiac!
>
> (Capp, p.123)

The common account of astrology is that it fell into decline from the end of the seventeenth century, and would not be revived until over a hundred years later. And it's certainly true that few astrology textbooks were published during the period, and serious astrology lost its position of respect. However, astrology never truly died and continued to be practised in simple forms.

By the eighteenth century, astrology had left the universities, and many educated people dismissed its practice as superstition. However, a huge amount of people outside intellectual circles continued to believe in and practise astrology.

Cunning folk, also known as wise women, wise men, conjurors and wizards, were an integral part of English society right up until the early twentieth century. They were consulted about a wide range of problems, and one of their skills was astrology. Their practice was based on oral tradition that went back centuries, and they were largely independent of the intellectual magicians and their writings. As well as making charms and amulets, healing ills and casting spells, they commonly believed in life being bound up with the movement of the planets and the phases of the Moon. In the nineteenth century, there were several thousand at work across the country.

Popular astrology never truly went away. Almanacs continued to sell, and people continued to consult fortune tellers, who used astrology alongside other techniques. Gradually, in the nineteenth century, astrology was to undergo a revival and regain popularity among some of the more educated members of the population.

# 7

# Astrology's Golden Age

The golden age of astrology occurred in the seventeenth century and the story of popular astrology at that time is mainly that of the almanac. Although the English government had come down hard on astrologers making predictions during the sixteenth century, by the second decade of the seventeenth century its authority had weakened and astrologers had begun to take on a consciously political role. They had a wide variety of views and allegiances. The seventeenth century also saw the birth of the newspaper and the most renowned astrologer of the period, William Lilly, was also the author of the first astrological newspaper column.

Lilly, known as England's greatest astrologer, the 'English Merlin', was born in 1602, in Diseworth village, Leicestershire. He arrived in London in 1620 and became a servant and secretary to Gilbert Wright on the Strand, where he remained for seven years. After Wright's death, Lilly married Wright's second wife and the house where he'd lived as a servant became his property and money was no longer an issue.

After meeting the astrologer Rhys Evans, Lilly became hooked on astrology. He bought astrological textbooks and read them day and night, until within six weeks he could cast and read a horoscope.

Becoming more and more interested in the occult, Lilly began to teach and practise astrology in 1624. A scholar pawned to him a manuscript that taught how to invoke spirits. Soon afterwards, David Ramsay, the King's clockmaker (and the father of future astrologer William Ramsay), announced a search for

45

treasure supposedly buried under Westminster Abbey. John Scott and Lilly agreed to help him. In front of thirty spectators they dowsed for the treasure. They dug beneath the spot marked and found a coffin. A wild wind arose and Lilly had to dismiss the demons while listening to the laughter of spectators.

Following a number of lawsuits relating to property, Lilly rented a house at Hersham in Surrey, burned his magical textbooks, and lived quietly in the country for five years. By 1641, he was ready to return to London, and resume his astrological studies. In 1643, Lilly impressed the MP Bulstrode Whitelock with his accurate prediction of the course of an illness. Through Whitelock he met many members of the Long Parliament and was soon embroiled in the politics of revolutionary England. His first almanac was published in 1644 and sold out within a week.

Lilly advised many leading politicians and soldiers. He was consulted by Royalists, notably Lady Jane Whorwood, who secretly visited him three times when plotting King Charles's escape from imprisonment. Lilly suggested a place in Essex and was paid £20 (£2,500) for his work. After an attack by the avowed Royalist, and astrologer, George Wharton, Lilly became a declared Parliamentarian.

His prediction of the King's defeat at the Battle of Naseby in 1644 established his reputation as England's leading astrologer. However, Lilly's predictions, and his support of army complaints, led to his being summoned before the Parliamentary Committee of Examinations, although charges were not pressed.

Lilly's seminal work, *Christian Astrology* was published in 1647, and in the same year he had to defend himself from a charge of having brought about a marriage by undue means – in other words of conjuring. Although by 1648 Lilly was claiming to support Parliament, he sent a saw to King Charles to help him to escape from Carisbrooke Castle.

In 1652 he was imprisoned for predicting that the army and the common people would combine to overthrow the new government. Fortunately, he managed to amend his writing before appearing in court and so was only imprisoned for thirteen days.

During Cromwell's Protectorate, sales of Lilly's almanac rose to around 30,000 a year. Lilly was consulted by Cromwell's son-in-law, John Claypole, and through him secured for Whitelock the post of English ambassador to Sweden. He ventured into international politics in 1658 by urging an English alliance with Sweden and received a gold chain and medal from the Swedish King.

Lilly was constantly at odds with the law. He was involved in a case in 1655 where he was indicted for having unlawfully given judgment concerning the recovery of stolen goods, although he was later acquitted. During the Restoration, Lilly was examined about his knowledge of King Charles' execution. He knew, and spent time with, the diarist Samuel Pepys at this time. He was arrested again in 1661 in a general roundup of 'supposed fanatics,' but sued out a pardon and pledged his allegiance to the King.

Lawsuits relating to his properties took up much of his time in 1663 and 1664, and in 1665 Lilly left London to escape the plague and settled at Hersham, having been appointed churchwarden at the parish church of Walton-upon-Thames. Lilly had made many enemies, but his reconciliation with the new regime was made easier by his friendship with the eminent Royalist, Elias Ashmole, who worked behind the scenes on his behalf. Ashmole was fascinated by magic, alchemy and astrology, and befriended many astrologers regardless of political allegiance. He first met Lilly in 1646 and was impressed when he spoke up for George Wharton in 1650. They had been firm friends ever since.

In October 1666, Lilly was summoned to appear before a committee investigating the causes of the Great Fire of London, which he had predicted in 1651 in the form of a coded drawing, although he was later exonerated of all blame. At the trial the following year of a number of men who were accused of setting the fire, it was stated that the date had been chosen owing to Lilly's predictions.

Afterwards he lived quietly at Hersham and studied medicine, gaining a licence to practise in 1670. He became a physician/astrologer and every Saturday rode to Kingston to give advice to the poor. At the start of 1681, Lilly's health declined and, although his health later began to improve, he lost his sight. After suffering a stroke Lilly died of paralysis on 9 June 1681 and was buried in St Mary's Church, Walton on Thames.

Astrologers had a steady stream of clients who sought answers to questions. At the height of his career Lilly dealt with two thousand questions a year. In 1662 he was said to be making £500 a year (about £44,500).

One reason for the rise in popularity of astrology in the seventeenth century was the collapse of censorship in 1641. Publications on every subject imaginable appeared at an almost alarming rate. Hundreds of newspapers arose from nowhere, in which there was more than enough space for astrology. The Company of Stationers no longer held the power it had previously, and whereas astrological texts had previously appeared in Latin, a number were now published in English. The first of these was Lilly's *Christian Astrology*. Although many texts drew heavily on older literature, they presented the work to a completely new audience.

Astrology still maintained a strong presence in medicine. It was during this era that Nicholas Culpeper's famous herbal was published in 1652, bridging the gap between academic medicine and the practices of cunning folk.

From at least 1647 onwards, the Society of Astrologers in London held regular feasts. Around forty astrologers attended these gatherings held at least annually in London.

Astrology was now a profession and had separated to a great extent from the folk astrology represented in almanacs. However, the astrologers who worked alongside Lilly were part of the London elite. The vast majority of the population of England was still rural. Although huge in comparison to other cities, London could still only claim about eight percent of the population. Literacy was lower in the provinces and, although learned texts in astrology abounded, their readership was still a very small proportion of the population.

Astrology permeated all levels of society. The distinction between astronomers and astrologers didn't yet exist and astrology was still a matter for serious study, while at the same time continuing to appeal to the population in general at a more simplistic level.

Although in public many intellectuals would decry the validity of astrology as it became more and more fashionable to laugh at astrologers, in private many of them were serious students of astrology. But gradually, as the century drew on, astrology began to lose its hold on the public imagination.

The oft quoted 'death' of astrology in the eighteenth century can be calculated as March 1708, and the death blow was delivered by none other than the satirist Jonathan Swift.

Today, Swift is remembered for his book *Gulliver's Travels*. Although it's now often treated as a childish fantasy, *Gulliver's Travels* was a biting satire in the eighteenth century. Swift took it on himself to adopt the pseudonym of Isaac Bickerstaff, and under that name wrote an almanac, the main purpose of which was to render the life of the astrologer John Partridge a living hell.

John Partridge was originally a cobbler by trade, who later took up astrology and published a number of almanacs from 1680 onwards. This often-given description however, reduces Partridge to a humble shoemaker out to make a fast few shillings. In reality, Partridge had managed to teach himself enough Latin, Greek, Hebrew and astrology to enrol at Leiden University in Holland from where he graduated in medicine. By 1682 he was able to style himself 'Physician to his Majesty'. Although one of the sworn physicians of the court, he apparently never attended the king or received any salary.

In one of his almanacs, Partridge challenged his readers to try their hands at prophecy to see if they could beat his own prophetic abilities. Partridge had attacked the Church of England, and in 1708, Swift, who was ordained into the Church of Ireland, objected to Partridge's stance as well as his propensity for using his almanacs to further the Whig cause.

In February 1708, *Predictions for the Year 1708* went on sale. One of the events predicted was the death 'by a raging fever' of Partridge. Bickerstaff predicted that Partridge would die at exactly 11 pm on 29 March of that year.

> My first prediction is but a trifle, yet I will mention it, to show how ignorant those sottish pretenders to astrology are in their own concerns: It relates to Partridge the almanack-maker; I have consulted the stars of his nativity by my own rules, and find he will infallibly die upon the 29th of March next, about eleven at night, of a raging fever; therefore I advise him to consider of it, and settle his affairs in time.

Almost immediately Partridge issued a reply, claiming that Bickerstaff was nothing but a fraud.

> His whole Design was nothing but Deceit,
> The End of March will plainly show the Cheat

The curious in London waited to see who would be proven right. On the night of 29 March Swift issued a black-framed *Elegy*, containing his famous epitaph.

> Here, five Foot deep, lies on his Back,
> A Cobler, Starmonger, and Quack;
> Who to the Stars in pure Good-will,
> Does to his best look upward still.
> Weep all you Customers that use
> His Pills, his Almanacks, or Shoes;
> And you that did your Fortunes seek,
> Step to his Grave but once a Week:
> This Earth which bears his Body's Print,
> You'll find has so much Vertue in't,
> That I durst pawn my Ears 'twill tell
> Whate'er concerns you full as well,
> In Physick, Stolen Goods, or Love,
> As he himself could, when above.

A day or two later, an anonymously authored pamphlet was also circulated around London titled *The Accomplishment of the First of Mr. Bickerstaff's*

*Predictions*. Swift maintained that he had been told by a taxman who knew Partridge of the astrologer's death and that with his last words Partridge had admitted to being a fraud. Apparently, Partridge had only written his predictions in order to earn enough money to support his wife. The pamphlet declared that the prediction had come true, but noted that its timing had been off since Partridge had died at 7:05 pm, not 11 pm. The news of Partridge's 'death' only became generally known throughout London on 1 April, April Fool's Day.

In 1709, Dr Thomas Yalden, posing as Partridge, published *Squire Bickerstaff detected: or the Astrological Imposter convicted,* in which he described his problems in combating the belief that he was dead.

According to this, on 1 April Partridge was woken by the sexton outside his window who wanted to know if there were any orders for his funeral sermon. As he walked down the street, people he knew stared after him or stopped him to inform him that he looked exactly like a deceased acquaintance.

> The maid, as she was warming my bed, with a curiosity natural to young wenches, runs to the window, and asks of one passing the street, who the bell toll'd for? Dr. Partridge, says he, that famous almanack-maker, who died suddenly this evening: The poor girl provoked, told him he ly'd like a rascal; the other very sedately reply'd, the sexton had so informed him, and if false, he was to blame for imposing upon a stranger.
>
> Pray sir, says I, not to interrupt you, have you any business with me? [...] Sir, says I, my name is Partridge: Oh! the Doctor's brother, belike, cries he [...] With that I assumed a great air of authority, and demanded who employ'd him, or how he came there? Why, I was sent, sir, by the Company of Undertakers, says he, and they were employed by the honest gentleman, who is executor to the good Doctor departed; and our rascally porter, I believe, is fallen fast asleep with the black cloth

and sconces, or he had been here, and we might have been tacking up by this time.

[J]ust as I was putting out my light in order to it, another bounces as hard as he can knock; I open the window, and ask who's there, and what he wants? I am Ned the sexton, replies he, and come to know whether the Doctor left any orders for a funeral sermon, and where he is to be laid, and whether his grave is to be plain or bricked? Why, sirrah, says I, you know me well enough; you know I am not dead, and how dare you affront me in this manner? Alack-a-day, replies the fellow, why 'tis in print, and the whole town knows you are dead; why, there's Mr. White the joiner is but fitting screws to your coffin, he'll be here with it in an instant: he was afraid you would have wanted it before this time.

In short, what with undertakers, imbalmers, joiners, sextons, and your damn'd elegy hawkers, upon a late practitioner in physick and astrology, I got not one wink of sleep that night, nor scarce a moment's rest ever since.

Partridge published a pamphlet in which he insisted that Bickerstaff was a fraud. Swift responded by arguing that Partridge was obviously dead, since no living man could have written the rubbish that had appeared in his last almanac. He kept the joke running by publishing a critical account of 'Bickerstaff's' predictions and challenging Partridge to refute them.

Yalden described how Partridge went into hiding for three months to escape the furore, which didn't help at all. When he did emerge, he was the subject of endless jokes.

I could not stir out of doors for the space of three months after this, but presently one comes up to me in the street; Mr Partridge, that coffin you was last buried in I have not been yet paid for: Doctor, cries another dog, How d'ye think people can live by making of graves for nothing?

Lord, says one, I durst have swore that was honest Dr. Partridge, my old friend; but poor man, he is gone. I beg your pardon, says another, you look so like my old acquaintance that I used to consult on some private occasions; but, alack, he's gone the way of all flesh - Look, look, look, cries a third, after a competent space of staring at me, would not one think our neighbour the almanack-maker, was crept out of his grave to take t'other peep at the stars in this world, and shew how much he is improv'd in fortune-telling by having taken a journey to the other?

Not only was Partridge 'dead', but when he did manage to convince anyone he was alive, he was now seen as nothing more than an opportunistic cobbler. Various stories circulated. His certificate of burial was requested by the parish again and again. His wife had to put up with being addressed as Widow Partridge. An opportunistic astrologer, whose name is unknown, announced himself as now living in the house of the dead Partridge. He had to prevent a gravestone being erected in his name. One rumour that has sustained is that the Company of Stationers took him off their lists as they thought he was dead. A completely unrelated dispute with the Company (without whose licence Partridge was unable to publish his almanacs) did mean that his almanacs failed to appear for three years.

Swift continued to assert that Partridge was dead, citing the fact that almanacs continued to be published under their original authors' names long after their deaths - so why should this situation be any different?

The identity of Bickerstaff soon became known throughout Europe. The episode is often cited as symbolising the death of astrology. However, Partridge's almanac suffered no loss in sales once it reappeared in 1713, and the imprint was continued until the end of the century. Partridge's 'death' showed the death of astrology as a respectable metropolitan pursuit. Astrology itself survived.

# 8

# Eighteenth and Early Nineteenth Centuries

By the start of the eighteenth century, astrologers were less interested in the intellectual or empirical truths of the claims of astrology than their forefathers. No longer part of academic life, and unfashionable in the metropolitan centres, astrology had gradually moved downmarket.

A notable development during the eighteenth century was the appearance of almanacs directed specifically towards women readers. The *Ladies' Diary* appeared in 1704 and had articles on famous women, recipes and riddles as well as astrological items. By the 1750s, it sold 30,000 copies a year.

Astrologers continued their everyday work as they offered advice about illness, love, lost property, and money to their clientele, many of whom were found from advertisements in the provincial press. Although they made a living, doubt about the efficacy of astrology can be seen in the published rebukes of those who came to see them merely for amusement, and the advice that was given to colleagues to get their hands on the fee before beginning to cast the horoscope.

The major British astrologer of the eighteenth century was Henry Season (1693-1775), a doctor and surgeon from Wiltshire, who was self-educated. He taught himself medicine and astrology and gained a licence to practise as physician and surgeon. His almanacs are filled with his personal views, including his opinion that it was a good thing man would never be able to visit the Moon for he would corrupt its inhabitants.

In America, astrology was still studied at some universities at the turn of the century. Although the fortune-telling aspects of astrology were denied, the connection between the planets and meteorology, and the influence of their movements on the human body and mind was still a respectable course of study. As late as 1762, Harvard accepted a master's thesis that argued that "the heavenly bodies produce certain changes in the bodies of animals," and asserted that the time was coming when Virginians would surpass the Chaldeans in astrology. Yale similarly tolerated astrological studies. Judicial astrology tended to be dismissed as superstition, but natural astrology had an air of respectability.

However, most astrologers, on both sides of the Atlantic, relied on the popularity of their almanacs to keep them afloat. Astrology had declined in status during the eighteenth century. Its revival in more intellectual circles began in the 1780s. It coincided with a newly developed interest in ancient Hermetic beliefs such as magic and alchemy. A number of astrologers now saw their art as a science, founded on strict mathematical principles.

Astrology had also survived in the world of freemasonry. Freemasonry had begun in earnest on 24 June 1717, at the Goose and Gridiron Tavern in London, when four local lodges joined to form the Grand Lodge of England. Although an occult tradition still existed, it had gone underground, marginalised by the progress of rationalist and empiricist modes of thinking.

Ebenezer Sibly (born 30 January 1751 in Bristol) frequented affluent social circles in England and Europe. He was a member of the Mesmer Harmonic Philosophical Society (which promoted Franz Anton Mesmer's theories of animal magnetism) and became a freemason in 1784, the same year that saw the publication of the first volume (of four) of his The Complete Illustration of the Celestial Art of Astrology. Sibly had studied surgery and in 1792 graduated from King's College, Aberdeen. His title Chirurgus Londinensis, indicates that he may have completed his degree by correspondence while living in London, on Upper Titchfield Street.

He is best known amongst astrologers for his famous horoscope of the United States published in 1787. Although Sibly published new texts, his work was mainly plagiarised from the works of seventeenth century authors.

Sibly was behind the first magazine in any language to be solely concerned with astrology – *The Conjurer's Magazine,* which appeared in 1791. The earliest issues included articles on subjects such as conjuring tricks and chemistry experiments as well as astrology. A year after it first appeared, in August 1793, the magazine changed its name to *The Astrologer's Magazine,* and from then on devoted itself completely to astrology. *The Astrologer's Magazine* ceased publication in January 1794 and Sibly died in October 1799. It looked for a while as if there was no-one to take up the astrological mantle in England.

One of Sibly's students was Francis Barrett who was born in London on 18 December 1774 (probably). Barrett lived only a street away from Sibly in Norton Street (now Bolsover Street). Little is known about Barrett's early life, apart from the fact that in 1802 he had several disastrous balloon ascents, but he is remembered for his book *The Magus* – a compendium of magic. An advertisement in the book indicates that he also set up a school of occult studies. Barrett practised horary astrology and made astrological talismans. *The Magus* was a compilation of slightly amended selections from Agrippa's work, Robert Turner's translation of the *Heptameron* of Peter of Abano, and Giambattista Porta's *Magia naturalis* and was published in 1801. Barrett travelled the country lecturing about the occult, for example, in Penzance, Cornwall in 1806. He also advertised a school for students of occult philosophy from his home in London until at least 1806. What happened to him next is unclear, although it was rumoured he published at least one more anonymous text. Barrett died in about 1828 (certainly before 1830).

There were a few abortive attempts to launch new astrological magazines. John Corfield's (born in London, 1767) *The Urania* lasted one issue in June 1814. The copy in the British Library is full of Corfield's annotations pointing out how he'd made up all the letters in it and had lost all the money he'd invested in it because no-one wanted to read it. And *The London Correspondent* ran to eight monthly issues from January 1814.

Although Sun sign astrology did exist in the eighteenth and early nineteenth centuries, the simpler forms of astrology, found in popular fortune telling books and the press, often gave equal – if not greater – weight to people's rising sign, or ascendant. The most common form of popular astrology remained lunar based.

Because of how individuals' horoscopes were cast and analysed, the available descriptions of zodiac signs were much shorter than readers would consider useful today. The descriptions that did appear tended to be based on physical appearance rather than character or personality.

> This sign produces a dry, lean body, middle stature, strong limbs, large bones, long and meagre face, sharp sight, neck rather long and scraggy, dark eyebrows, swarthy complexion, hair reddish and wiry, thick shoulders; disposition, angry and violent as the ram.
>
> (Zadkiel, *Grammar*, p.159)

However, generalised predictions were made. In the mid nineteenth century, Raphael's *Prophetic Messenger* included forecasts for each day of the year, notable for their lack of frills:

> 23 May 1852: Engage in wedlock.
>
> (*Raphael's Almanac* 1851, p.72)

Although there had been little published on the subject throughout the eighteenth century – less than half a dozen new manuals appeared between 1700 and 1780 – astrologers continued to practise.

In 1795, two men were born within nine days of each other who were to lead the revival of astrology in the nineteenth century – Robert Cross Smith, who was to become known as Raphael and Richard James Morrison, who adopted the name of Zadkiel. Morrison was less interested than Smith in appealing to the public at large. As far as the history of Sun sign astrology goes, Smith has far more relevance.

Smith began to study astrology at an early age by taking lessons in his home city of Bristol. He moved to London with his new wife in about 1820, to work as a clerk with a builder in Upper Thames Street, London. One of his acquaintances was the balloonist George W. Graham, who numbered astrology and alchemy amongst his interests. Balloonists and occultists commonly rubbed shoulders in the early nineteenth century. Graham introduced Smith to his friends and helped him financially. Smith decided to leave his job and begin a new career as an astrologer.

In 1824, Smith was appointed editor of a new periodical, *The Straggling Astrologer*. He introduced a weekly feature predicting planetary effects on love and marriage, finance, business, and travel. These were the first weekly predictions in astrological journalism, and a clear forerunner to the modern horoscope column. He did go a bit far at times – an article on how a man could discover astrologically whether his fiancée was a virgin caused enough offence to warrant an apology in the next issue.

*The Straggling Astrologer* didn't last long; it ceased publication in October 1824, although it was republished in bound form under different titles on two occasions. Smith had better luck with *The Prophetic Messenger*, first published in 1826, which on his death in 1832 was taken over and continued until 1858.

In 1827 the *Prophetic Messenger* became the first astrological almanac to offer predictions for every day of the year. Raphael became extremely well known, not only in England, but also in the US and continental Europe. He died in 1832, but his name was handed down to a succession of astrologers who maintained his tradition.

Although Raphael also produced a number of serious astrological books, he was unpopular amongst scientific astrologers who objected to his efforts to present astrology in a popular form. At least some of their objections may have been based on the fact that Raphael was a close friend of John Harries, and for a while worked with him.

Harries, a qualified surgeon, was well known as a cunning man or wizard in Carmarthenshire, Wales and came from a family with a long history of producing cunning men. Raphael was perfectly aware that astrology had survived in this popular form, and if it were to be revived, that this needed to be acknowledged. Wales appears to have been the area of Britain where cunning folk were the most numerous. Raphael was brought up in Bristol, relatively close to the Welsh borders, and would have been familiar with the work of cunning men from an early age.

Popular astrology survived throughout the eighteenth century primarily through the work of these cunning folk. And one facet of this astrology was Sun sign astrology. Occasional references to this appear in fortune telling books in the early nineteenth century, for example in *This Instructing Gypsy or the True Fortune Teller* of 1804, which describe 'zodiology' as:

> The science of foretelling events and characters by the signs of the zodiac and the planetary system.
>
> (Ward)

And continues:

> As the Sun is the most powerful and conspicuous, we shall proceed to work his way through the different signs of the zodiac, and to show the effect of his revolutions, beginning, for the sake of enabling our readers more readily, with the month of January, although the ancients began their year in March.
>
> Aquarius – About the 20$^{th}$ of January the Sun enters this sign: a man born at this period will be of an unruly, restless, fickle and boisterous disposition, will be given to odd whims and strange fancies. A woman born at this time will be of a studious, industrious and sedentary disposition.
>
> (Ward)

Other fortune telling books relied on the traditional way of making predictions according to the Moon's phases or days of the Moon. Although lunar predictions were more common, Sun sign predictions and analyses certainly existed, and appeared at regular intervals throughout the nineteenth century, not only in England, but also in the US. For example, in 1840 Thomas Hague wrote in his *The Horoscope*:

> Sol Aquarius. On traditions relating to the fate of those born from the 20th January to the 20th February...

There's a tendency to see the type of astrology that appears in almanacs and chapbooks (cheap, pocket sized booklets made from a single folded sheet) as a corrupt version of astrology, a discarded remnant of a science that had fallen out of favour. However, a form of natural astrology has always existed alongside its more technical and complex form.

Natural and Sun sign astrology were dependent on the calendar and associated with almanacs, and there isn't always a clear division between the two. Natural astrology applied information about planetary motion and lunar phases to phenomena such as the growth of crops or administration of medicine. An association between lunar cycles and agriculture was extremely old and thought of as being self-evident.

Lunar phases could be understood by anyone, and no astrologer was needed to make predictions of this type. The necessary information was always present in the calendar, as the Church based its movable feasts, such as Easter, on lunar phases.

During the eighteenth century, natural astrology was widely known and practised. Some forms of natural astrology, especially as it related to the weather, were widespread well into the nineteenth century.

In the nineteenth century, antiquarians often referred to natural astrology as 'Moon lore', and gave the impression that it survived only amongst isolated rural populations. The data included in almanacs makes it clear that it was, in fact, much more widespread than this.

The more technical form of astrology vanished from almanacs by 1805, but natural astrology was the mainstay of almost all popular almanacs. Using lunar phases to predict the weather required little or no education. It also wasn't true that almanacs were only consulted by the least educated members of society. There were members of the middle classes who subscribed to Moon lore. And the middle classes would lead the next revival of astrology.

# 9

# Nineteenth Century Revival

The mid to late nineteenth century was a time of enormous change. The industrial revolution had reconstructed the European economy, the new scientific method of inquiry had challenged accepted religious norms, and international communications had removed geographical barriers. Socialist organisations proliferated and in 1859 Charles Darwin published his *Origin of Species,* a work that shattered many people's religious beliefs. The combination of these and other events led to a revival of the occult traditions that had been discredited during the Enlightenment. The intellectual ferment of the Victorian era provided alternative explanations of the world and enabled a space to open in which alternative beliefs could flourish.

The roots of the modern spiritualist movement were laid in the late eighteenth century after Emmanuel Swedenborg's work reached London in 1749, and the Swedenborg Foundation was established in 1849. Swedenborg was a Swedish engineer, who turned to theology at the age of fifty-five. He communicated with angels and spirits and followed a philosophy in which the spiritual realm was more real than the physical world. Swedenborg saw a correspondence between everything in the spiritual and physical realms.

Franz Mesmer popularised the concept of animal magnetism in the late eighteenth century, and Andrew Jackson Davis became the first theorist of spiritualism through the 1847 publication of his *The Principles of Nature, Her Divine Revelations.*

## Nineteenth Century Revival

In 1848, mysterious spirit rappings were reported by the Fox family in their home in Hydesville, New York. The story of two young girls who could contact the spirit world flew around the globe and ignited a revival of occult interest and activity that became the modern Spiritualist movement.

By 1851, there were about one hundred mediums in New York City alone. Séances became the vogue in Europe and mediums were in demand to entertain guests with physical and mental phenomena at private parties. Spiritualism rapidly became part of an alternative lifestyle including vegetarianism, feminism, dress reform, and homeopathy.

Numerous spiritualist groups were formed and Hermetic, Rosicrucian, magical and occult societies sprang forward in an almost unseemly hurry. Scores of people took it upon themselves to investigate psychic phenomena, many of them forming their own societies. Spiritualists, theosophists, Kabbalists, palmists - each and every field of the occult had its adherents. And alongside them were the astrologers of a new generation.

There was a sizable enough audience to warrant the inclusion of astrology in the popular press from the late nineteenth century onwards. In Britain, a number of astrologers tried their hands at writing regular columns. In 1887, R.H. Penny contributed a column, under the name of 'Neptune', to the *Society Times*, which was later taken over by the astrologer Sepharial. This comprised answers to correspondents who sent in their birth details and a small fee. Sepharial later wrote for *Pearson's Weekly* and the *Evening News,* and contributed a regular astrological forecasting column to *The Star* before WW1, as well as contributing features to the *Tribune.* The national press occasionally featured astrological stories when news was thin on the ground.

Plenty of more general and popular astrology also appeared, offering predictions if you were lucky enough to have your birthday that day, especially in American newspapers. In fact, by the end of the nineteenth century these columns were standard features of the press. So much so that in 1898 the astrologer Luke Broughton commented:

> Within a few years there will scarcely be a respectable newspaper in the United States or Canada, which will not have an Astrological or Horoscope column.
>
> (Broughton, p.18)

And newspapers insisted that there was a 'fad' for astrology:

> Astrology is the dominant occult attraction in London at the majority of West End "At homes"... In New York the art is practiced sub rosa... Intimate friends form a coterie which meets once a month...
>
> (*Washington Times*, 2 January 1895, p.18)

> Astrology threatens to replace palmistry as a social diversion...
>
> (Anaconda Standard, (Montana), 6 February 1898, p.10)

There were reports of astrology's revival and how it was a new fad every few years. In the UK, the *Daily Mail* was especially fond of reporting this, ominously pointing out in 1904:

> Nothing must be attempted, nothing done, without a consultation of one's signs and dates. It is upsetting social arrangements, and in many cases causing positive mental depression.
>
> (*Daily Mail,* 3 June 1904, p.4)

The *Daily Mirror* joined in to comment:

> Having your horoscope drawn is now quite a common diversion among credulous people who have more money than brains.
>
> (*Daily Mirror,* 23 June 1904, p.7.)

The *Mirror* had carried advertisements from astrologers since its launch in 1903. In an attack of complete contrariness, shortly after making the above comment it launched into enthusiastically offering astrological content at the drop of a hat. On 27 August 1904 it reported that it had sent a representative to speak to an astrologer who was consulted by business men.

He was impressed, but worried. He walked back to the office as if the burden of Saturn was already on his back. He felt that at any moment he might become a meteor or something, and fall with a flash into somewhere else.

Most references tell how the first American astrology column appeared in the *Boston Record* in 1931. The earliest columns may well have appeared in Boston, but they were around much, much earlier. On 21 January 1894 the *Boston Post* announced 'It's all in the Stars' and that it had employed a well-known astrologer to make daily predictions plus a few individual readings that would appear in the column. More demanding readers could pay $1 for a personalised horoscope of between 250 and 500 words.

> Wednesday—The influences are unfortunate for business, mental efforts, correspondence, travelling; for the political, office-holding, ruling, literary, educational and saturnine classes; but for pleasures, domestic affairs, etc., the configurations are more favorable.

And a series of readers were told firmly how their lives would go wrong:

> NOT A HAPPY LIFE. C. B.—You were born under the sign Scorpio; Mars is your ruling planet; there are three gentlemen by whom your social and matrimonial prospects and conditions will be affected: two of these are short, thick set persons, one being rather darker than the other, the other is a stranger and traveller, or one whom you may first see at the time of your taking a long Journey: you are not to lead a very happy life, for some of your greatest troubles and misfortunes will be in part caused by these persons; you will gain money by Inheritance. honors by deaths, and knowledge from your intelligent friend.

On 25 February 1894 the *Post* pointed out that their column was written by a woman astrologer. From the earliest days, such columns tended to appear on women's pages or next to content intended to appeal to women, such as fashion articles. Almost all bylined early astrology columns in the US were written by women. Some titles had their own astrologer but the majority of columns in the US were syndicated material, primarily from the McClure syndicate. Such columns were general in nature and didn't usually refer to the zodiac signs – except perhaps for the one that applied that day. It was common to devote the greatest space to people who had their birthday on the date in question:

> SUNDAY, Feb. 10. 1895. Rather favorable for common affairs, up to 1 p. m., but decidedly evil afterward. Unfortunate to either marry or propose marriage, or to commence anything new or important. A child born before 1 p. m. will be careful, plodding and industrious, and gradually rise by its own efforts. From 1 p. m. until midnight will be very refined and intelligent, fond of the fine arts, but will be extravagant and generally poor. A male born before 1 p. m. will marry a careful, industrious, but cold and distant lady, who will treat him with coldness and neglect, but they may not separate. From 1 p. m. until midnight will marry a refined, intelligent lady, but she will be extravagant, and they are likely to separate. A female will better her condition by marriage, live happy and her husband will become wealthy.
>
> (*Courier-Journal,* Kentucky, 9 February 1895, p.10)

> A good day to deal with lawyers and to travel. Those whose birth data this is are threatened with Illness during the year and some disappointment. The greatest danger in their business will be danger from lending money or going as security for others. The child born today will have a most interesting, but not easy life. It will meet great reverses, but will achieve equally great successes. Its mind will be a kingdom to itself – clever, clear and high spirited.
>
> (*Buffalo Times,* New York, 11 August 1907, p.28)

This doesn't mean Sun signs weren't mentioned. Lists often appeared with the corresponding dates so readers knew what sign they were born under, and there were numerous articles about which birthstone was associated with which sign. And Sun signs mattered when it came to 'MAKING LOVE BY THE SIGNS IN THE HEAVENS':

> How to be happy, though married, is an interesting theme. It always will be; but the advice that is frequently given to attain so desirable a condition is not always easy to follow. There should be no difficulty, however. in following the new rule—How to make love by the signs in the heavens....
>
> It is suggested that if a man born between March 21st and April 18th – which is under the zodiacal sign of Aries, whose domain is Fire – should marry a woman who was born between October 23rd and November 21st which is under the sign Scorpio, whose domain is Water—the marriage will be one of splutter and [illeg], of hiss and steam, just as it is when water is thrown on fire. Fire and Earth get along better together than the last two and so will married couples, one of which is born on a date under the zodiacal sign whose domain is Fire, and the other under a sign whose domain is Earth..
>
> <div align="right">(<i>Pearson's Weekly</i>, 19 February 1897, p.7)</div>

In both the US and the UK, articles commonly appeared explaining what the zodiac signs meant and how they described your character.

> From the 20th of May to the 21st of June we are under the sign of Gemini the Twins, the first sign of the air domain, some definite characteristics attach all born under the influence this particular sign of the Zodiac. They are a teasing, "contrary," contradictory temperament. Says an old authority on the subject:—"They are filled with opposite desires and emotions. They are kind to others, clever with their hands, but hate to think for themselves. Children under this sign are usually well formed, with dark hair. They are filled with the spirit of unrest. It is essential that such children should live with calm, restful persons.

> They are often thrown into fits excitement nervous disturbance. These children frequently become ill with no apparent cause. They should be guarded carefully, for one their characteristics is imagining evil. If allowed to continue, it ripens in later years to distrust. The gems are beryl, aquamarine, and blue stones. The astral colours are red, blue, and white.
>
> (*Dundee Evening Telegraph*, 22 May 1907, p.6)

However, astrology columns that offered predictions before World War I were aimed towards the new generation of astrologers and featured the same details of planetary configurations as could be found in astrological texts:

> An unfortunate day according to astrology. The Sun is in a place strongly aspected for evil, while Neptune and Saturn are also adverse in their influence...persons whose birth date it is may have anxiety concerning their health during the coming year. They should be extremely cautious in business and domestic affairs.
>
> (*Washington Post*, 5 December 1913)

A number of subscription only astrological magazines also existed offering similar forecasts:

> Moon in Second Quarter. Increasing. Saturday, 1$^{st}$ - Moon square Venus and Mars, sextile Jupiter. Moon 11 degrees 21 minutes in Sagittarius. Sun 8 degrees 22 minutes in Leo. Excesses in pleasure and sports with danger of accidents or trouble. Good for spiritual and educational matters.
>
> (*Astrological Bulletina*, 1914)

Popular though these forecasts appeared to be, they would be largely unrecognisable to today's readers. Astrology still made no concessions to those without basic astrological knowledge - or so it appeared. In fact, things were quietly changing in the background and the gradual introduction of a new astrology, based on Sun signs alone, began to emerge in cheap, popular, fortune telling books.

From the 1880s the mention of Sun signs in these fortune telling books began to increase. Some offered character analyses, some lucky and unlucky days and some predictions based on your Sun sign. What they all had in common is that they were rarely described as astrology books, but held titles such as *The Birthday Book of Fate* and *Zolar's Fortune Teller*. Sun sign astrology was seen as an old, revived tradition.

> What is said here is not new. It is the wisdom of ages culled from the minds of ancient and modern philosophers.
>
> (Walter)

> Long ago, a system of astrology was drawn up, which requires no great stretch of the imagination to accept today. People born in certain months when certain stars ruled, were found to correspond in great measure in temperament, where they differed ... was ascribed to the working of other stars.
>
> (Hyland)

The detailed explanations of the signs and the periods they cover make it clear that Sun signs were not necessarily general knowledge. There was a general awareness that the month you were born in could make a difference, but a number of books and pamphlets ignored the zodiac signs and instead offered interpretations for the month, which were usually based on the sign that was active for the major part of that month.

The concept of being born 'on the cusp' – at a date when the Sun was changing signs – was mentioned in columns from time to time.

> Women and men born between now and April 16th are on the cusp of Aries and Taurus and will probably be much influenced by Mars, being inclined to aggressiveness which, without self-control, may become

violent. They are able to wrest success from conditions that defeat weaker natures.

(*Buffalo Times,* New York, 21 April 1909, p.4)

As Sun sign astrology gained in popularity around the turn of the century, more and more people became aware of the zodiac sign they were born under.

The signs of the zodiac are more or less known to everyone.

(Omar)

You could also put a coin in a fortune telling machine if you wanted to know more about your zodiac sign. Coin operated machines are much older than you might expect, dating back to 1615 when a machine was invented where a box opened when you put in your coin and you could take a pinch of snuff – only a small one if you obeyed the honour system, although there was no way of regulating delivery at that time. More sophisticated machines followed, and J. Parkes obtained a patent for his mechanical fortune telling machine in 1867. By the late nineteenth century, they appeared in arcades, on seaside piers, at stations, in hotel lobbies and languishing on the street in front of shops. By choosing your month of birth (sometimes your date of birth as delineations were often offered according to which week you were born), you'd receive a tightly-rolled scroll or a card that described your sign.

However, the word 'horoscope' itself often didn't apply to astrology at all – although it *could* be used to describe a popular astrology column and was used when discussing someone's full chart, it was more often a word that meant 'forecast' or 'prediction' in general. For example:

*The London Times* is not given to rainbow chasing in its financial and commercial horoscopes.

(*Galveston Daily News,* Texas, 9 January 1895, p.4)

There is no cloud in the circle of the political and social horoscope.

(*Dublin Weekly Nation,* 17 June 1865, p.8)

'Social horoscope' was a particularly common expression from the mid-nineteenth century, and appears in American, British and Australian English. 'Horoscope' was also used as a synonym for 'relationship' and the 'fashion horoscope' was often discussed on women's pages in newspapers. While in the future 'horoscope' would describe Sun sign astrology, another word was needed at this point. And by the turn of the century, books that discussed Sun signs included a new term – solar biology.

> This little book is an introduction to the interesting subject of horoscopes...covers only the *Sun's* position in the *twelve signs* of the *Zodiac* and its effects on human life...a system of solar biology.
>
> (Caterina)

This book is typical in that it analysed the character of those born under each zodiac sign, listed associated birth stones and body parts and offered names of celebrities born under each sign. Many writers took care to point out that they were offering a system of solar biology. What was solar biology? It certainly sounded modern and a more scientific term than 'zodologia'.

Solar biology was often used in the same way as we would use the term 'Sun sign astrology' today. But when it first came into being it had a far more specific meaning. Solar biology was born out of early theosophy and to trace its origins we need to consider the effect that theosophy had on astrology in the late nineteenth century.

# 10

# Theosophy

The late nineteenth century was a time filled with spiritual turmoil – especially in England. Despite the image that sustains of Victorian Britain being a God-fearing society, only a small percentage of the population actually attended church. Growing doubt about Christine doctrine was accompanied by the advancement of natural science.

There were numerous religious revivals during the period, but now they tended to identify true spirituality with mysticism or occultism rather than traditional Christianity. The spiritual was gradually moving away from religious institutions. Though the established churches were in decline, interest in religion itself had never been stronger. People were obsessed with the search for a single key that would unlock the mysteries of the universe, and constantly searched for *the* way to find unity in diversity.

The fascination with spiritualism and psychic phenomena had reached a high point in Britain and the USA during the late nineteenth century, when interest in the subjects transcended the boundaries of class. The possibility of divining the future intrigued the idle rich throughout the Edwardian period and became highly fashionable. Fortune-telling effectively took the place of charitable good works.

The professional middle class were also numerous in the divinatory and psychic fields. In fact, the most active practitioners and espousers were drawn from the middle and educated working classes.

The Theosophical Society was only one of many organisations formed to fill the growing need for new ways to make spiritual connections. It was founded in New York in 1875 by Helena Blavatsky, William Quan Judge and Henry Steel Olcott.

Helena Petrovna Blavatsky was born in Russia in 1831 of an aristocratic family. She ran away from her first husband, Nikifor Vassilievitch Blavatsky, after three unhappy months of marriage. Blavatsky then reputedly travelled the world, spending some of her time in Tibet studying with men she called the Brothers. In 1858, she returned to Russia, later to leave with Italian opera singer Agardi Metrovich, by whom it's rumoured she had a son. After spending some time in Cairo, where she formed the occult Societe Spirite, Blavatsky emigrated to New York City in 1873. She soon established a reputation for her psychic abilities, performing levitation, clairvoyance, out-of-body projection, telepathy, materialisation, and clairaudience. In 1874, she met Henry Steel Olcott, a lawyer, agricultural expert, and journalist who covered spiritualist phenomena. Olcott later became known as the first prominent person of Western descent to make a formal conversion to Buddhism. The third of the trio primarily responsible for the early TS was lawyer William Quan Judge, born in Dublin in 1851. His family had emigrated to New York in 1864.

Blavatsky wasn't the most appealing of people and arguments continue to this day about her honesty and whether or not she was a fraud or one of the greatest modern mystics we've ever known. What was certain is that she had a powerful effect on everyone she met, and her strong personality persuaded many to ignore her character flaws. Elliot Coues described her as:

> Remarkably small, pretty hands and feet for such a curiosity, though with long, dirty nails; suspicion of pug in the saucy nose; pale, restless eyes; flossy yellow hair, tending to kink; Tartar face with high cheekbones, fat chops, and a dewlap, the latter always hid by hand or fan in her photographs; stature medium; weight perhaps 250 pounds; harsh, strident voice; conversation profane and witty; temper

> abominable; odor of tobacco abiding; dress a sort of a compromise between the robes of a Norma and a *robe de nuit* ...
>
> (Coues)

There was no reason at the time to suppose that this particular occult society would be more important than any other. However, theosophy, and the Theosophical Society were to prove hugely influential – especially in the field of astrology.

The word 'theosophy' itself is derived from the term 'theosophia', meaning 'knowledge of the divine'. The Theosophical Society aimed:

> To form a nucleus of the Universal brotherhood of humanity, without distinction of race, creed, sex, caste, or colour; to encourage the study of comparative religion, philosophy, and science; to investigate the unexplained laws of nature and the powers latent in man.
>
> (Ransom, p.5)

The Theosophical Society reached England in 1878. Charles Carlton Massey had opened the first European branch of the Theosophical Society in London that year and was the first president of the British Theosophical Society. However, he resigned in 1884 after finding that his discovery of what he thought to be a precipitated letter had been staged. The Society's early meetings were held at the London home of the British National Association of Spiritualists in Great Russell Street, London. Many of its early English members were claimed from amongst spiritualist circles. Within a few years, theosophy was firmly established and strong enough to withstand the numerous accusations of fraud and trickery that were aimed in its direction.

Theosophy taking off in England was due to the efforts of journalist Alfred Percy Sinnett. Sinnett was a journalist, and worked on a newspaper, *The Pioneer,* in Allahabad, India from 1872. On a trip home in 1875, he attended his first séance and became totally convinced of the veracity of spiritualism. After he wrote a note in *The Pioneer* about Blavatsky and Olcott's imminent visit in

1879, Olcott began a correspondence that led to Blavatsky and Olcott visiting Sinnett. Although from the outset Sinnett spoke of Blavatsky as getting on his nerves, and they argued frequently, he became a staunch supporter of theosophy. By 1882, the Theosophical Society was an international organisation.

Sinnett's enthusiastic campaigning for theosophy lost him his job in India and he returned to England in April 1883 where he quickly made himself and his home a centre of theosophical activity in London. His regular 'at homes' were filled with:

> Astrologers, the mesmerists, the readers of hands and a few, very few only, of the motley spiritualist groups.
>
> (Waite)

The doctrinal core of theosophy was derived from Blavatsky's books *Isis Unveiled* and *The Secret Doctrine*. Theosophists believed that the world's religions were underpinned by divine wisdom that had passed down from the ancients. Their teachings borrowed from Buddhism, Hinduism, and Western esoteric thought.

Theosophists believe that nothing in nature occurs through chance. Every event happens because of laws that are part of a universal paradigm and everything is impregnated with consciousness. All is from one divine source. Human beings in their higher selves are immortal, but their personalities are unconscious of the link with their divine nature and perish unless they can join the two. The theory of reincarnation is a fundamental part of theosophy. In the theosophical system of reincarnation, it isn't possible for humans to reincarnate as animals or plants, except in rare cases of disintegrating lost souls. However, humans aren't considered to be the end stage of evolution, which continues for three further stages. Good and evil are the result of differentiation of spirit/matter in a cycle of becoming. There is a natural involution of spirit into matter followed by an evolution of matter back into spirit. The purpose of the Universe is for spirit to manifest itself self-consciously through seven stages. Human civilisation is measured in a seven age cycle of incarnation and spiritual evolution and the universe is ordered by the number seven.

The constant emphasis on the number seven was enough to convince some astrologers of a connection between theosophy and astrology as they could relate it to the seven classical planets. The borrowing of ideas from Eastern religions further cemented the association between astrology and theosophy.

The Society numbered many astrologers amongst its membership and it was common amongst theosophists to study astrology. After all, astrology was part of the ancient wisdom that theosophists held dear. Blavatsky herself thought that:

> Once the probability, or even the simple possibility, of an occult influence exercised by the stars upon the destiny of man admitted... astrology becomes no less an exact science than astronomy.
>
> (Blavatsky, *Stars*)

The cosmology of the theosophists gave the Sun a prominent role. Blavatsky knew that the Sun had been an object of religious veneration since earliest recorded history. She was profoundly influenced by the Hermetic heliocentric cosmology of the first and second centuries BCE, the structure of three heavens, and the centrality of the sun. She was equally aware of, and influenced by, the works of writers such as Max Müller who argued a solar basis for all religions. In referring to the "central Spiritual Sun," she echoed Hermetic teachings.

> (our) spirits...incorruptible and eternal, both emanate from the eternal central sun and will be reabsorbed by it at the end of time...
>
> (Blavatsky, *Isis*, p.502)

Theosophy became wildly popular and its influence permeated popular culture at all levels. Astrology benefited from theosophy in a number of ways. For a start, theosophy was socially acceptable in a way that astrology hadn't been since the seventeenth century. Though astrological works enjoyed a considerable following in the servant's hall, they were less popular amongst higher society. A few of the more prominent astrologers of the nineteenth century moved in society circles. But in general terms, astrologers were seen as:

Grubby little men and women hopefully trying to turn a reasonably honest penny.

(Russell, p.103)

Thanks to Sinnett, astrologers had a new meeting point – somewhere they could discuss astrology and its esoteric connections, instead of arguing about finer points of technique. They mixed with palmists and other occultists and all flung in their ideas into the great melting pot of theosophy. Some of the greatest astrologers from the late nineteenth century were staunch theosophists. For example, Sepharial (Walter Old) threw himself into theosophy with the same enthusiasm he applied to a number of modes of thought that took his fancy. He went down in theosophical history as holding Blavatsky's hand when she died – having previously predicted her death through examining her horoscope. He was also responsible for introducing Alan Leo to theosophy; Leo was to become one of the most influential – some believe the most influential – astrologers of the late nineteenth and early twentieth centuries.

But not all astrologers were happy with the influence that theosophy was having upon their art. A.J. Pearce, known as Zadkiel, declared theosophical astrology to be "nauseating" and E.H. Bailey in editing *The British Journal of Astrology* was later to develop what almost amounted to a personal campaign against the influence of theosophy on astrology. (This was only one of Bailey's campaigns – he also railed against Alan Leo and was responsible for the first astrologer's strike when working for Leo in 1903.) Robert Cross Smith (Raphael) appeared to be more bemused by theosophy than anything. However, theosophy was to wield a huge influence on astrology, whatever the objections of non-theosophical astrologers.

# 11

## Solar Biology

Theosophy was firmly entrenched on both sides of the Atlantic by 1887, and it should come as no surprise that a theosophist was responsible for resurrecting what we now know as Sun sign astrology. Hiram Erastus Butler, a 'sexual mage and astrologer' was the inventor of the system known as 'solar biology'. Why 'biology'? It hinted at a scientific (rather than mystical) practice, perhaps related to phrenology. Indeed, Butler was described as offering phrenology readings in some press reports. The term had first appeared in Robert Buchanan's 1883 novel *The New Abelard*. However, in *Lucifer* in 1889, Blavatsky referred to it as an invention of Butler's and he has been credited with it ever since.

Born in New York in 1841, Butler spent some years in Philadelphia where he married and subsequently deserted his wife and children. While still in Philadelphia, he'd managed a saw mill and spent time in prison on a charge of mismanagement. He later became a debt collector and was again arrested and imprisoned. Immediately after being released, Butler took up lecturing on Eastern religions and theosophy, which he combined with character reading. In the 1870s he made the press after establishing a sect near Laporte, Pennsylvania where he fasted for forty days and nights.

Butler had formed a group known as the 'Genii of Nations, Knowledge and Religions' – or, as Helena Blavatsky liked to call it, "Gulls Nabbed by Knaves and Rascals" – which he headed under the name 'Adhy-apaka, the Hellenic Ethnomedon'. Blavatsky railed against the sexual magic of Butler's group, equating it with the Hermetic Brotherhood of Luxor and saying that it simply repeated the tenets of the now defunct brotherhood.

The Hermetic Brotherhood of Luxor first came to note in 1884 when an advertisement appeared in the English edition of the *Divine Pymander of Hermes Mercurius Trismegistus*. Aspirants were invited to contact someone called 'Theosi' or 'Theon' and would then receive a letter asking for a photograph and a natal horoscope to see whether or not they were suited for occultism. There is no list of members in existence. Members received their material through the mail and corresponded with a mentor. The intention of the Brotherhood was to teach practical occultism to individuals and so it appealed to those who lived away from large cities. Its use of sex and drugs caused the Brotherhood to hide behind a veil of secrecy. The HBL told its neophytes that they were joining the Exterior Circle of a very ancient initiatic order, which had existed since the time of Hermes Trismigestus.

The Theosophical Society regarded the HBL as a rival from the start. From their point of view the HBL was a sinister order of low-grade occultism, newly invented as a mockery of the 'real' Brotherhood of Luxor, which had inspired the beginnings of the TS. The HBL stressed that it was a Western order and so unconnected with the esoteric Buddhism of the theosophists. It claimed to have started in 1870 and to have roots in the 'Brotherhood of Luxor'. No-one knows the truth of their claims.

It is true that the HBL developed as a powerful rival of the TS, even though numerous people joined both organisations. The HBL's existence was one of the reasons that Blavatsky founded an esoteric school within the TS. Although there were large numbers of members in England, France and the US, it was in the US that the HBL was most successful, after the founders of the TS decamped to India and Blavatsky decided to spend her last years in London.

Despite later assertions to the contrary, Butler was indeed a member of the Theosophical Society, having joined a branch in Rochester, New York in

1885, then controlled by Josephine Cables, the head of one of the lodges of the Hermetic Brotherhood of Luxor.

> "Are the theosophists throughout this country favorable to this movement?" "No, they hate us," responded Butler. "They hate us for our many virtues."
>
> (Godwin, p.147)

Butler published his book *Solar Biology* in 1887, comprising a new system of astrology invented by him. The basic premise of his work is that the Sun is central to this system of character analysis. He described how the varying positions of the planets, and more specifically the Sun in the zodiac signs, produced:

> Not only ...different seasons and stages of fruitfulness, but different human types and qualities...
>
> (Butler, *Solar Biology*, iv.)

Although Butler claimed that his system was based on heliocentric astronomy, and not astrology, it's difficult to see his work as anything but astrological, although there's much theosophical sounding talk of 'solar fluids' and the ether.

Rather than describing the Sun entering the zodiac signs, Butler outlines the Earth entering the signs:

> This portion of the earth commences at the autumnal meridian about the 22$^{nd}$ of September and continues to the 23$^{rd}$ October.
>
> (Butler, *Solar Biology*, p.33)

The reader may struggle through discussions of fluids and ethers to find with relief straightforward descriptions of each zodiac sign and each of the planets in the signs, with the greatest emphasis placed on what we now see as Sun signs. There was no system of houses, no planetary aspects to contend with. The technical aspects of traditional horoscopic astrology were completely ignored.

Butler focused on delineations of planets in signs. Your time of birth was unimportant in this system, except for working out precisely what sign each planet fell in. There was no room for prediction, this was about delineating character, and despite its esoteric overtones much of the text is indistinguishable from simple, Sun sign astrology texts of today.

A whole new system of astrology deserved more than one textbook, so a magazine, *The Esoteric,* was launched at the same time as *Solar Biology* was published and Butler founded the Society for Esoteric Culture which offered different tracks of instruction for men and women and secret initiations into an inner order. *The Esoteric* focused on one Sun sign per issue. The first issue published in July 1888 discussed:

> The nature of people whose birthday falls between July 22$^{nd}$ and August 22$^{nd}$.
>
> It is quite evident that people differ widely in character and functional adaptability; but it is not generally understood that this difference has any relation to the period of the year in which they were born, and consequently to a specific sign of the zodiac. But observation and experience demonstrate that such is the case and, commencing with the present number, we shall each month give the general characteristics of all the persons born during the period represented by the sign in conjunction with which the number is issued.

Claims were made again and again that this was an astronomical system, and so had nothing to do with astrology. Astrology was to do with telling the future and the system of solar biology did not allow for this.

> This work... makes no pretence to tell the future, having no relation to astrology, though employing well-defined and accepted astronomical facts.

A series of articles entitled 'How to Study Solar Biology' described how the ether through which the Sun moved was divided into twelve distinct oceans with the Earth immersed in them. The combinations made were what produced physical and mental conditions. Apart from the Moon, the planets were considered by their heliocentric positions. The lines of the ether radiated from the Sun to the orbit of the planets, on each side of which different qualities of ether flowed. The constellations had nothing to do with it, and therefore issues of precession and accuracy of star positions were irrelevant in solar biology.

However many times Butler and his followers claimed to be advocating a heliocentric system of character analysis, what the reader could see was a clearly and simply laid out system of astrology that bypassed the need for tortuous calculations and arcane mathematical knowledge. With a brief set of tables, anyone could set up their horoscope. In fact, even without tables, anyone could delineate their Sun sign, enough for the large numbers of those who only wanted a cursory look at the possibilities of astrology.

So how come if a prominent theosophist was promoting Sun sign astrology in the late 1880s, and gaining numerous adherents to his theories, astrological history seems to be unaware of him? The problem was that Butler's other activities were nefarious enough to overshadow any of his astrological successes.

Butler's activities in Boston were brought to an abrupt end soon after *The Esoteric* appeared, when, with his colleague Eli Ohmart, he was found guilty of fraud. Ohmart was an experienced financial swindler, long before he met Butler. The two had circulated a book in which *Vidya Nyaka* (Ohmart) said that he wanted to found a college in the US to teach its stockholders and students all the mysteries and the power of acquiring vast wealth. Subscribers were promised that after the college was organised, unlimited means would be at its disposal. However, to get the scheme going, the faithful needed to offer their financial support. Theosophists reached deeply into their pockets to do just that. Butler and Ohmart seemed to suddenly have an almost unlimited source of income, in exchange for vague promises.

The whole scheme collapsed with an exposé in the press. The press and public saw no difference between Butler's claims and those of the Theosophical Society and theosophists scurried to deny any connection with Butler and his ilk. This incident alone was enough to ensure that Butler was neatly deleted from theosophical history wherever possible, but the whole situation was made much worse by accusations of debauchery.

Butler's teachings were allied with those of the Hermetic Brotherhood of Luxor, which drew heavily from the magico-sexual theories of Paschal Beverly Randolph, an African American born in New York, in 1825. Like all good occultists of the era, he spent a great deal of time travelling the world. According to Randolph, at the age of twenty-one he became Supreme Hierarch of The Brotherhood of Eulis. In what seems to be almost admirable thoroughness, he also became involved in spiritualism, séances, and magic mirrors, he used mind-altering drugs and had numerous trance visions. Randolph knew all the great occultists of the time, and met such major celebrities as Napoleon III and Abraham Lincoln. It was on his travels through Palestine that he discovered what he was to be most remembered for – sexual magick.

> One night...I made love to, and was loved by, a dusky maiden of Arabic blood. I of her, and the experience, learned... the fundamental principle of the White Magick of Love; subsequently I became affiliated with some dervishes and fakirs of who, by suggestion still, I found the road to other knowledges; and of these devout practicers of a sublime and holy magic...
>
> (Greenfield, p.92)

In his privately circulated manuscripts, Randolph plainly laid out his system of sexual magick.

> The ejective moment, therefore, is the most divine and tremendously important one in the human career as an independent entity; for not only may we launch Genius, Power, Beauty, Deformity, Crime, Idiocy,

> Shame or Glory on the world's great sea of Life, in the person of the children we may then produce, but we may plunge our own souls neck-deep in Hell's horrid slime, or else mount the Azure as coequal associate Gods; for then the mystic Soul swings wide its Golden gates, opens its portals to the whole vast Universe and through them come trooping either Angels of Light or the Grizzly Presence from the dark corners of the Spaces. Therefore, human copulation is either ascentive and ennobling, or descensive and degrading...
>
> (Greenfield, p.94)

Randolph described "the marital office and function" as "material, spiritual and mystic," and he proclaimed that "my doctrine... alone declares and establishes the fact that the marital function is unquestionably the highest, holiest, most important, and most wretchedly abused of all that pertains to the human being." Amongst the abuses listed by Randolph were inconsideration (marital rape or non-satisfaction of one's partner) and "the murderous habit of incompletion of the conjugal rite." Sex was celebrated as a metaphysical and holy ritual, but only when it produced orgasms for both partners. The promised results of sex magick were telepathy, communication with discarnate spirits, increased wealth, forecasting the outcomes of financial transactions, rendering adulterous husbands and wives cold to others, improved health, the power of preparing amulets, the ability to secretly know others' designs and plans, the power to direct others, and the gift of spiritual revelations. And you were obliged to enjoy yourself at the same time.

Perhaps unsurprisingly, Randolph ran into trouble with the authorities and was briefly jailed for his distribution of free love pamphlets. In 1875, when his son was four months old, Randolph committed suicide.

How far Butler followed Randolph's tenets isn't clear. However, it was alleged by the *Boston Herald* on 18 February 1889 that Butler, Ohmart and perhaps other members of the Society for Esoteric Culture sexually assaulted women during their initiation into the inner order, claiming that this 'mortification of the flesh' was necessary to dampen lust and that at least one of these women had become pregnant. Butler claimed that abstinence was a prerequisite for joining his society and total continence in thought and deed was required for progress. Blavatsky, for one, was totally unconvinced by this assertion, and simultaneously sought to disassociate the Theosophical Society from any connection with Butler, while gleefully writing numerous letters about Butler's activities to *The Boston Globe*. In case Butler wasn't totally demolished, other accusations flowed in. He was accused of plagiarism, Ohmart's past financial cons were brought out into the open, and hints of strange dealings with disembodied spirits were thrown about.

> Thereby hangs a tale, a long, complicated, involuted, weird, mystical, scientific, hysterical tale – a tale of love and intrigue, of adventure, of alleged and to some extent of admitted swindling, of charges of a horrible and unspeakable immorality, of communion with embodied and disembodied spirits, and especially of money. In short, a tale that would make your head weary and your heart faint if you attempted to follow out all its labyrinthine details and count the cogs on its wheels within wheels. A tale that quite possibly may find its sequel in the courts, where judge, jury, and counsel will have a chance to cudgel their brains over almost every mystery in the known universe.
>
> (Judge, *Occultism for Barter*)

Butler initially took the fuss in his stride:

> If there are no arrests made, I shall go right on with the work; but if they make trouble, I shall stay and face the music.
>
> (Judge, *Occultism for Barter*)

But the scandal grew so much that he finally left Boston and headed west to California, taking his theories of solar biology with him. He had to move on from San Francisco when newspapers realised who he was and accused him of using his occult powers over the weak minded so he'd secure enough money to build an esoteric college. Butler established the Esoteric Fraternity in 1893 in Applegate, California, a community that existed (albeit on a very small scale) until the 1970s, The Fraternity published Butler's works comprising titles such as The Seven Creative Principles, The Revised Esoteric, Mind Control, and Practical Methods to Ensure Success. Butler died in the Applegate colony in November 1916.

Butler's followers remained faithful, and slowly, outsiders latched onto this 'new system' of astrology. Numerous books and pamphlets were published extolling its virtues and offering delineations by Sun sign, often carrying advertisements for lessons in solar biology.

By 1910 a new publication had appeared to extol the virtues of solar biology, The Occult and Biological Journal. With less talk about ethers and fluids, this much simpler magazine described the planets' meanings in zodiac signs, brought up the issue of planets on the cusp (where they are changing sign), and offered delineations for readers.

Solar biology was here to stay even if its king had lost his crown. Butler's assertions that his system didn't allow for forecasting did nothing to prevent astrologers from developing systems using his theories as a basis. However, despite the popularity of solar biology amongst a select few, it still hadn't reached a mass audience. It took the intervention of two astrologers who were to become the most famous in their respective countries to ensure that Sun sign astrology was placed firmly on the map – Evangeline Adams in the US and Alan Leo in England.

# 12

# Alan Leo

Alan Leo is commonly thought of as being the first modern astrologer and is revered by astrologers the world over. Born William Frederick Allen on 7 August 1860, Leo had already tried and failed at a number of professions and was managing a grocer's shop in Manchester when he met a Dr Richardson who taught him astrology in 1885. Two years later, Leo returned to the city of his birth, London, and found employment as a salesman for a confectionary firm. Shortly afterwards, he answered a letter from Frederick Lacey in the short-lived *Astrologer* magazine. Four others responded to Lacey's letter and they formed a group that met at Lacey's house in Brixton on Friday evenings.

Early in their friendship, Leo and Lacey joined an occult society, *The Celestial Brotherhood*, run by the Welsh seer and mystic John Thomas, better known as Charubel. Thomas had originally trained as a Methodist preacher, but by his early twenties had become a curative mesmerist, later progressing through herbalism, astrology, mediumship, and occultism. He was renowned for his healing skills, and often relied on precipitated letters from the spirit world for his methods of treatment. Thomas prepared hundreds of horoscopes in his time, taking the trouble to draw them in parchment. He also did a roaring business in talismans.

Each member of the Brotherhood adopted a mystical name derived from astrological significators, numerology, and geometry. Leo became known as Agorel and Lacey as Aphorel. Although the Society was never the success that Thomas had hoped, it had members all over the world and for much of his life he kept up lengthy and frequent correspondence with its members. Leo was a regular writer for the Brotherhood's magazine, *The Occultist*, which appears to have had a connection to the Hermetic Brotherhood of Luxor. In the mid 1880s, Leo spent much of his time travelling in the north and west of England, and took the opportunity to spend time with Thomas when he could.

Most astrologers of the period adopted pseudonyms – often with mystical overtones. Their audiences expected it, and they didn't want to risk their day jobs or attract police attention. Leo wasn't satisfied with the name bestowed on him by Thomas and needed an alternative. His birth chart showed he'd been born with Virgo rising, but only a minor tweak was necessary for his rising sign to be Leo, the same as his Sun sign. He was clearly a Leo, the sign much more suited to the king of astrologers, which is what he planned to become.

In 1889 – despite neither of them having any idea of what it entailed – Leo and Lacey decided to start an astrological magazine, the *Astrologer's Magazine* (renamed *Modern Astrology* in 1895), which they launched in July 1890.

Lacey had introduced Leo to Sepharial, already a theosophist at this time and a member of Blavatsky's inner circle. Leo took to theosophy like a duck to water. It was only a short step away from the studies he had already undertaken with Thomas and he joined the Theosophical Society in April 1890.

In 1894 Lacey gave up working on the magazine and Leo rented an office off Fleet Street to run it as sole proprietor. He finally gave up other employment to become a full time astrologer in 1898. By 1903 Leo employed nine members of staff at the Modern Astrology offices, including the astrologer Edward H. Bailey, who was later to become the editor of Modern Astrology's arch-rival *The British Journal of Astrology*.

Leo's occult training and involvement in theosophy persuaded him into building a more spiritual and psychological basis for astrology. He wanted to make it more effective as a tool for character analysis. As his later assistant, Annie Barley, said:

> His life work was to cleanse the Augean stables of astrology, and only those who worked in close touch with him know what an accumulation of filth there was in those stables, and what slime he waded through.
>
> (Leo, Life and Work, p.134.)

Being a theosophist informed every area of Leo's life. He said to those who opposed a theosophical style astrology:

> If you squeeze Theosophy out, you squeeze me out.
>
> (*Modern Astrology*, December 1901, p.183)

Leo made a fortune from mass produced horoscopes as well as publishing numerous books and running a correspondence course. He'd realised that there was a severe lack of affordable astrology textbooks. In 1901 the first of his small manuals of the *Astrology for All* series appeared. Alan beavered away, writing as much as he could himself, writing on average a book every three months. By 1915, he had authored or helped produce about thirty astrological books. They were frequently reprinted and many titles remain in print today.

He also wanted to sort out wayward astrologers and get them organised, which led to a number of astrological societies being set up and folding. In 1915, Leo founded the Middlesex Lodge of the Theosophical Society, later the Astrological Lodge of the Theosophical Society which would give birth to the Faculty of Astrological Studies and the Astrological Association. The Astrological Lodge continues to attract new members and still meets regularly.

From an early date, Leo included Sun sign delineations in his lectures. In 1899 he gave a lecture entitled 'The Unseen Law which Governs Humanity' at the Astrological Society's annual meeting. After some general comments about ruling planets, he proceeded to describe each of the Sun signs and what they meant.

> Aries, the ram, rules from March 20— April 21 Men born within those dates are pioneers. Aries influence is the highest of all but it MAY

BECOME PEVERTED and then you are a thief. How you can prevent Aries from becoming perverted was not explained at this time...

(*Evening News,* London, 11 February 1899, p.3)

Leo reformed astrology by making a number of revisions to astrological techniques to simplify matters. One of these changes was to make the Sun central to astrological interpretation. Like any astrologer of the period, Leo had read Butler's *Solar Biology* and apparently plagiarised the book happily when preparing his 'test horoscopes'. These were horoscopes sent to subscribers of *Modern Astrology* for a shilling fee, and made up of mimeographed sheets prepared in advance and compiled in the same way that a computerised horoscope is today.

> The whole of the mimeographed sheets comprising his test horoscopes were copied, in many cases verbatim, from Sepharial's *Prognostications from the Rising Sign* and H.S. Green's *Planets in Signs and Houses,* while the greater part of the other sheets of his system were copied and paraphrased from Butler's *Solar Biology.*
>
> (Bailey, *Destiny,* p.20)

Theosophy certainly exerted a major influence on Leo's astrology. However, it's debatable whether Leo was most strongly affected in his astrological approach by theosophy itself or by Butler's solar biology theories derived from theosophy. It may not be important. What is important is that Leo promoted a form of astrology to which the Sun was central. In fact, Leo wrote a Sun sign book in 1909.

The first edition of *Everybody's Astrology,* Volume 1 of Leo's *Astrological Manuals,* comprised chapters on the Sun in each of the twelve zodiac signs with no discussion of other astrological factors. In the second (and subsequent) editions, material was added to include Sun sign combined with Moon signs as well as short chapters on the other planets. This particular book apparently caused Leo a number of problems. His amendments to include other astrological information for the second edition led to complaints that the Sun sign interpretations were reduced in length. By the tenth edition an appendix was included to extend the Sun sign interpretations. Apparently, Leo could not decide whether to write a Sun sign book or a standard astrological textbook.

The *Astrological Manuals* were intended for beginning astrologers, whilst most of Leo's works were aimed at those more competent in astrology and so treated the subject in greater depth. Leo's prime motivation was to encourage people to interpret their own horoscopes rather than pay someone to do it for them. To this end, he offered a never-ending series of classes, lectures and lessons.

Leo gradually discarded almost the entire list of zodiacal attributes, which had been accumulated from the first to seventeenth centuries. He ignored physical characteristics to focus on inner character. His descriptions of the signs set the tone for future descriptions of signs – or arguably, Butler's descriptions repeated through Leo's work did so. For example, he wrote that Aries:

> Represents undifferentiated consciousness. It is a chaotic and unorganised sign, in which impulse, spontaneity, and instinctiveness are marked features. Its vibrations are the keenest and most rapid, but without what may be called definite purpose, except towards impulsiveness and disruption. It signifies explosiveness, extravagance and all kinds of excess. Its influence is more directly connected with the animal kingdom, in which life is full and without the directive power of fully awakened self-consciousness.
>
> (Leo, *Nativity*, p.17)

Making the Sun the focal point of a horoscope added strength to the concept of a simplistic astrology based on the zodiacal position of the Sun alone. Although Sun sign astrology was already being used in many quarters, Leo's writings moved the description of such astrology from solar biology to Sun sign astrology. Leo argued that as life-giver, the Sun is the single most important factor in the zodiac and therefore the birth chart. Astrology would never be the same again.

> The Sun-sign philosophy is an enormous departure from what went before it. It completely disregards the world-view, which held from classical times through until the seventeenth century, which was that Man stood on top of the Earth but below the stars, while God was above all. Instead, it suggests that Man is at the center of all things... it rejects fatalism and predestination, and it celebrates freedom and the qualities of the individual... The Sun-sign philosophy of Alan Leo has given astrology what it needed to survive and to grow through the twentieth century... (it) took astrology away from a privileged elite and gave it genuine mass appeal...
>
> (Eccles)

Leo wasn't the only astrologer moving towards a solar-centred astrology. However, his work ensured that in England at least, Sun sign astrology was no longer restricted to the 'lowest' form of astrology, but could be valid as a part of 'higher' astrology.

In the USA the story of Sun sign astrology ran in parallel. Although Leo's work was known and widely read there, it was the work of Evangeline Adams, and her adoption of a form of solar biology that ensured Sun sign astrology would be firmly placed on the map in America.

# 13

# Evangeline Adams

The story of astrology in the American press is similar to its British counterpart. *The Boston Globe* regularly interviewed Catherine Thompson, Boston's most renowned astrologer in the 1890s, and one of Evangeline Adams' teachers. Thompson was born in England and moved to the US after marrying a wealthy businessman. They had homes in New York and Newport, where Thompson became a well-known hostess. Abandoned by her husband, and left alone with two children, Thompson took up astrology, studying under Luke Broughton. Thompson met Adams in 1888 after her teacher, J. Heber Smith, wasn't able to continue with his tuition owing to his other obligations.

Evangeline Adams has been acknowledged as one of the most important influences on the development of American astrology. Born in 1868, she arrived in New York in 1899. Adams obtained instant fame as an astrologer after a successful prediction she made to the proprietor of her hotel. She told Warren Leland that he was in imminent danger. Leland assumed that this was to do with his investments on the stock exchange and pointed out that as the following day was a holiday, nothing too untoward could happen. Adams questioned him further. After listening to Leland describe his experiences when similar astrological configurations had occurred, she warned him of the danger of fire. Leland's hotel did indeed catch fire. A day later, the press headlined articles with Leland's statement across the front page proclaiming that the fire was predicted by Evangeline Adams the day before it happened.

Adams' career took off and over the years she did readings for many rich and famous personalities. It almost came to a halt in 1914 when she was arrested for fortune telling for the second time. She decided to fight the charges.

In 1916 the editor of *The New York World*, an Irishman named Cosegrave, invited Evangeline Adams to dinner – partially to introduce her to the occultist Aleister Crowley. They discussed the possibility of Crowley ghost writing a book on astrology for Adams. Unfortunately, their relationship broke down and the planned book was never completed, although Adams kept Crowley's original manuscripts. Crowley tells the story in his autobiography, *The Confessions of Aleister Crowley*, but Adams makes no mention at all of Crowley in her own autobiography *Bowl of Heaven*.

Many people believed that Adams' books *Astrology, Your Place In The Sun*, and *Astrology, Your Place Among The Stars* were almost entirely written by Aleister Crowley. When *Your Place Among The Stars* was first released, Crowley sent the publishers Dodd, Mead and Company of New York a letter, pointing out that much of the book was his work. Crowley's authorship was finally recognised in law in 1999.

The involvement of Crowley and Adams may not have been relevant to our discussion if it weren't for a comment made at the start of *Your Place In The Sun*.

> Part 1 of the book is largely based on Solar Biology, which concerns itself only with the influence of the sun...

It isn't clear whether the comment about solar biology stems from Crowley or Adams. The imoprtant thing was that it was the Sun that really mattered when you got down to it, and by saying solar biology was different to astrology, Adams wasn't bringing astrology into disrepute – she was doing something else entirely.

> THE sun is sometimes called the "daddy" of the stars. And in a strictly scientific sense, this is a fairly accurate definition. For in astrology as in

> nature, the sun is the center and giver of all life and strength this parent of the entire solar eystem. It is so important a factor in determining our individuality that there has been built around its influence a science of its own, often confused with astrology, called solar biology. From one viewpoint, aolar biology is merely a poor relation of the greatest science, but from another viewpoint it is the basis and foundation stone.
>
> (*Indianapolis Star*, 12 April 1931, p.61)

Whether or not Adams' Sun sign work was directly derived from Butler's solar biology theories doesn't alter the fact that she produced a large number of Sun sign booklets that offered character readings similar to those found today. She ran a large mail order horoscope business and her Sun sign booklets evolved from that. They were widely distributed through Woolworth stores in the US, and bore the trademark of Adam's work by including Sun sign analyses of popular celebrities of the day.

The booklets referred to "your solar horoscope" and didn't bear the names of the relevant zodiac signs on the cover but instead were headed with the relevant dates. The text described the characteristics of the featured sign, using celebrities' charts as examples. The names of the signs were still not completely familiar to Adams' readers:

> Don't let these strange names frighten you. All you need to know at first is that each sign governs a special part of the year.
>
> (Adams, *Your Place in the Sun*, p.9)

And still not completely familiar to Adams' readers:

> If you read one booklet, you learn about one group of friends. If you read all twelve booklets, you learn about *all* your friends.
>
> (Adams, *Own Book of Astrology*, p.10)

She needed to explain what Sun sign astrology was, although this wasn't a term Adams used. However, she did refer to "your stars" as her booklets were subtitled 'What the stars say about you'. It's hard not to view these booklets as a quick money-making venture, considering that later versions contained large amounts of text extracted from her earlier books.

It's difficult from this distance to appreciate how revered and popular Adams was as an astrologer. When she visited England two of the foremost astrologers of the day, Sepharial and Alan Leo made sure they had an audience with her. Adams had numerous wealthy and prominent clients, including John Pierpoint Morgan, Franklin Roosevelt, Tallulah Bankhead, Joseph Campbell and Enrico Caruso.

In the late 1920s she was charging $50 (equivalent to over $800 today) for a consultation. Almost single-handedly she created a market for Sun sign astrology in the US. As well as having a huge personal clientele, Adams hosted a three times weekly astrological radio show from 23 April 1930 which thousands of listeners tuned into. She received up to 4,000 letters a day and employed more than twenty-five assistants in her New York offices. It was rumoured that commuter trains between Washington's Union Station and Pennsylvania Station in New York were run as a convenience for her clients.

Adams reputedly predicted the stock market crash of 1929 (in fact she predicted in February 1929 that the markets would rise), World War II, the deaths of King Edward VII, Rudolph Valentino, Enrico Caruso, and herself.

Her writing on astrology commonly featured in newspapers from 1914, focusing on the meaning of Sun signs. However, rather than simply giving character delineations, from the start she used Sun signs as the basis of her predictions, although she rarely referred to the signs, simply listing relevant dates.

> JUPITER. For persons whose birthdays occur during the last ten days of January, first thirteen days of February, last week in May, first half of June, last week in September and first half of October. Jupiter is favorable to your sun, an aspect which gives you buoyancy, magnetism and health. You will be conscious of high aspirations. What you

undertake you are likely to succeed in. Opportunities for advancement will open to you. This is your time. Go in and win.

(*Pittsburgh Press,* Pennsylvannia, 11 January 1914, p.47)

Adams justified her focus on Sun signs as a means of making astrology more accessible:

Horoscopes For Everyone ... THATS a large order, isn't it?

But it can be done in today's article if we stick only to the influence of the sign of the zodiac under which you were born... Of course, that isnt all there is to astrology.... For the thing which gives zest to existence on this globe is that every man is different from every other man and every woman even more so. Astrology accounts for these differences, too. But in this week's article, we are not concerned with them. We are thinking only of the general characteristics which all people born under any one sign are likely to share...

(*Akron Beacon Journal,* Ohio, 30 December 1930, p.12)

Those who made astrology more accessible to the population at large, were responsible for restoring astrology to its rightful position, said astrologer Katherine Taylor Craig:

Astrologers too have become more scientific. Men like Alan Leo and women like Miss Evangeline Adams have convinced the world of the accuracy of their calculations of their logarithms their arcs and radii. Under these circumstances we may all live to see 'the foolish sister of astronomy' exchanged for the soubriquet of the 'stay-at-home sister' the one who watches our lives and firesides even as the dog-star of Egypt protected the homes of Egyptians by warning the herdsmen of the coming inundation of the Nile.

(*Brooklyn Daily Eagle,* New York, 5 March 1916, p.40)

Adams continued her work until her death in 1932 having refused a lecture tour scheduled for the autumn which she turned down because her astrological chart had indicated that her imminent death would make such a trip impossible.

Adams was also a palmist. And it was to be another palmist who took the baton from Leo in England and further promoted the concept of Sun sign astrology – her teacher, a man known to the world as Cheiro.

# 14

# Astrology and the Law

One of the difficulties in practising astrology, until relatively recently, was that it wasn't actually legal. For centuries, a variety of laws had ruled against the practices of fortune-tellers, astrologers, and necromancers, in an attempt to protect the gullible. The story begins with the Vagrancy Act of 1597. This ruled that:

> All fencers, bearwards, common players and minstrels, jugglers, tinkers and... persons pretending to be Egyptians... were rogues and vagabonds and if caught they were to be stripped naked from the middle upwards and be openly whipped until his or her body be bloody... thence taken to the House of Correction there to be kept till they are employed or banished.

On the face of it, this doesn't appear to have much to do with astrology. However, the individuals targeted by the Vagrancy Act were gypsies – England's traditional fortune-tellers and folk astrologers. An amendment to the Act came in 1604 when it was added that any such rogues as were:

> Adjudged incorrigible or dangerous shall be branded in the left shoulder with a hot burning iron the width of the breadth of a shilling with a great Roman R upon the flesh.

It was much more likely however, that anyone seeking legal redress against an astrologer would turn to the Witchcraft Acts. These laws could be used against anyone suspected of practising witchcraft and prevented anyone from:

> Upon him or them by witchcraft, enchantment, charm, or sorcery, to tell or declare in what place any treasure of gold or silver should or might be found or had in the earth, or other secret place; or where goods, or things lost or stolen should be found or be come; or shall use or practice any sorcery, enchantment, charm or witchcraft to the intent to provoke any person to unlawful love.

Under this Act, the practice of using horary astrology for finding lost or stolen items would place an astrologer in the same category as a conjurer seeking to raise people from the dead. Under the 1542 version of the Act, the punishment for such offences was death – although there are no records suggesting that this sentence was ever carried out on an astrologer, and in any case, it was repealed in 1547. The Elizabethan Act of 1563 proscribed one year's imprisonment and four stints in the pillory for a first offence, life imprisonment for a second offence, and death for those who conjured up evil spirits.

If the Vagrancy and Witchcraft Acts weren't sufficient, it was also possible to prosecute astrologers for fraud. When witchcraft and conjuration ceased to be a crime, following the Witchcraft Act of 1736, that same law ensured that pretended witchcraft or magic remained a punishable offence. This meant that from 1736 onwards it was no longer possible to prosecute people for what they said they could do, but for what they could not do. In other words, witchcraft and magic became legally defined as fraudulent beliefs and practices.

There had been a number of laws against vagrants in the past (including the 1494 Vagabonds and Beggars Act) but the 1713 Vagrancy Act sought to put together all the laws relating to rogues, vagabonds and beggars into one Act. This was repealed in 1740 but swiftly followed by another similar statute. This Act applied until 1822, when the laws were again consolidated and amended, resulting in the 1824 Vagrancy Act. During the early nineteenth century, few prosecutions of astrologers appear to have taken place, although it's clear that a variety of legal means were available if the authorities wished to take action. The Vagrancy Act was the most straightforward to use against astrologers. In 1807 an astrologer called Robert Powell was convicted of being a "Rogue and Vagabond". He was charged with:

> Otaining money under false and fraudulent pretences from one Thomas Barnes, a footman in the service of Surgeon Blair, of Great Russell Street, Bloomsbury, and taking from him two shillings and sixpence under pretences of telling him the destinies of a female fellow-servant, by means of his skill in astrological divination.
>
> (*Newgate Calendar*)

Powell advertised his services through a handbill, the text of which appears below.

Sciential Instructions

A. B. PROFESSOR OF THE SIDERAL SCIENCE

No. 5 SUTTON STREET, SOHO SQUARE

*Teaches Astrology and Calculating Nativities, with the most Precise Accuracy, at 2s. 6d. per Lesson*

APPLICATION TO THE COURTEOUS READER

WHO will not praise and admire the glory of the sun and stars, and the frame of heaven, and not wish to know their influence and operation upon earth? For fear of the ridicule of revilers and vilifiers of the science, who understand it not, and so deem it fraud and iniquity.

Oh, happy world! if they were not a hundred thousand times more hurt by the baits of pleasure, honour, pride, authority, arrogance, extortion, envy, covetousness and cruelty ! and thereby make or ruin themselves, by grasping and wantonness ; and others by deception, craft, fraud and villainy ! but that is all gilded over, and so such pass for good respectable people. Some may start and rave at this, but who can confute the truth of it?

Can any suppose that the stars, the celestial bodies, are designed for no other purpose than for us to look at heedlessly, as being of no worth, nor having any effect on us?

Daily experience, and the most learned of all ages, have proved it, and testified it to us that they have, and in a great degree do determine our fate; which I and all other professors have experienced and proved in thousands of different nativities. Who then, by means of such a noble and inestimable science, would not wish for a precognition of the events of their most sanguine hopes and fears, which alternately alleviate or depress their minds? Is the praising and magnifying a work a wrong to the workman? Is knowing, manifesting and experiencing, the power and operations of the created, wronging or dishonouring the Creator?

Though this be a persecuted science, yet happy world I how blest a state, if nothing worse was practised in it! No letters, unless post paid, will be taken in.

The handbill was posted through doors and one morning a copy appeared on the breakfast table of a Mr Blair. On reading it, Blair was incensed enough to contact the Society for the Suppression of Vice and with their help decided to entrap Powell. Blair dictated a letter to his footman, Barnes, saying that he wanted to know the future destiny of the cook-maid, and what sort of husband she was to have. The letter was delivered to Powell's address, who responded saying he could either supply an answer immediately or the footman could return the following day when Powell would have had time to prepare a written answer. Barnes chose to return the following day and paid Powell with a marked half crown. Just in case there was any doubt, Barnes also accepted the signed receipt, which Powell offered him. As soon as Barnes returned, Blair told him to report the incident to the local magistrate, a man named Trott. Trott rushed to Powell's premises where he found:

> The sage absorbed in profound cogitation, casting the nativities of two plump and prurient damsels, and consulting the dispositions of the stars as to the disposition of the lasses, and the kind of sweethearts or husbands they were destined to have. Not only were the planets consulted, but all the eminent authorities, from Moore's Almanack up to the Ptolemies, which composed the 'seer's' library, were shrewdly scanned on the subject. All the conjunctions of course were found to be copulative, and the omens propitious...
>
> *(Newgate Calendar)*

Powell was searched and the marked half crown found on him – although you may wonder why anyone bothered, he was hardly keeping his activities secret. Powell had already been convicted of fortune-telling and repeatedly warned against practising astrology again. He claimed that he had resorted to astrology through sheer desperation. With no money, and being unable to find work he had to find a way of supporting a miserable lunatic wife –

> For the moon was still worse to him than the stars
>
> *(Newgate Calendar)*

– and "three naked, famishing children." He didn't want to resort to begging for fear of being convicted as a vagabond. Unfortunately, he was convicted on this occasion, and imprisoned for a year as well as being openly whipped "at the cart's tail from the end of Mutton-lane to the end of Aylesbury-street."

Being prosecuted for practising astrology at this time appears to have been relatively unlikely. It certainly didn't worry Powell too much. After his 1807 trial, he resumed his astrological career and continued undisturbed in his work until he was again convicted in 1814, and found guilty of fraud and deception.

> JOSEPH POWELL was indicted for that he... on the 10th of October, in the 48th year of his Majesty's reign, been adjudged an incorrigible rogue... having made use of a certain subtle craft, pretending to have skill in Astrology, to deceive and impose upon James Weston, to tell future events that would happen to him...

A Benjamin Smith had called on Powell to ask if there was any likelihood of his wife returning. It appears that Powell cast a horary chart to answer Smith's question as:

> He then took a slate, and drew some figures on the slate, and when he had drawed the figures, he signified I might possibly see my wife on the 1st of November; if I did not see her on that day, he thought I should see her at the latter end of that month: and if I did not see her at the latter end of that month, he thought I never should see her again.
>
> <div align="right">(<i>Proceedings of the Old Bailey</i>)</div>

Smith paid Powell two shillings and sixpence for his work and was given a handbill to offer other potential customers.

> POWELL, late Professor of Astrology, & Physic.
>
> Respectfully informs his friends and the public, that he now sells the invaluable articles, viz. a liquid that is a certain cure for the scurvy in the teeth and gums, being only used with a brush it makes the blackest teeth clean, and white in a few days; an eye-water which has restored the sight when almost lost; a tincture for curing the torturing pain of the tooth-ach, at two shillings and sixpence per bottle. Also the scurvy, rheumatism, consumptions, old coughs, colds, and various other diseases safely and speadily cured, on very reasonable terms; any commands by letters (post paid) will be punctually attended to at No. 64, Queen-street, Soho, near Greek-street, first doors up one pair of stairs.

(No questions asked)
A Penegeric on the Starry Systom,
How great the Glorious of the Skies,
The Sun, the Moon, the Stars likewise;
The frame of Heaven transpend out spread,
With brilliant beauties spangled;
Without these orbs past all relate,
Here's no light, nor life, nor state,
If they give life and wealth create,
Then sure they must ordain our fate.

Smith appears to have been a little confused as to the purpose of his testimony at Powell's trial. He didn't feel that he'd been deceived but had simply paid the asking price for the answer to a question. A police officer produced Powell's slates, some books, and a set of letters with questions to be answered as evidence. Powell maintained that Smith had simply asked his opinion and he wasn't trying to predict anything. When Smith insisted on paying, Powell asked him to take back a shilling. The court was completely unconvinced. Powell was fined one shilling and imprisoned for two years, at the age of seventy. Whether he continued to practise astrology after his release is unknown, but it seems likely.

Powell's case was relatively unusual, but it wasn't the only one of its kind. In 1813 Thomas White, the author of *The Celestial Intelligencer* was approached by a police informer who asked for a reading and then paid with marked money. White was arrested, his books and papers were seized, and he was convicted under the Vagrancy Act. White died after three months in Winchester jail.

Although it wasn't unheard of for astrologers to be prosecuted as vagrants, it wasn't until fortune-telling was made prominent in the 1824 Vagrancy Act, that astrologers felt themselves to be in substantial danger. Rather than simply assuming an astrologer to be a rogue or vagabond, use of the 1824 Act specified that it applied to:

> Every Person pretending or professing to tell Fortunes, or using any subtle Craft, Means or Device, by Palmistry or otherwise, to deceive and impose on any of His Majesty's Subjects.

Astrologers were now in greater danger of prosecution and imprisonment than they had been for years. Prosecutions were actively sought by the constabulary and judiciary. They often used paid informers to entrap the astrologer, and the penalty was usually severe: a prison sentence of up to three months, accompanied or followed by hard labour. Appeals weren't usually allowed.

Amongst the Act's casualties were James Bradshawe from Manchester who was imprisoned for a month in 1842 and Francis Copestick, who in 1852 was trapped by a policeman masquerading as a client and sentenced to a month's imprisonment with hard labour.

After Bradshaw's conviction, the then-Zadkiel, Richard James Morrison, set up the snappily-named *British Association for the Advancement of Astral Science &c., and the Protection of Astrologers*. Following his appeal, Bradshaw was released and the magistrate forced to pay him £35 in compensation. Others were less fortunate. Unfortunately, this society soon folded. Morrison didn't give up. He hoped to make it legal for enfranchised householders to practise professionally in their own homes, and on the advice of Christopher Cooke, a solicitor and astrologer, in 1852 he wrote a petition which MP William Ewart presented to Parliament as a private members' bill. It sank without trace.

The case of Richard Henry Penny took place in June 1886. Penny had been advertising his services in local newspapers and had adopted the name of 'Neptune'. There was no doubt as to the type of services he offered.

> Wanted, everyone to have their nativity cast; yearly advice given and astrological questions answered.
>
> (*Weekly Dispatch,* 6 June 1886, p.11)

Penny was defended by Charles Carlton Massey, who valiantly tried to argue that Penny was simply an astrology enthusiast and had no intention of deceiving anyone. However, Penny's extensive price list told against him and the magistrate refused to hear more evidence, saying that it was unnecessary as Penny had clearly professed to tell fortunes. As a belief in astrology was absurd, Penny couldn't possibly have been acting in good faith. He was offered the choice of a fine of five pounds or twenty-one days imprisonment.

Astrologers were now in greater danger of prosecution and imprisonment than they had been for years, as prosecutions were actively sought by the constabulary and judiciary. They often used paid informers to entrap the astrologer, and the penalty was usually severe: a prison sentence of up to three months, accompanied or followed by hard labour. Plus, appeals weren't usually allowed.

A solicitor from Halifax, Joseph Dodson, recognised the need for a united front. He also needed someone who knew how to attract publicity and wasn't scared of losing his job. In short, he needed Alan Leo. The first meeting of the *Occultist's Defence League* was held 9 May 1899 at Leo's house. Despite its grand plans, and much pontificating by its members, the League only effectively comprised Dodson. But to be fair, Dodson was unstoppable and continued to defend occultists wherever he could find them. In 1904 he was involved in his biggest case to date – defending the 'Keiros', palmists Charles Stephenson and his wife Martha. Although found guilty of fraud, the Stephensons were bound over once they promised not to practice palmistry again.

By 1912, the number of fortune-tellers in London had risen rapidly. It was estimated that between six and seven hundred were operating at that time. The Metropolitan Police Commissioner responded by issuing an order that fortune-tellers of all types within his jurisdiction must remove all words such as 'palmist', 'clairvoyant' and 'astrologer' from their doorplates, window signs and other public advertisements. Public concern was heightened enough for questions to be asked in the House of Commons in 1911 and 1912.

Although regular clampdowns against fortune-telling took place at the start of the twentieth century, this did nothing to prevent it becoming a fashionable amusement amongst the middle and upper classes where it was seen as a harmless form of entertainment.

The last major case against an astrologer under the Act was that against Alan Leo in 1914. Leo pleaded not guilty and gained the support of numerous peers. The case attracted enough public interest for the press to attend. Alan Leo's first problems with the law occurred in 1911 while he was in India. A man giving the name of Hugh McLean called at the Modern Astrology offices and said that complaints had been made that work was being sent out while Leo was abroad. Although Leo was informed, he didn't think it was anything to worry about. At that time, there was no way that he could have known that Detective Inspector Hugh McLean was acting on behalf of the City of London Police.

McLean's name was to intrude in Leo's life a second time. In April 1914, Leo received a summons to attend the Magistrates court at Mansion House, London to answer a charge of fortune-telling.

> Information has been laid this day by Hugh McLean of the City of London Police for THAT YOU on the 27th day of February 1914 did UNLAWFULLY PRETEND TO TELL FORTUNES to DECEIVE and IMPOSE upon the said Hugh McLean and others of his Majesty's subjects contrary to the Statute... YOU ARE THEREFORE hereby summoned... at the MANSION HOUSE on Wednesday the 6th of May at 11:15 am.

By 1914, Leo had been working as an astrologer, and publishing magazines and books, for almost twenty-five years. He had no reason to think that he was likely to fall on the wrong side of the law at this late stage of his career. Leo had been completing his jury service when he received the summons and assumed that the visit on 29 April from two "gentlemen" who had called "from the Jury" was related in some way. Leo asked that the men be shown in whereupon they handed him the summons. He was a little taken aback and asked who Hugh

McLean was. The detective handing over the summons said that it was him and Leo responded:

> I have never seen you before: I do not tell fortunes.
>
> (*Belfast Telegraph*, 20 May 1914, p.4)

He then opened his office door to see the men out. Although Leo didn't consider himself to be in any particular danger, after thinking it over, he decided to consult Kingsley Bayley, his solicitor. Bayley took the matter seriously and advised Leo that going to prison as a martyr for the cause was probably not the best idea he'd had. They were too many prison martyrs already.

On 1 May, Leo gave instructions to the solicitors firm of Mann & Cramp, and agreed to W.R. Warren being appointed as barrister. He turned up to Mansion House on 6 May, ready to fight the charges. Journalists and a large crowd of character witnesses, including Annie Besant and A.P. Sinnett were in attendance.

Mansion House was a magistrate's court, presided over by the Lord Mayor of London, the chief magistrate. Numerous high profile cases were heard here. The official residence of the Lord Mayor, Mansion House is fronted by six fluted Corinthian columns and is an imposing and grand enough building to worry even those confident of their innocence. Leo was charged with having told fortunes on both 27 February and 8 April 1914. He pleaded not guilty.

Mr Vickery, the prosecuting solicitor, began by pointing out that three years ago Leo had been cautioned by the police. When the police found out he was in Madras, they told Leo's clerk, who was working in the office, that he should tell Leo that casting horoscopes and fortune-telling through astrology was an offence. Nothing further happened until in February 1914, when McLean wrote to Leo asking for a list of charges for horoscopes. He received in response a letter and a booklet entitled *The Stars and How to Read Them*. The letter outlined the various charges for horoscopes, ranging from five shillings to five guineas, the latter offering forecasts for ten years. McLean sent off for a ten shilling horoscope. For his money McLean received a *Delineation of*

*Nativity*, and the advice that he could either purchase a more detailed judgment or add to it himself by studying Leo's books *The Key to Your Own Nativity* or *The Progressed Horoscope*.

The section of the report entitled *Future Prospects* was read out in court. Warren, acting for Leo, pointed out that when the letter was sent, Leo was abroad and couldn't have written it. It didn't help that McClean assumed the name of 'William Hammond' in his correspondence. The case was dismissed, but costs were refused. The second summons was then considered. Again, Warren pointed out that there was no evidence that Leo had any knowledge of the horoscope sent to McLean, or that it was sent under his authority. The Lord Mayor felt obliged to dismiss the charge, although he said:

> I am fully convinced in my own mind that there is no doubt that it is endeavoring to tell fortunes.
>
> (*Times*, 7 May 1914)

Costs were again refused. Oddly, Leo developed a liking for McLean, and actually said that he felt sorry for him when he lost the case. Leo's trial was covered widely in the press and an issue of *Modern Astrology* was devoted to discussing its ramifications. Although Leo wasn't convicted of fortune-telling, it was a weak victory to have the case dismissed on a technicality. Eventually the fuss died down and it seemed that everyone could simply get on with the business of supplying horoscopes – except that in 1917 Leo was again summonsed to appear at Mansion House and again pleaded not guilty to the charge of fortune-telling.

> A 'bomb' more cruel that the German air raider's bomb fell into the astrological camp at 11.5 a.m. on July 2nd, when we were served with a summons to appear at the Mansion House at 11:30 a.m. on July 9th on a charge of 'pretending and professing to tell fortunes.'
>
> (*Modern Astrology*, September 1917, p.257)

As soon as Leo sought legal advice, he was told to find people who would be willing to act as character witnesses. In response to the hundred letters he sent, Leo received seventy-three replies during the week before the case was heard. A number of people agreed to speak on Leo's behalf in court, amongst them the theosophists A.P. Sinnett and Maud Sharpe.

The case was broadly similar to the one brought in 1914. An Inspector Nicholls had ordered a five guinea horoscope, which when it arrived was found to contain predictions for the next ten years. This time the case against Leo was treated more seriously. Despite the efforts of Leo's defence, the magistrate refused to allow discussions as to the validity of astrology. Leo was defended by Ernest Wild and the same Mr Warren who had appeared for him previously.

Leo's defence was that his report showed only tendencies and shouldn't be defined as fortune-telling as that involved making a specific statement about the future. This approach may have succeeded if it weren't for one sentence in the report sent to Nicholls:

> At this time a death in your family circle is likely to cause you sorrow.
>
> (*Times*, 7 May 1914)

Was the death a tendency, or was there a tendency towards death? The prosecution wasted no time in asking this question. Although the remainder of the hundred-page report adhered to the tenet that the stars inclined rather than compelled, this sentence lost the case for Leo.

The hearing, which was adjourned for a week, ended in a nominal fine of £5 and £25 costs, over £1000 in today's terms. At that time, the maximum sentence possible was three month's imprisonment – including hard labour, so Leo got off a lot more lightly than he might have done. There was no doubt in the mind of the press that he was guilty and that his conviction was just:

> The result of the prosecution should make clear beyond any doubt that in the eyes of the law the scientific astrologer is just as much a rogue and vagabond as any gipsy woman who asks you to cross her hand with

a piece of silver. There is, of course, a vast gulf between Mr Leo and the majority of the horoscope merchants. The element of imposition was lacking in his case. He could and no doubt did draw up horoscopes scientifically accurate. Where he went wrong was in interpreting his maps for money. Rightly, I think, our laws decrees this to be an offence, for whether such interpretations are honest in intention or otherwise, they are equally likely to be harmful to persons credulous enough to believe them. Mr Leo or any other astrologer has, of course, a right to believe in and practice astrology, but he must not make his living by it.

(*Modern Astrology*, September 1917, p.259)

Leo originally planned to appeal against the decision, but decided against it as his chances of success were low. Instead, Leo travelled with his wife Bessie to Bude in Cornwall for their annual holiday. While there, he was taken ill and died on 30 August 1917. Many of his supporters blamed the case for his death and viewed the authorities as murderers.

The situation was no different in the USA, where Evangeline Adams was prosecuted for fortune-telling in 1914 for the second time. Adele Priess, who was part of the Detective Bureau of the New York Police, visited Adams on 13 May 1914 and had her horoscope read. Priess stated that Adams had written on a circle marked on a piece of paper. She then read Priess' palms. Adams also drew up horoscopes for Priess' two daughters and her son, described their characters and made predictions. She charged five dollars for her work saying that she would perform a reading for Priess' daughter for three dollars if they called back that evening.

When challenged in court, Adams was more specific in her description of what happened. She described how she had used books of tables to estimate Priess' ascendant, although she agreed that she read her palms. Adams gave an analysis of Priess' horoscope and described in court the details of the planetary positions she considered. She said that she hadn't drawn up Priess' daughter's chart but had simply looked at the planetary positions in her ephemeris and made a few comments. Adams was extremely careful to explain that she could only describe possibilities and did not say what was going to happen. Rather than trying to foretell an event, she said that all she did was to explain the positions of the planets and read their indications. She treated astrology as a science and went about her work in a mechanical fashion.

According to Adams' counsel, although fortune-telling was clearly against the law, not every astrologer was a fortune-teller. There was a difference between someone who told the future and someone who explained what ought to happen. Adams was finally acquitted. The oft-quoted story that Adams prepared a horoscope of the Judge's son and impressed him so much that he dismissed the case is simply not true. This version of events didn't emerge until ten years after the case.

And then came the war and the world changed forever. Fortune-tellers and their activities were a low priority over the years following Leo's and Adam's trials. Although astrology regained its popularity in the post war years, it seemed that people had forgotten that it was technically illegal. There were more important things for most people to worry about. But astrologers themselves hadn't forgotten.

# 15

## Popular Astrology in the 1920s

In the unsettled years following the horrors of World War I, Europe entered 'The Age of Anxiety'. Although the military crisis was over, the economic crisis remained, along with a crisis of the mind. No longer did people dwell on the growing enlightenment of their times, but instead they focused on the anxiety they felt about their existence, their culture, and their destiny. This sense of despair, bitterness, and anxiety led to a literary revolution and numerous artistic movements springing up. In all of these, the theme was broadly similar – to abandon tradition, experiment with the unknown, change the rules, dare to be different, and innovate. The values of Western civilisation were seen as a sham and, in a world devoid of values, all that was left was to try something new.

With the radical change in society, many of the earlier boundaries had broken down. In the late 1920s and early 1930s there were about a quarter of a million practising spiritualists and almost two thousand spiritualist societies in the UK. A number of prominent figures who adopted spiritualism, including the physicist Oliver Lodge and writer Arthur Conan Doyle, fostered the cause still further. Although numerous people turned to spiritualism anew following the war, others sought something less religiously and spiritually based. Fortune-tellers were regularly consulted, and astrology, having been made more accessible by the works of writers such as Leo and Cheiro, had grown into a form that could be as disposable and simplistic as palmistry and card reading.

Throughout Europe, interest in astrology increased, especially in Germany. Astrology was now regarded by many as a science, and while the Germans experimented with new theories designed to bring astrology into the twentieth century, the French tried to justify astrology on a statistical basis. The nature of science itself had undergone a rapid change. Relativity and quantum theories had shattered the purely materialistic universe and anything seemed possible. Astrologers were worried about what the public at large understood of their science.

> When I speak of the science of astrology I mean the real and true science, that which is based on the laws of nature and is therefore of Divine Origin, and not that mass of superstition which is paraded before the world by people who pose as astrologers, and have not the faintest idea of the subject they pretend to use.
>
> (*British Journal of Astrology*, July 1930, p.200)

But while students of astrology fought to gain respect and disassociate themselves from any suggestion that their work was related to fortune telling, the public at large were unbothered by such nuances and were hungry for astrology in whatever form they could get it.

Books that listed the zodiac signs and outlined how they described your character had been around for years but started to become more popular. They were, and are, largely unchanged in the information they offered abut each sign, although modern readers might be a little surprised to find that as an Aquarian your colours are green and pink (specifically, Nile green and salmon pink). Today they'd be firmly told it's electric blue or turquoise.

This British press was to either report on astrology seriously, often with a delineation of a chart, or to devote a few column inches to how terrible it was that people were taken in by such bunk – the most common derisory term applied to astrology. In the US newspaper astrology hardly changed in the 1920s, although it became even more widespread. So widespread that everyone knew that Americans were hungry for popular astrology.

> It is amazing how widespread is the astrological hokum let loose on America. I know a love-sick fellow who consults the daily horoscope in a newspaper to see when Venus is in the ascendant; and, when she is, he writes or telephones the girl who continues to reject him in favour of a rival! He will not take "no" for an answer and he intends to work in harmony with the stars until she changes her mind...
>
> (*Liverpool Echo*, 6 December 1924, p.12)

It was almost impossible to find a newspaper that *didn't* feature an astrological column. Lengthy articles describing what your Sun sign meant and what gems you should wear also became common. Some astrologers featured in the press were renowned in astrological circles, such as Grace Ellery Williams who was part of the Academy of Astrologians and was acquitted of fortune telling in 1928. Some were journalists who'd slipped into writing an astrology column. These women – because they were all women – became celebrities. For example, Elsa Allen wrote for the Bell Syndicate from 1922 and her columns appeared in the *Philadelphia Inquirer*, *Brooklyn Daily Eagle*, *San Francisco Examiner* and the *Akron Beacon Journal* (Ohio) until 1934. Writing about what you should expect if today was your birthday, she mentioned Sun signs in her columns.

> Indeed, you are intensely sensitive to all Zodiac forces, and should restrict your dealings to those born under your congenial signs – Aries, March 21 to April 19, and Sagittarius, November 22 to December 21...
>
> (*San Francisco Examiner*, 6 February 1922, p.11)

Mary Blake's columns appeared in the *Buffalo Courier*; *Miami News*; *Times* (Louisiana); *Evening Star* (Washington); *San Francisco Examiner*; the *Missoulian*; *Tuscon Citizen*; *Knoxville Journal*; *Courier Journal* (Kentucky) and the *Salt Lake Tribune*. Her columns continued to appear until the 1940s. Also offering birthday predictions, her columns were headed with the name of the relevant sign and often contained a lot of astrological detail. She was still writing her columns unchanged until at least 1941.

Scorpio.

The planetary aspect of today is a good influence developing from Venus, reaching its greatest degree of power at eventide.

(*San Francisco Examiner*, 18 November 1924, p.12)

Doris Blake's columns first appeared in 1915. Actually the journalist Antoinette Donnelly (1887–1964), she wrote for 45 newspapers served by the New York *Daily News* and *Chicago Tribune* syndicate. Originally from Ontario, Donnelly moved to New York in 1898 and later became a stenographer. She became an assistant to the woman's page editor on the *Chicago Tribune* in 1919 and later took over the beauty column and problem page. Her first astrology columns in October 1921 were unattributed but by December they were bylined 'Doris Blake'. After mentioning an astrological configurations, she proceeded to make numerous predictions for the day, focusing on business and politics.

This is a rather uncertain day according to astrology. While Jupiter and Mercury are in benefic aspect, Saturn is adverse... Sensational speeches and renewal of power are foreshadowed for a man prominent in politics...

(*Washington Herald*, 9 December 1921, p.20)

People expected to be told what their birthday meant, and Donnelly didn't disappoint them:

If your birthday is today you are

PRACTICAL

You are intensely interested in the practical things of life. You have to fight this side of nature to get the best out of life. Even when you marry it will be done after a practical commn sense deliberation in which romance does not have to be dominant. You are inclined to melancholy at times, as too much of the practical and not enough of the lighter vein will eventually make one.

(*Daily News*, New York, 2 January 1922, p.33)

She wrote a number of articles describing the Sun signs through the 1920s, pointing out:

Whether you believe in astrology or not, there are few who are not interested in the characteristics accredited by astrologers to their birth month.

(*Daily News*, New York, 27 January 1929, p.57)

Donnelly wrote the column 'Beauty Answers' for the *Daily News* and other papers and in 1920, she wrote one of the first books about weight loss – *How to Reduce: New Waistlines for Old*. She also wrote numerous advice articles. Doris Blake's five times weekly radio shows for WMCA, New York reached audiences of more than 10 million by 1940. By the end of her career, Donnelly had been featured in 422 newspapers. She went down in history for her problem pages and beauty tips. However, her astrology columns are rarely mentioned. It was no secret that she wrote them, although she didn't call herself an astrologer – the *Daily News* referred to her as a 'characterologist' and 'personal advice editor'. Donnelly retired in 1962 and died in Greenwich, Connecticut in 1964.

More charismatic than the above was Belle Bart (Belle Dulany born 18 August 1892 as Bella Flam; Bart was her first husband's name). Her astrology columns appeared in the *Detroit Free Press,* and she ran the American Academy of Astrology with her husband (William) J. Clark Dulany and Edward Daniels. She'd been taught astrology by Evangeline Adams, saw numerous moneyed clients and gave lectures on astrology as well as writing her columns. Her reputation wasn't helped when in 1926 she predicted that Edwin S. Vare would be elected to office in 1927. The problem was that he'd died in 1922.

Belle offered mail order horoscopes from May 1922, and in 1923 when she became an astrology columnist, she was announced as the youngest astrologer by removing several years from her age and claiming to be nineteen. She immediately launched into giving radio shows and Belle's first astrology articles were long and detailed, delineating full charts and discussing planetary configurations. She soon settled into providing daily predictions accompanied by a delineation of the Sun sign for the day, and her columns were syndicated from 1926.

> TODAY IS inauspicious for dealing in any new ventures or attempting risks of any kind. There is a tendency toward upset conditions, making it more profitable to put off important work until a later date... If you were born on November 16, you have an intense mystic nature with marked insight into any scientific and mechanical fields. It will be necessary for you at all times to indulge in music as this will give you the equilibrium essential for your best activities. You will be more successful when following your intuitions than when guided by the advice of others. You should avoid forcing an issue until you are positively sure that the road is clear for so doing, since obstacles may have the tendency to cause a laxity of interest in a particular venture...
>
> (*Windsor Star,* Ontario, 16 November 1916, p.2)

Belle spent huge amounts of money and a lot of time in court. In 1928 she was cleared of embezzlement after being accused of stealing a diamond ring worth $18,000 that belonged to her stepdaughter. Charges of forgery and that she and her husband were confidence tricksters were also brought. Belle's husband was in court in 1930 after not paying child support to his second wife – Belle being his third. He said he hadn't made any money in the last two years and relied on Belle's income. She commented:

> When I married Mr. Dulany... I told him my chart was definitely the stronger and that he must follow my direction.
>
> (*San Francisco Examiner,* 7 April 1935, p.107)

He did at first, and they bought a large house in New York City, filled it with expensive antiques and set up the American Academy of Astrology. But when Dulany stopped listening to Belle's astral guidance, their money problems began in earnest. Falling bankrupt in 1931, Belle decided the influences in California would be better and moved there. It was a complete coincidence that by doing so she avoided prison. The $400,000 worth of notes Belle and her husband had issued against property was found to be insufficient security. After $300,000 worth had been sold, a court order was issued restraining them from selling more. Belle and Dulany ignored this and were found guilty of contempt of court. In 1935 she returned to New York where she spent three months in prison, which she accepted stoically. Belle continued to make predictions and appear on radio throughout the 1930s. She divorced Dulany in 1936 and continued to work as an astrologer until the early 1940s. It's unclear when she died.

Possibly the most famous of them all was Genevieve Kemble. Born 13 July 1867 in San Francisco, California as Genevieve Hogan, she married Paul Kemble (brother of the illustrator Edward Winsor Kemble) in 1889 and moved to New York. In 1901 Kemble disappeared – it appears that he simply walked out on Genevieve. A year later it was reported that he'd died of a heart attack at a station while with his 'wife' and nine-month old child. (This unidentified wife claimed to have married him two years prior and is clearly Genevieve's replacement.)

It was around this time that Genevieve took up astrology, and in 1904 she married John Hazelrigg. An ex-actor who'd studied with Luke Broughton, Hazelrigg was already renowned as an astrologer and is often credited with being one of the revitalisers of astrology in the US. Both Genevieve and Hazelrigg were part of the Temple of the People, a theosophical offshoot that was formed in New York but moved to Halcyon, California in 1903. Astrologers primarily remember Hazelrigg as one of the founders of the *American Academy of Astrologians* in 1916. And in August of that year, Genevieve's article 'What do the Stars have to do with it?' was syndicated throughout the US and

Canada. In 1917 her horoscope columns began to appear and were featured in the appearing in the *Washington Post, Dayton Herald, Indianapolis Star, Tulsa Democrat, Calgary Herald, Arizona Daily Star* and elsewhere. They comprised a paragraph or two outlining planetary configurations for the day in question.

> THIS being the day of the new moon it is auspicious for undertaking near ventures of whatsoever nature. Never begin a thing with the moon on the wane as it is then losing in magnetic attraction, tending to dissipate and diffuse and not to promote or increase. Therefore, push all interests especially new deals and undertakings but use cool judgment as the quarrelsome Mars tends to rashness haste and disputes...
> (*Lexignton Herald*, Kentucky, 18 February 1917, p.23)

From time to time, Genevieve also wrote about Sun signs in feature articles, but she primarily focused on daily predictions. In the late 1920s, she headed her columns with quotes from Hazelrigg's work but by then they'd separated. Genevieve reverted to her previous name and Hazelrigg, who lived with his twin brother Oliver, claimed he'd been widowed, suggesting theirs wasn't a totally amicable separation. Genevieve's horoscopes continued to appear, and were widely syndicated (initially by the Newspaper Feature Service and later by Associated Newspapers), until the mid-1950s. They were largely unchanged throughout, although in 1937 she produced a twelve-sign column. She claimed never to have cast a horoscope but to have focused solely on producing her columns, but she did occasionally write lengthy astrological features. Genevieve died 20 December 1958 in Alameda, California.

Although Sun sign astrology occasionally featured in the British press (especially in the *Daily Mirror*), it was usually limited to character readings for people born that day.

> Are you a November child? If your birthday is in this month – that latter part of it at least – your lucky star is Saturn. Saturn people are

supposed to be quiet and rather reserved, but have deep feelings and love to spend their days surrounded by the people they love.

(*Daily Mirror* 18 Nov 1924, p.11)

A rare example of a British newspaper column that made predictions in this period was from C. E. (Charles Everard) Mitchell (1883-1967) who wrote for the *Halifax Evening Courier* in the late 1920s. He'd previously sold the 'desketter' a 'useful desk companion and message recorder'. When his company failed at the end of 1924, he needed something new to do and happened on astrology, which he often used to give financial advice. After sending his astrological views to the *Courier* in 1926, he (initially under the name of 'Havarah Durkee' based on the names of nearby places) produced a column that ran through 1927-8. After that his predictions, mainly centred on local politics, continued to appear at intervals. He gained some (mainly local) fame for correctly predicting a plane accident in 1933. However, Mitchell's 'daily horoscope' was also a Sun sign reading for people born on that date:

> If to-morrow (April 2) is your birthday, you are altogether too non-provokable, and long-suffering for your own good: you allow others to browbeat you and take advantage, in many different ways, of a thrustfulness beyond belief, a credulity that is rare, and a patience that out-Jobs that of Job.
>
> (*Halifax Evening Courier*, 1 April 1927, p.4)

Mitchell's column was sensible (if sometimes on the dull side), and it surely couldn't be such astrology that provoked the *Daily Mail* to say in 1928:

> Investigations made during the last few weeks by The Daily Mail have disclosed the practice in London of the ancient art of fortune-telling, now thinly disguised by pseudo-medical terms, and on a scale believed to be unprecedented in modern times.
>
> (*Daily Mail*, 11 June 1928, p.13)

Serious astrologers were equally as disapproving. The interests of the public at large weren't their concern and they sought to defend and retain the quality of astrology. They shivered with horror at the thought of being called 'fortune tellers' and desperately tried to dissociate themselves from clairvoyants and palmists. The law didn't recognise the difference. In a report on the Astrological Congress of 1927, the *British Journal of Astrology* described:

> A very spirited protest against the prosecution of astrologers for fortune telling and urged the meeting to take steps to obtain a repeal of the Clause of the Vagrant Act, which is put into operation, and wrongly so, against astrologers.
>
> (*British Journal of Astrology*, September 1927, p.7)

The legal status of astrology continued to be a problem, and the outcome of this type of campaigning will be addressed further on. However, a greater worry for many astrologers was the effect of the newly arising Sun sign astrology that they ran into at every turn.

> It is quite popular teaching, but one which is diametrically opposed to astrology that people with the Sun in one sign should always marry another with the Sun in a signs that is sextile or trine to it. No genuine astrologer would ever put forward such and utterly erroneous or unscientific theory.
>
> (*British Journal of Astrology*, July 1928, p.1)

Not everyone who was new to astrology, and whose interest had been piqued through reading Sun sign interpretations, was satisfied to restrict their knowledge to that level. Anxious to learn more, a number of fledgling astrologers discovered the astrological societies that had been quietly working away in the background all along. They soon found that they weren't always welcome amongst the middle and upper middle class astrologers who made up the bulk of those involved in serious astrology.

> I am told that certain people will not come to astrological meetings because they have to sit with people who are dowdily dressed and not in the same social 'set' as themselves. Also insinuations are made that those who take an active part in these meetings are 'neglectful of their personal appearance' and come in their 'working clothes'.
>
> (*British Journal of Astrology*, August 1929, p.161)

This class barrier was observed by many, including the clairvoyant and writer Nell St John Montague (we will meet her properly in the next chapter). Although she mixed in society, and came from a wealthy, colonial family, Nell's career didn't so much as open doors, but often slammed them in her face. In her memoirs she described turning up to give a reading as requested at a smart house, to find that she was treated with derision and told:

> I always thought clairvoyantees [*sic*] were black.
>
> (Montague, p.267)

Although clairvoyance, palmistry, astrology, and similar practices were becoming acceptable in some circles, it would still take some time before they gained any sort of respectability, no matter how hard practitioners tried to attain it.

> There are deep rooted prejudices in the minds of many people against the encouragement of clairvoyants, mediums and all who are supposed to practice the superstitious arts or deal in 'black magic'.
>
> (p.176)

One of the most deep-rooted of all prejudices came to the fore in Britain when popular astrology found a new home. It featured in story magazines aimed towards young working women. It was written by women and for women. Just as in the US, popular astrology was women's business.

After the First World War, the women's press changed drastically. The earlier magazines directed towards the upper classes, which had dominated the industry, gave way to an increasing number of magazines that catered for the middle and working classes. Amongst these were story papers. Boys' story papers continued to sell in their original form until after the Second World War but were gradually replaced by comic books. The last remaining boys' story paper, *The Rover*, ceased publication in 1973. However, those aimed towards a female readership joined the ever-increasing number of women's magazines.

Women's magazines had a huge audience in the 1920s. Sales figures were high – for example, *Woman's Weekly* sold about 380,000 and *Home Chat* 200,000 issues a year. The readership was even higher – magazines were commonly shared. As George Orwell said:

> The women's papers... are read for the most part by girls who are working for a living. Consequently they are on the surface much more realistic. It is taken for granted, for example, that nearly everyone has to live in a big town and work at a more or less dull job. Sex, so far from being taboo, is the subject. The short, complete stories, the special feature of these papers, are generally of the 'came the dawn' type: the heroine narrowly escapes losing her 'boy' to a designing rival, or the 'boy' loses his job and has to postpone marriage, but presently gets a better job... The idea is to give the bored factory-girl or worn-out mother of five a dream-life in which she pictures herself — not actually as a duchess (that convention has gone out) but as, say, the wife of a bank-manager...
>
> (Orwell)

From the end of the First World War, such magazines frequently included fortune telling content – including astrology. (Aspirational, fashion, home maker and society magazines rarely carried such content.) Unlike today when a horoscope column often hides at the back of a magazine, such content was often in a prominent position, often in the first few pages, and could be a full page or more in length.

*Home Companion*, which had been launched in 1897, contained a column giving daily predictions in 1922, headed 'The fortunes of the days', a clear forerunner of the modern horoscope column, although it didn't describe it as astrological.

> January 10th – An excellent day for a journey, especially one by road. Blue-eyed people who were born in April may expect to meet long lost friends.
>
> (*Home Companion*, 4 January 1922, p.12)

In December 1922 it also offered 'birthday readings' for the following year, based on Sun signs. Like all such magazines, *Home Companion* featured a variety of fortune-telling articles. Like most magazines of its type, *Home Companion* offered dream interpretations and a free dream book in 1928. In an attempt to be different, it also offer red 'Gypsy Zillah's fate balloons' as a free gift on 13 August 1922. Precisely how you used these balloons with numbers on to tell your fortune is unknown as they and their instructions haven't survived.

But Gypsy Zillah probably knew what she was doing. Numerous fortune telling articles were written either by 'gypsies', or at least by a young woman who wore a headscarf and large hooped earrings, assuming the drawings that headed such columns were true.

Madame Astral of *Betty's Paper* was represented in this way. First published 11 November 1922, *Betty's Paper* featured on its cover a sheikh looking smoulderingly at the swooning woman in his arms and readers were promised 'a thrilling story of love and passion in the mystic east'. It was an added bonus that Madame Astral could tell you if your dreams would come true if you wrote to her. She also offered card readings, advised on lucky colours (according to your birthdate) and could analyse your handwriting or read your palm. She was always ready to use her clairvoyant skills to help you solve your problems. Of course, Madame Astral knew her Sun signs.

> If you were not Born in November, you are sure to have a Chum who would just Love to Read this Article
>
> Girls who are lucky at this season of the year have this gift: they can get nearly all their wishes granted if they practise self-restraint and do not become too sure of themselves. The fair November girl is luckier in love than in business, but once she marries the man she truly loves, Providence will guard her from money troubles...
>
> (*Betty's Paper*, 24 November 1923)

In *Pam's Paper* of 1923, Zarah offered to consult the stars on your behalf if you sent in a coupon and pointed out:

> I was born under a star which gave to all born under it wonderful powers.
>
> (*Pam's Paper*, 1 December 1922)

Zarah also read cards and interpreted dreams in her column 'What do the stars say?' *Pam's Paper* additionally included articles on charms you could use to increase your luck and advised you how to read your tea leaves.

*Home Chat* in 1924 discussed your nativity and birth number. It also offered hidden Sun sign interpretations. In January 1930, you could receive an analysis of your character if you sent in a clip of your hair – accompanied by your birth date.

*Poppy's Paper* offered a free birthday book with its 23 February 1924 issue. It already featured regular articles about palmistry and dream interpretation when on 2 August 1924 it announced its new astrology column by 'Greta, the chief witch of Wembley'. Greta briskly explained your character according to your Sun sign in a series of articles.

> The girl whose birthday falls between July 21st and August 21st is born under Leo, the Lion, and her ruling planet is the sun. ...
>
> (*Poppy's Paper*, 9 August 1924)

By October 1924 you could read your daily predictions:

> November 2nd – One of the few really unlucky days this month. Wear a piece of ivory as an amulet against danger.
>
> *(Poppy's Paper*, 1 November 1924)

Although the content suggests this column was based on Sun sign predictions, it wasn't described as such. It was a short-lived column, replaced by a series of articles about the meaning of your name on 17 October 1925.

*Poppy's Paper* featured numerous offers to read your fate, even roping in film stars to share their mystical knowledge – for example, on 8 February 1924 Ramon Navarro offered his 'Persian dream book' as a free gift.

The symbols we are used to seeing for the zodiac signs didn't commonly appear in these articles. However, *Red Letter* in its column 'When is your birthday?' on 26 January 1924 used the illustrations were familiar with today, for example, a set of scales for Libra.

In 1927 *Girls' Mirror*'s 'Mystic Myrella' began to produce its astrological calendar:

> November 19 (Monday) – No special influence is connected with this day.
>
> 20 (Tuesday) – Not good.
>
> 21 (Wednesday)- Good for buying and selling.
>
> 22 (Thursday – Be careful. Do not start any fresh undertaking.
>
> The influence of Sagittarius begins
>
> *(Girls' Mirror*, 5 November 1928)

Mystic Myrella also helpfully contributed articles on palmistry, ghosts, handwriting, and reading moles.

In *Woman's Life* of 1928 Madame Zizma offered a free birthday forecast, and that same year *Woman's Weekly* featured a set of articles that explained your character by your birthday. *Red Star Weekly* embraced astrology with enthusiasm from its launch in 1929, and Madame Zodiac advised you which type of man to marry according to your sign as well as your lucky number and colour in a series of lengthy articles entitled 'Follow Your Star'.

But all the above fade into insignificance when we consider the hugely popular and influential *Peg's Paper*.

*Peg's Paper* first appeared in 1919 and continued until 1940. Aimed at young working class girls, it featured lurid fiction with sheikhs and viscounts bumping into girls on their way to the shops. From the start, fortune telling and prediction made up a large part of its content. 'Your Woman of Mystery' provided character readings using a variety of methods, including analysing the shape of your nose. But most importantly, she wanted to know 'is your birthday this week?' If it was, Your Woman of Mystery had plenty to tell you.

> Those girls who were born during this week from the 30th of May to the 5th of June are generally very lucky in their love affairs...
>
> (*Peg's Paper*, 29 May 1919)

In addition to its regular columns, *Peg's* Paper also offered astrology in its numerous free gifts. For example, its fortune telling book that was given away with the 4 December 1929 issue pointed out:

> The January girl ... should be very careful whom she marries, for she was not born under a very lucky star, and should she marry a man born under similar astral influences, or under any other which will not affect her future beneficially, great misery would be the result. She should never marry a sailor...and she should never choose a man born in March, June or December. She should particularly avoid a man whose eyes are not straight, or who squints in the very slightest degree...

On 18 May 1921 Your Woman of Mystery replaced her Sun sign character descriptions with daily predictions.

> Wednesday 11th May This is a lucky day for the business girl and she should chose to-day to ask for any special privilege. It is unlucky for

lovers, and especially so for a meeting near running water, or for an excursion on the river.

(*Peg's Paper*, 17 May 1921)

Although the format of the column changed from time to time, it consistently offered Sun sign astrology, although it was referred to by such terms as 'your birthday luck'.

On 4 December 1923 the first column appeared by Nell St John Montague. Nell used an impressively comprehensive number of methods to tell your fortune over the coming week. She often gazed into her crystal or read cards or dominoes, but if you sent in a coupon to ask for her personal attention, you generally needed to include your birth date. Although usually described as a clairvoyant, Nell sprinkled Sun sign interpretations throughout her articles.

Born Eleanor Lucie-Smith in India (27 June 1875), Nell married Irish judge Henry Standish-Barry in 1899. Her working life began when she wrote *The Irish Lead* (1916), a play she directed and acted in to raise funds for Irish prisoners-of-war. This led to a brief acting career and she starred in *An Interrupted Divorce* and her own plays *The Barrier* and *Room 7*. She later appeared in silent films including *The Glorious Adventure* (1922) and *A Gipsy Cavalier* (1923).

It was shortly after this that Nell emerged as a professional 'clairvoyante', although she was already known for her skills. She claimed her powers had been learned from the Maharajah and mystic fakirs from her early years in India. One of her most famous predictions was that Lord Kitchener would die at sea. He was drowned a few weeks later in 1916.

Nell wrote for multiple magazines, including *Woman's Friend* in 1924, *Poppy's Paper* in 1925, *Lucky Star* in 1935 and *Prediction* in 1936. She was so popular that in one week in 1927 she received over 10,000 letters. She even made inroads into television – in 1932, she appeared on a BBC programme as a palmist.

In addition to her magazine and newspaper writing, Nell made personal appearances, dressing up as a gypsy. She was instantly recognisable at the many society events she attended, always wearing her black satin headband and often carrying her pet monkey, Judy, which she said brought her good luck. She died in 1944, reputedly after predicting her own death. Nell was so famous that the war memorial in the East Sussex village of Bishopstone includes both her real name and her pen name. Many people believed she had been a spy.

Nell's columns continued in *Peg's Paper* into the late 1930s, after it had merged with *Glamour*. But she never displaced Your Woman of Mystery, who continued to offer daily predictions and Sun sign character readings throughout the 1920s.

> Those whose birthday falls this week are often gifted artistically, many poets and musicians having been born under this week's ruling planet.... The lucky number is eight and lucky day Monday... this is a lucky week for marriages but not for widows, who should put off a second marriage until luna rules the heavens
>
> (*Peg's Paper*, 14 August 1928)

It was also Nell who provided the answer to the question as to why popular astrology featured so heavily in these magazines. Right from the start, women's magazines featured problem pages. (Indeed, the first ever magazine aimed towards a female audience, the *The Ladies' Mercury* in 1693, featured a problem page.) All the magazines discussed above featured problem pages. Magazines intended for a higher class readership that didn't carry astrology or fortune telling articles also didn't carry problem pages.

Sometimes the answers to those problems featured astrological solutions, based on the reader's Sun sign. The association was made more obvious on 7 January 1928 when *Woman's Friend* featured the first of a regular column where Nell answered readers' problems using her 'second sight'. Nell would go on to write problem pages in *Peg's Paper* and *Lucky Star* in the mid-1930s. Other writers for women's magazines also crossed over. Jill Craigie, the documentary film maker and future wife of MP Michael Foot, wrote for *Betty's Paper* in the early 1930s. She was both the astrologer 'Professor Philastro' and the writer of the problem page.

Astrology was both entertainment and a way of solving your problems. It sat happily amongst beauty, fashion and domestic tips, offering insight into how you could resolve your personality issues and learn to better understand yourself.

By the end of the 1920s, women (and their men friends who made up a substantial number of readers of these magazines) were already familiar with Sun sign delineations, and were used to receiving promotional gifts of cheap jewellery, lucky charms and books based on Sun signs. Sometimes it was called numerology, sometimes clairvoyance or fate reading. But it was Sun sign astrology and there was plenty of it.

# 16

# Cheiro

Cheiro was the greatest seer of modern times; the greatest palmist ever known, mixing with the good and the great. Legends abound about his predictive abilities, including those he supposedly made about the abdication of King Edward VIII, the deaths of Queen Victoria and Edward VII, the fate of the Czar of Russia and his family, the assassination of Italy's King Humbert, the assassination attempt on the Shah of Persia, and the death of Lord Kitchener. In his lifetime, Cheiro was an international celebrity.

His life is shrouded in myths of his own invention. Cheiro began life as William John Warner born in Bray near Dublin, Ireland on 1 November 1866. He was the son of William Warner, a schoolteacher who believed he'd traced his family back to the Hamons of Normandy – hence Cheiro's later use of the title 'Count'. The myth surrounding 'Count Hamon' became powerful enough for Cheiro to be listed under that name in *Who was Who* as the son of William de Hamon and Mlle Dumas. Cheiro called himself 'Louis'. In the late 1890s, he was 'Leigh de Hamong', which he later changed to its French form of 'Louis Hamon', the name he adopted legally in 1918.

Several versions of Cheiro's early life circulated: apparently he was kidnapped by gypsies when young and they exploited his clairvoyant gifts. Or his mother had been a palmist and interested in astrology, passing on her skills to her talented son. Alternatively, or perhaps additionally, he spent some time in India studying palmistry and astrology, where he viewed an astrological book written on human skin that was more than a thousand years old. While in India he survived on a diet of fruit and rice while living for two years in a cave temple. And another time he was trapped within an ancient Egyptian tomb. There's no evidence he visited Egypt or India, but these tales were part of Cheiro's identity and are really good ripping yarns. He did, however, own a mummy's hand.

Cheiro claimed he met Helena Blavatsky in March 1889.

> I received a message saying Madame Blavatsky would like me to call on her that evening at nine o'clock. Without a moment's hesitation, I accepted. I considered myself highly honoured in being asked to meet such a remarkable woman, of whose doings the papers had been full for many years.
>
> (Cheiro, *Mysteries*, p.170)

According to Cheiro, Blavatsky informed him that he was a reincarnation of Cagliostro, the eighteenth century occultist. She then went on to make a number of predictions about Cheiro's life, saying he would travel widely and influence royalty. On his second visit, the next day, Blavatsky asked Cheiro to predict the date of her death. He forecast that she would die a little beyond the age of fifty-eight – in other words she hadn't long to live. Blavatsky died two years later at the age of sixty. Cheiro said he refused her invitation to join the Theosophical Society, although he did accept a letter of introduction to Annie Besant. Maybe he really did meet Blavatsky – it wouldn't have been much of an achievement as Blavatsky met an enormous number of people.

In reality, Louis moved permanently to London in 1891 and joined the Princess's Theatre company as an actor, playing small roles that demanded an Irish accent. Things were going well when he was cast in the play *Strathlogan* in 1892. The production ate money that didn't exist and was simply terrible – it closed suddenly leaving the cast unpaid and out of work. Louis couldn't even think of taking a holiday as the world was in the midst of a cholera pandemic. But Americans who'd planned a summer adventure in Europe shifted direction to the British south coast, and they were willing to pay for entertainment.

Louis had already been reading palms for friends and fellow actors, so on 18 July 1892 in Eastbourne, Cheiro was born.

Louis used his contacts to engineer a meeting with actress Sarah Bernhardt to read her palm. The press loved the story. Then in October 1892 he met Oscar Wilde – Wilde knew Edward Heron-Allen, the man who'd revived palmistry in the mid-1880s, and when he said a palmist was good, you knew they were *really* good. Louis upgraded his wardrobe, wearing a mystical ring coordinated with his skull and crossbones scarfpin, and decorated his consulting rooms with so many exotic drapes, statues, and mystical items that it was hard to fit people in. Finally, he needed a book, so he hastily completed *Cheiro's Book of the Hand* in late 1892.

With London at his feet, Louis first toured America in September 1893. He was on his second trip in 1896 when Evangeline Adams attended his palmistry classes. In 1902 he bought the *American Register* newspaper and moved to Paris. After running a failed bank and facing embezzlement charges, he was forced to flee France and later owned a factory in Ireland that converted peat into carbon. After his factory was burned down, Cheiro was obliged to return to London. He spent much of the 1920s writing until he moved to Hollywood in 1929 where he tried and failed to sell his screenplays and worked as a celebrity palmist. He died there in 1936. Many of Cheiro's books are still in print today.

Although best known as a palmist, Cheiro knew his astrology and knew Alan Leo with whom he corresponded in 1899 about the nature of Saturn. He used a combination of palmistry, numerology, and astrology in his readings, coupled with the ability to say just what his clients wished to hear. However, his predictions were almost completely astrological in nature.

Cheiro saw the benefits of focusing on Sun signs early on in his career and there are accounts of him attending parties where he made predictions based on people's birthdays. At this time, Sun signs weren't widely enough known to be used as we do today, and so Cheiro's writings at the start of the twentieth century comprised character descriptions and forecasts grouped by month of birth, with no mention of the relevant zodiac sign. Books that gave character delineations and predictions based on months of birth were common at this time, and don't immediately appear to be Sun sign astrology. However, a closer look soon reveals that this is precisely what they were.

For example, in *When were you Born?* (1930) Cheiro recommends reading character and disposition by the period of birth – in other words according to your Sun sign. Although the individual sections were divided into calendar months, statements such as the following for people born in January makes it clear that these were Sun sign interpretations:

> This period commences on December 21 and last until January 20. (the student must allow 7 days at the beginning of the Sign for it to come into its full strength, and 7 days at the close for it to gradually die out)...
>
> (p.1)

Cheiro regularly used the word 'period' when referencing Sun signs, at this stage the expressions, 'Sun sign' or 'sign' hadn't fallen into general usage.

> The period or sign is so called from the fact that the Sun enters into a fresh sign of the zodiac at each of these periods and so alerts the electric radiations of the Planets and Zodiac.
>
> (p.5)

And it was Cheiro who has the honour of being responsible for instigating the concept of being born on the cusp of a sign - at the time when the Sun is moving from one sign to another. With the Sun entering the zodiac signs on slightly different dates each year, people weren't always clear which sign they were born under. For a mass popular astrology it was important to take account of this without worrying the reader about the technicalities of horoscope calculation.

> The 'cusp' lasts for seven days, consequently the full influence of this sign comes into power about the 28th December and lasts until the 21st

January, when another seven days 'cusp' begins under the influence of the next incoming sign.

(Cheiro, *You and Your Stars*, p.9)

Cheiro's aim was to "interest and educate the masses." He knew that the type of astrology he was promoting wasn't what other astrologers would view as 'serious' astrology, but was rather a simplified version, designed to be accessible to as many people as possible. This was precisely his intention.

> The system I am about to explain in the following pages is not one based on what may be called the rules of ordinary astrology. To make a map and erect a horoscope from the exact hour and possible minute of birth, is a mathematical operation requiring considerable training and application.
>
> (Cheiro, *You and Your Stars*, p.9)

Although Cheiro isn't usually renowned as one of astrology's greats, he had a huge influence on how ordinary people saw astrology, and was instrumental in increasing its popularity. It wasn't his astrological skills that brought him to the fore, but rather his magnetic personality and celebrity status. Fred Gettings wrote of him in his *Book of the Hand*:

> Count Louis Hamon, better known as Cheiro, is one of the most remarkable figures in the history of cheiromancy. His ability as a palmist is legendary and so many people testified to it that it cannot be doubted. The difficulty in assessing Cheiro is that his theory was unsound, his knowledge of the history of the subject ludicrously inaccurate, his sense of honesty sadly impaired, and his sense of importance verging on megalomania.
>
> (Gettings, p.209)

Perhaps he did verge on megalomania – but he was also responsible for ensuring the popularity of palmistry in the modern Western world, introducing numerology to the public at large and simplifying astrology in such a way that Sun sign columns, as appear in newspapers today, became possible. A man who had such a major influence – and was perfectly aware of the fact – had little reason for modesty. His status as an international celebrity, coupled with an ability to write for an audience, brought Sun sign astrology into a much wider arena, free from the esoteric – and somewhat baffling to a general audience – associations with solar biology.

Only a quirk of fate prevented Cheiro from becoming known as the man who changed the face of popular astrology. In 1930, he turned down a request from the *Sunday Express* to write an astrological feature on the newborn Princess Margaret on the basis of being too busy. Instead, he passed it on to his assistant – a young man who called himself R.H. Naylor.

# 17

# Popular Astrology in the 1930s

The 1920s had seen publishers consolidate their positions and expand, with circulations climbing steadily, but the economic depression soon put an end to the abundance of the twenties. The financial downturn following the stock market crash in October 1929 sharply affected the practices of publishers. Advertisers who had spent lavishly in the 1920s were forced to cut back their budgets drastically in the 1930s. Most people's worries were centred around their financial insecurities. However, the early 1930s was also a time of radical change and instability, similar in many ways to the late Victorian era.

The press expanded drastically in the 1930s, especially in the U.S. Cheap magazines were ideal for an America in which people had plenty of time for recreation, but little money to spend. There was an explosion of new titles in the pulp magazine industry during this decade. Women's magazines were already plentiful, but new ones sprouted throughout the decade, while older magazines increased their circulation. The growing popularity of radio and movies spawned an increase in fan magazines for both. Although a typical American bought and read few books, they spent much of their time reading. In 1938, there were an estimated 1,200 weekly magazines with a circulation of around fifty million and about 2,000 monthly magazines going to approximately one hundred million buyers. In Britain books were more commonly bought, but the story was similar. Thousands of publications fought for a readership to help them sustain their existence.

Astrology was ideal for filling the spaces on those many pages. As the 1930s opened, astrological features continued to appear in the press with more emphasis on Sun sign character analysis:

> According to astrology the month of May is governed mostly by Taurus. Those born in May according to astrology have fine memories, are not easily aroused to anger, but when goaded they may become furious. The horoscope of those born in May promises a patient plodding nature that makes persistent application more possible and this often carries with it more of the elements of success.
>
> <div align="right">(<i>Key West Citizen</i> (Florida), 8 May 1930<i>)</i></div>

Although astrology had always appeared in the press, the situation was to change drastically, to a point where it was almost obligatory to include astrology in every newspaper. This brings us to the story of R.H. Naylor, the man commonly attributed with the responsibility for inventing Sun sign astrology.

Born 2 August 1889 in London at 9:15 am (which he later rectified to 9:16 to give himself Libra rising and a Cancer MC), in his early life Naylor answered to the name of Harold Thropp (although he was registered under the name of Richard Harold Naylor.) Naylor was his mother's maiden name. His father was a hardware manufacturer, and legend has it that Naylor decided to become an astrologer in 1910 after his father gave up trying to persuade Naylor to enter the family business. In 1914 he joined the York and Lancaster Regiment as a second lieutenant and is recorded as R H Thropp. In 1916 he married Ellen Catley (born 9 February 1893), a tailor's daughter from Leeds. Naylor was wounded in France in 1917, after which he was promoted to lieutenant. Records show he had addresses in both Harrogate and Maida Vale immediately after the war. As soon as he began his new life, he used the name R H T Naylor—he later dropped the T.

Naylor came across astrology as a boy when he found a copy of Joseph Simmonite's *Key to Scientific Prediction* in a second-hand bookshop. Originally published in the 1840s, Simmonite's work had been republished by Joseph Story who was a practising astrologer and happened to live in Sheffield, close to where Naylor lived at the time. At the suggestion of the bookshop owner, Naylor went to meet Story and his life changed forever.

By 1919 he was running Memphis Occult Products in Derbyshire. Part of his business was selling horoscopes, and he pointed out in his advertisements that he was now attending personally to all business, suggesting a previous venture when perhaps he wasn't. By 1922 Naylor lived in Harrogate from where he offered to do your horoscope in as little as four days 'free from pseudo mystery or ambiguity.' He also had an office in New Bond Street and insisted:

> You may not believe in astrology but it pays intellectually and materially!
> (Occult Review, June 1922, p.379)

In 1923 Naylor moved with his family to Crouch End in London and sold Memphis Occult Products. Although still practising as an astrologer, he also ran a bookshop in Oxford Street. At least, he sold books from his 'salon' on the fourth floor along with a selection of incenses, jewellery and 'requisites of every kind for the student of occultism and astrology.'

It's unclear when Naylor met Cheiro, but during the 1920s he acted as his agent (which might have been a grand description for collecting his mail). He wasn't exactly Cheiro's assistant as is often said, although they worked together. *Cheiro's Year Book* for 1929 (which appeared early that year) contains the credit 'Astronomical and astrological computations by R. H. T. Naylor'. This book was successful enough for another edition to appear in 1930 which Naylor also collaborated on. By now, Naylor was gaining a reputation amongst astrologers—he spoke at a meeting of George Wilde's London Astrological Research Society in May 1929 and it clearly wasn't his first talk there.

Princess Margaret, the younger daughter of the future King George VI, was born at Glamis Castle on 21 August 1930. When the *Sunday Express* was preparing its issue for 24 August the news was already old. The editor decided to give the story a fresh angle by publishing a story about the Princess's horoscope.

As the foremost astrologer of the day, Cheiro was the obvious choice to write the feature. As he was unable to do so, the job passed to his assistant – Richard Naylor. Naylor was happy to oblige. Along with the requested analysis of the Princess' birth chart, he added general political predictions and comments based on readers' dates of birth. (Although it's generally accepted that Naylor was responsible for the first Sun sign forecasting newspaper column, his columns in the *Sunday Express* didn't take this form until 1936.) Naylor's article has been so often cited as the first Sun sign newspaper feature, and so has passed into astrological history, that it's worth quoting in full:

> Here is the 'horoscope' of the Baby Princess. In convenient form we have here the sphere of the heavens at the moment of birth, cut open for inspection, as an orange is bisected. The upper half of the figure stands for the visible heavens, the bottom half for the heavens beneath our feet. The symbols scattered over the figure are a sort of astronomical shorthand showing the position of the twelve Zodiacal signs and the Planets.
>
> Applying the age-old lore of astrological doctrine to these figures, what deductions can be made?
>
> The babe is truly a 'royal' one, a fact which will prove true in more senses than one, for she is born when the sun is passing through Leo – the traditional 'royal' sign of the zodiac.
>
> The Princess will share certain basic characteristics common to all people born in the present month - hence in a sense she is an astrological cousin of all readers of *The Sunday Express* whose birth anniversaries fall about the same date.
>
> These basic characteristics are loyalty, pride, an intensely affectionate nature, in turn depending on affection, but with a strong will. There is

a love of the beautiful, great frankness – a scorn of restrain. As the race needs Madonnas – not Mimes – the Princess will nobly fulfil that need.

The infant Princess is also born under the sway of three planets, Uranus (the Awakener), Saturn (the Star of Service), and Venus (the Star of Love).

The rays of these three planets will greatly modify the basic characteristics already mentioned.

Uranus will give the Princess extreme originality of mind, an unconventional vein, a keen interest in everything that is up to date, original and novel. She will insist on seeing life at an early age.

Saturn, on the mid-heaven of the horoscope, will give the child something of her father's intense devotion to duty; her whole life will be spent in the conscientious service of her family and country.

From Venus which is setting in the figure, will come a vivid emotional nature, which insists on following the dictates of the heart rather than those of the head, but this royal child, when she reaches maturity, will be essentially a woman of the new age.

In one sense her life will be a series of episodes rather than a coherent sequence.

In the great times that are coming on the world, she will have to face sweeping changes affecting the Royal House of England, which will grow stronger, rather than weaker, while the world is in a melting pot.

The indications as to health are fairly good, but the physical organism will be extremely sensitive. In the course of life there will probably be some minor injury to the face or head, for people so born usually carry a mark or mole on the scalp or face.

The Princess will lead an eventful life. Events of tremendous importance to the Royal Family and the nation will come about near her seventh year (1937), and these events will indirectly affect her own fortunes. She will marry rather suddenly, about the 24$^{th}$ or 26$^{th}$ year, but as a result of an attachment of long standing.

The film of fate will flash across the screen rapidly during the next few weeks, and this week in particular will see the beginning of great happenings.

A sudden outbreak of revolutionary activities may be expected in Germany almost at any time now, and most probably the last week in September will see notable developments in this direction.

The first lapping of the wave of intense industrial depression which is now gathering strength and which will shortly engulf the world will be felt in the first three days of this week, though values on Change and otherwise will appreciate after Thursday morning.

Readers of the *Sunday Express* who are lucky enough to be born about the first week of July in any year should now enter on a really favorable period. Money will come their way and – to them more important – an easier time! If you were born at the beginning of July, the beginning of November, or the beginning of March, even bank managers will look kindly on you!

Under the general heading "And a few hints on the happenings of this week," Naylor included forecasts for each birthday:

August 27... you will find life romantic and interesting.

A flood of appreciative letters persuaded the editor of the *Sunday Express* to commission a feature "Were You Born in September?" for the following Sunday. This too, was received with acclamation and Naylor was asked to provide a

144

series of articles beginning 5 October. A week later a new weekly article began entitled, "What the stars foretell for this week."

Naylor's success was secured when one million readers read his prediction in the *Express* that British aircraft were in serious danger. The BBC announced that day that the R01 airship, on its maiden voyage from Cardington to India, had crashed in Northern France. A week later, the *Sunday Express* crowed over Naylor's success, and from then on allocated a full page for his weekly articles which became one of its permanent features. Naylor became famous overnight. His horoscope column in the *Sunday Express* was published weekly from this date, except for breaks in 1936, when Naylor was in court, and 1942, when the reputability of Sun sign astrology was called into question by an article in *Picture Post*.

The *Express* was clearly delighted with the popularity of Naylor's columns. An editorial note introducing his second feature on 31 August 1930 reported that "enormous interest was aroused" in Naylor's predictions and treatment of the Princess's birth chart. Arthur Christiansen, the entertainment editor of the *Express* who was responsible for the decision to hire Naylor later wrote:

> Naylor and his horoscopes became a power in the land. If he said that Monday was a bad day for buying, then the buyers of more than one West End store waited for the stars to become more propitious.
>
> (Christiansen, p.65)

Naylor continued to work as a consultant astrologer and in 1931 he abruptly left Ellen and set up home with Phyllis Poulton in Bishop's Stortford. She immediately started describing herself as Phyllis Naylor. Their son Roger was born in December 1931.

The following year was busy for Naylor. The Filmaphone company struck a deal with him for exclusive recordings of *What the Stars Foretell* - a free horoscope was offered with every purchase. And instead of ghostwriting Cheiro's predictions, Naylor issued his own yearbook in 1933. Ellen filed for divorce in 1932. The case was heard in 1933 and gained press attention -

although not as much as might be expected; perhaps few people knew Naylor's real name. Lord Merrivale who granted the decree nisi had clearly not heard of Naylor (who Ellen had said was an astrologer) as he commented:

> A somewhat absurd description has been given of the husband's occupation. I see he describes himself an author and publisher.
> 
> (Lincolnshire Echo, 31 July 1933, p. 6)

That same year the *Sunday Express* heavily promoted a series of films based on 'What the Stars Foretell' which Naylor narrated. A film was made for each zodiac sign and they open and close with a scene where a newspaper editor and his secretary discuss Naylor and his forecasts. At the end, a closing title advertises the upcoming film for the next sign. Woolworth's also issued a series of records under the same name. He was still working as a consultant astrologer as if it hadn't occurred to him to give it up.

Astrology was now everywhere. Advertisers used astrological terms and shop window displays used the signs of the zodiac. Daily forecasts were made on the radio. The Gas, Light and Coke Company in London promoted themselves with the slogan "If you want to know the time ask the zodiac" in 1938. They also displayed a giant astrological clock outside their building on the Edgeware Road, placing Aries in the nine o'clock position. Lunn Travel Agency in the Haymarket, London added a bronze zodiac globe, belted with signs of the zodiac in blue, to their new premises in 1938. Popular songs such as *It's in the Stars* contained lines like "It's in the stars, that you were meant for me." As Naylor said:

> Everywhere appear articles, books, gramophone records and films on Astrology.
> 
> (Naylor, *Year Book* 1934, p.8)

The *Weekly Horoscope* pointed out the same in 1938.

> Astrological terms and symbols are passing into everyday parlance. The subject is introduced on the stage, in the films, over the wireless – in fact in every sphere where men forgather.
>
> (*Weekly Horoscope*, 26 March 1938, p.787)

If we want to see how popular astrology was at this time, we only need to look at one area of the media. In the 1930s, the most dominant leisure activity that cost money was going to the cinema. It accounted for two thirds of all entertainment admissions and expenditure in the UK. Although the 1927 Cinematograph Films Act required a quota of British films to be shown in the UK, the seven high volume Hollywood producers contributed almost half of the market supply. And that's without taking into account those films produced by American companies in the UK as 'quota films'. Visits to the cinema in the early half of the 1930s weren't a luxury. Between 1934 and 1938, most people went to the cinema more than once every three weeks.

Before the main feature, cinema-goers watched newsreels. The newsreel dated from 1910 with Pathé's *Animated Gazette* and was born out of the rising popularity of cinema. A newsreel was a piece of film lasting about five minutes that showed four or five stories covering the week's news. By 1912, newsreels had settled into a pattern of two issues a week, matching the change of cinema programs. They became hugely popular in the 1920s. Those from Pathé, Gaumont and Topical were dominant, with a fourth reel, *Empire News Bulletin*, joining them in 1926. Newsreel companies also issued cinemagazines that covered more light-hearted or ephemeral topics.

The first British sound newsreel was the American owned *British Movietone News*, which began life in June 1929. The changeover to sound was gradual and Pathé, Gaumont and Empire issued silent as well as sound reels for a few years. With the advent of sound, newsreels became longer, running for ten minutes or more, and became increasingly influential.

Considering how popular Sun sign astrology was in the press, it's not surprising that it featured in newsreels. In 1931, Pathé launched a series of astrological reels featuring the astrologer Gabriel Dee. Under the titles *Birthday Luck* and *When were You Born?* the reels offered interpretations of Sun signs and discussed the characteristics of those born under a specific sign. For example, in the film about Scorpio, released in March 1932, Dee sat in a darkened room and told how the scorpion and eagle represented the sign of Scorpio and suggested that good occupations for someone born under this sign would be the army, navy, surgery, and working with iron or steel and machinery of all kinds. Nothing new so far as the astrology went – but certainly new to the cinema. Dee produced a number of fortune telling books from the late 1920s to mid 1930s, including sections on astrology and her own ephemerides.

Dee wasn't the only newsreel astrologer. In 1936, Edward Lyndoe appeared in Pathé's *What of the Future?* a reel that contained predictions for the first half of 1937. Lyndoe authoritatively sat at his desk and discussed unemployment, military movements and the budget in terms of astrological patterns.

Astrology was also often contained in the main feature and formed the key part of the plot of a number of Hollywood movies in the 1930s. Possibly the most well known is *I'm No Angel* (1933), featuring Mae West and Cary Grant, remembered for West's immortal lines, "Well, it's not the men in your life that counts, it's the life in your men." and "Come up and see me sometime." In *I'm No Angel*, West plays Tira, a showgirl who becomes a lion tamer because she's bored with her life. The script was partially written by West. After one of her shows, Tira consults an astrologer:

> Rajah: You were born in August.
>
> Tira: Yeah, one of the hot months.
>
> Rajah: It was on the 17th under the sign of Leo, the Lion.
>
> Tira: Aw, King of the Beasts, huh.

West's own birth date was 17 August. Tira asks about her future and is warned to be careful that night, because she might be unlucky:

> Rajah: Ah, you have a wonderful future. I see a man in your life.

Tira: What, only one?

Rajah: But this is one very particular man. He is very wealthy, enormously wealthy.

Tira: ...What does he look like?

Rajah: I see he has brown eyes. In fact, I see two men... two different men. In the near future, I see a change... I see a change of position.

Tira: Sitting or reclining?...

Rajah: The horoscope. Keep this where you may consult it frequently.

Tira: All right, I'll take it to bed with me.

Tira keeps the horoscope and it's mentioned again during the course of the film, and she says:

My whole life is ruled by astrology.

*I'm No Angel* was a huge success and one of West's most popular films, being made before censorship was strictly enforced. In 1934, West was the fifth most popular star in the US and earned more than any woman in America.

If this had been the only film during the period featuring astrology, it would barely warrant a mention. However, it was not only one of several but wasn't even the first. *Stepping Sisters* of 1932 features an astrologer who tells his competitor in love that he is astrologically unsuited to the girl they are both chasing. In *Thirteen Women*, also in 1932, astrological predictions come true when a series of characters die, no matter how hard they try to avoid it.

And there is also the 1935 movie *Circus Shadows*, in which the main character, Dale, confides to his girlfriend, Elaine that he has learned about his aunt's astrologer, Zirillo, and his female assistant, who he knows are out to get his aunt's money; and *The Great Jasper* (1933) where the main character is befriended by Madame Talma, an alcoholic astrologer. He finally becomes a great astrologer himself. *When's Your Birthday?* (1937) features a busboy who moonlights as a boxer in order to pay for instruction in astrology. *Turn Off the Moon* (1937) features department store owner J. Elliott Dinwiddy who has waited ten years for the perfect astrological moment to propose to his secretary, Myrtle Tweep. His astrological advisor, Dr. Wakefield, has told him that if he can unite a boy and a girl in true love before midnight, he can propose to Myrtle the following night at 3:15 a.m. and she will accept.

*Personal Secretary* (1938) is about the trial of Flo Samson, who is accused of poisoning her husband. Newspaper reporter Mark Farrell assures his reading public that Flo is guilty, while his rival, the "Comet," whose true identity is unknown, insists that Flo is innocent based on her astrological charts. Finally, in *When Were You Born* (1938), Mei Lee Ling, an astrologer, tells one of her fellow passengers on a ship that he will die within two days - and the next day he is dead. As she is under suspicion, she offers the police her help. Ling, played by Anna May Wong, helps to question the suspects and uses their charts to find out further information. Each of the twelve characters in the film represents a different zodiac sign and the film opens with the astrologer Manley P. Hall, the writer of the original story, explaining the characteristics of the signs.

Astrology also appeared with the same regularity in novels, advertising images and songs. Sun sign astrology was so deeply planted in the public consciousness that in years to come practically everyone would at least know what sign they were born under.

With the popularity of Naylor's writings, and the eagerness of other astrologers to leap on the bandwagon, serious astrologers became increasingly worried about what was happening to their science:

> The present state of astrology is really deplorable.
> (*British Journal of Astrology*, March 1932, p.101)

Deplorable it may have been to this small select group. Not so for the astrology hungry public, or the many astrologers who now had a way of not only making a regular and respectable income, but also the opportunity to gain celebrity status.

# 18

## The Legal Challenge

Anything associated with the occult was fashionable in the 1930s. Clairvoyants, spiritualists, and palmists had a steadily growing clientele. By 1934, the popularity of such practices had grown to such an extent that the *Sunday Pictorial* hired the novelist Andrew Soutar to produce a series of articles about his experiences with fortune tellers. Soutar agreed with the public at large – astrology was simply another practice that could be thrown into the fortune telling basket.

> For the life of me, I cannot differentiate between the astrologer, the palmist, the psychoanalyst and the fortune teller. They belong to one family so why prosecute one member as a vagrant and raise your hat to another?
>
> (Soutar, p.22)

Fewer people today would suggest that psychoanalysts should be regarded as vagrants – although it's an attractive concept. But in general, despite the protestations of astrologers, this was the general view of the public. They could see no difference between a palmist, a psychic, and an astrologer. Indeed, many practitioners combined their skills and muddied the waters even further. Soutar was alert to the legal status of fortune tellers. In the early 1930s, they still risked prosecution under the Vagrancy Act. Their fears of persecution weren't based on a strange fortune telling paranoia, but were rooted firmly in reality.

> The prosecuting of fortune tellers comes in waves or cycles. There is a lull in the general atmosphere and it is as though someone in authority says: "It's a fine day with nothing happening, let's go out and shoot something, even if it's only a fortune teller". The authorities ...stress the contention that they do not object to anyone delving into the past, but they will not tolerate even one who professes to foretell the future... claim they are safeguarding the peace of mind of the public. They say that this fortune telling business leads, not infrequently, to blackmail.
>
> (Soutar, p.20)

Who the people were who were open to blackmail, and what they were being blackmailed about, has never been clear. No records can be easily found that describe this ever happening. Granted, it isn't totally impossible that a prominent politician may have told his favourite clairvoyant state secrets, or that an individual confessed a crime to an astrologer, and that they both then had to make regular payments in a darkened alley, but it doesn't appear to have happened.

By March 1936, Naylor was a world famous astrologer and happily claiming responsibility for inventing Sun sign astrology and bringing it to the masses. He was also facing charges of vagrancy.

It would be easy to think that by the 1930s, practising astrology in any form was unlikely to cause legal problems for anyone. There were many laws on the statute books that had become disused and outdated, and the relevant section of the Vagrancy Act seemed to be no different. From time to time, astrologers worriedly discussed the matter and whether they risked prosecution, but that was about as far as it went. At least until Maurice Barbanell, editor of the spiritualist newspaper *Psychic News*, brought his case.

Initially, Barbanell intended to bring action against the *Express* itself, but soon realised that it was impossible to charge a limited company with being a 'rogue or vagabond'. He amended his action to bring charges against Naylor along with the editor of the *Sunday Express*, John Gordon.

Barbanell brought the case because at this time spiritualists were under immense legal pressure. Numerous members of their ranks had been arrested and charged under the Vagrancy and Witchcraft Acts. Barbanell contended that the Vagrancy Act should be used impartially, and enforced against everyone who infringed its provisions, instead of being used to attack spiritualism. Charges against such a high profile astrologer as Naylor ensured maximum publicity for his case.

The most prominent spiritualist to suffer legal persecution was the medium Helen Duncan. Duncan had been tested by the Society for Psychical Research and they found it likely that she was a fraud. She was tried and fined under the Vagrancy Act in 1933.

Born in Callander, Scotland in 1897, Duncan practised both mental and physical mediumship, meaning that she could bring through materialised forms of the deceased, as well as communicating with the spirit world. A policewoman attending a séance in 1933 had grabbed a vest that was claimed to be Duncan's spirit helper. After being convicted, Duncan was fined £10. Most people involved in the case knew what Barbanell was trying to achieve with his action. There was nothing to indicate that he bore Naylor any personal animosity.

> The summonses were issued upon information by Mr Maurice Barbanell... The motive was altogether immaterial, but it might be admitted that he had a feeling that the law, having been enforced against spiritualists, such enforcement should be impartial.
>
> (*Times*, 14 October 1936)

Naylor appeared at Mansion House Justice Room, 13 March 1936. The charge read:

> For that he, on February 9, 1936, unlawfully did pretend to tell fortunes contrary to Section 4 of the Vagrancy Act 1824.

The summons against John Gordon was for aiding and abetting Naylor. Both men pleaded not guilty. Naylor was defended by Christmas Humphries, a barrister who had his place in history reserved for being not only the founder of the London Buddhist Society, but also the future prosecutor of Ruth Ellis, the last woman to be hanged in Britain. Journalists rubbed shoulders with spiritualists and astrologers in watching a case that promised great entertainment. Barbanell hired the renowned barrister, Gilbert Beyfus, to plead his case. Beyfus had previous experience in successfully prosecuting fortune-tellers.

The *Express* decided to play it safe and suspended Naylor's column. The press industry watched the case with avid interest. The majority of newspapers were printing Sun sign columns and a decision against Naylor would mean that they were all open to attack. The legal status of such columns had never been certain.

The tiny courtroom was filled with well-known spiritualists and interested journalists. Everyone recognised the strangeness of the case. After all, as Beyfus stated, Sun sign columns like Naylor's had been appearing in the press for a number of years and no objections had been seriously raised before. However, that did not necessarily mean it was legal – simply acceptable. The hearing focused on an article that appeared in the *Sunday Express* of 9 February, entitled, 'What the Stars Foretell'. By specifying dates of birth through his birthday predictions, Naylor could be seen to be fortune-telling in the same way as if he had approached the readers directly. In any event, this was the prosecution's argument.

Beyfus was particularly indignant that Naylor predicted that a girl born on 14 February could be about to meet her Mr Right. He indignantly pointed out that she may end up with the wrong man *entirely* if she heeded this prediction.

It could obviously be argued that a number of readers would be born on the same day and so read the same prediction, making it less personal. Beyfus contended that this made matters worse, rather than the predictions more vague:

> The mere fact that he does it a hundred or a thousand times, because he does it for every person whose birthday is on one of those days, merely means that the offence is a hundred or thousand times repeated.
> (*Psychic News*, 21 March 1936, p.2)

> He was not there to say that the articles... were written with any intention to deceive the public, but the view he put forward was that in the case of anyone putting himself forward to tell fortunes, the more honest and sincere he was, the more of a danger he was to the public. The effect upon the minds of weaker persons might be that they would regulate their lives by alleged predictions rather than the facts surrounding them.
> (*Times*, 14 October 1936, p.1)

The crux of the argument centred on the use of the word 'foretell'. The prosecution argued that this word showed that Naylor intended to impart foreknowledge from his readings. One sticky moment came for Beyfus when on reading Naylor's column he was forced to comment that his predictions had turned out to be correct. But accuracy in prediction was no defence against a charge of fortune-telling. Until 1921, it had been argued that the honesty and sincerity of the reader mattered. In the case of Stonehouse vs. Masson it was laid down that the offence of professing to tell fortunes was complete without any allegation or proof that the defendant did not believe in the possession of the powers claimed. Telling fortunes was an offence in itself according to this ruling.

Humphries argued that Naylor's column could not be construed as fortune-telling, as it was not directed towards an individual. He had problems in seeing how a Sun sign forecast could be relevant at all, considering the possible numbers of people born on any particular day. Astrology of this sort was, in his view:

> Harmless and interesting.
>
> (Psychic News, 21 March 1936, p.7)

He wondered aloud how it could compare with:

> People who use messages from the dead to tell people what they should do.

– which, of course, was precisely what was on Barbanell's mind. The magistrates were completely bemused by the whole event. After lengthy and lively discussions about the role of astrology, and whether the BBC could be seen as fortune-tellers for issuing weather forecasts, a ruling was made in Naylor's favour. However, the magistrates refused to allow costs as they thought there was a slight chance that weak minded people might be induced to act on Naylor's predictions.

> I have come to the conclusion that the statements in Mr Naylor's article are of such a vague and general character that there is nothing that can be said to amount to the telling or professing to tell, any person's future so as to come within the terms of Section 4 of the Vagrancy Act of 1824.
>
> (Times, 14 October 1936, p.1)

The *Express* reinstated Naylor's column and Sun sign forecasting continued as if nothing had happened.

The case went to appeal on 13 October 1936, where it was again dismissed. Beyfus contended at this hearing that because Naylor addressed people born on a particular day that his column was as much fortune-telling as if each person had received a separate letter making the prediction.

The *Daily Express* of the following day was filled with articles about Mosley's blackshirts and fights in the East End of London. Political unrest was the order of the day. Tucked away on page eleven was a short article announcing that the case had been dismissed.

The *Express* didn't report the Lord Chief Justice's comment that Naylor's articles were "a collection of imbecile and repulsive twaddle." Barbanell wrote in fury about the outcome of the case. His view that spiritualists would continue to be prosecuted under the Vagrancy Act was borne out by later events. He was left with costs of £300 (equivalent to over £15,000 in 2002), and forced to ask for contributions from sympathetic spiritualists.

Naylor had been vindicated. Puffed up with self-importance he claimed to have invented modern astrology, but he never really got the hang of being a celebrity. In the 1940s he could be found appearing at Butlins in Skegness as part of variety shows. He died on 17 May 1952. His son, John Naylor, took over his column in the *Sunday Express,* later becoming the astrologer for the *Daily Mail* until his retirement in 1986. Phyllis became a renowned astrologer herself and wrote the horoscope column for *Woman* in the 1950s. She died in 1988.

The legal situation with spiritualism remained the same for many years, with large numbers being prosecuted. The situation culminated in 1944, when Helen Duncan and three others were charged with conspiracy. Bail being refused, Duncan spent four days in prison. The case was transferred to the criminal court at the Old Bailey, where various charges were brought including vagrancy, conspiracy, and charges under the Witchcraft Act of 1735. The trial lasted seven days, during which many people testified to Duncan's abilities. However, she was finally sentenced to nine months imprisonment in Holloway prison.

Duncan found herself in trouble because she had a psychic message about the name of a ship that had sunk, but which had not been announced by the War Office. An off-duty naval officer had been in her audience and reported her. Duncan's defence was that she was calling up real spirits, not faking it – but this claim to be calling on real spirits was an admission of guilt on the charge of witchcraft. She submitted to a large amount of testing, including having her stomach x-rayed to prove it was normal.

Spiritualists immediately began to fight for the repeal of the 1735 Witchcraft Act, using Duncan as their figurehead. An appeal was considered and refused, mainly on Biblical and sixteenth century precedents. Another trial took place in 1950, and in 1951 the Witchcraft Act and Section 4 of the Vagrancy Act were replaced by the Fraudulent Mediums Act. This didn't end Duncan's legal problems as she was raided again in 1956, although charges weren't pressed. She died soon afterwards.

Section 4 of the Vagrancy Act finally disappeared as part of the Statute Law (Repeals) Bill on 16 November 1989, after the Law Commission's working party reported "widespread agreement" that it should be repealed without replacement. Astrologers didn't even notice its disappearance until early 1991. After all, astrology was now legal and this was no longer their problem.

# 19

# Astrology and the Press in the 1930s

Naylor's popularity as an astrologer was unassailable. Modesty was never one of his failings and, aware of the public's change in attitude towards astrology as a whole, he was eager to take the credit.

> In 1930 I commenced a series of Astrological articles which have entirely altered the orientation of the public mind towards Astrology. I am aware all this sounds egotistical and perhaps boastful, but it so happens it is true.
>
> I do still feel that Astrology awakened in London in AD 1930 and will stay awake!
>
> (*Prediction* , 1 May 1936, p.162)

Although not all readers could be assumed to be aware of their personal sign, Naylor was able to develop his Sun sign writing by introducing his readers to Sun signs as a character type, including profiles for the sign of the month, featuring Mr and Mrs Taurus, for example. The success of Naylor's column led to the *Daily Express* launching a daily column in 1934 by an anonymous writer. This consisted of about one hundred words for the birthday of the day and twenty words to sum up the day as a whole for all other readers.

Naylor had noticed that his Sun sign forecasts, which by now were also appearing in book form, did nothing to increase his popularity amongst serious astrologers. He began a series of justifications that have continued to appear amongst Sun sign astrologers ever since.

> Much discussion has raged around the Astrological birthday forecasts published by myself in the Press and this annual volume...when exploring unknown country a rough sketch map is better than no map at all.
>
> (Naylor, *Year Book*, p.13)
>
> We are not surprised when lambs born unusually early in the year are not so strong as those born in the lambing season proper. It does not strike us as curious that roses should bloom in June and not in October. We expect wasps to manifest themselves at a certain time of year and not at any other. Why then should we regard it as improbable that individuals born of certain seasons of the year will have certain distinctive characteristics that we can identify with the month of birth.
>
> (Naylor, *Year Book*, p.221)

Control of their science seemed to be slipping from the grasp of more serious astrologers. In spite of their valiant efforts to keep astrology on an even keel, they could no longer ignore the fact that to most people, Sun sign astrology now was astrology.

> One of the most misleading aspects of the newspaper articles is the extraordinary importance given to the sun in the sign, as though there were no other influences worth considering. The possibility is that the writers have evidently got hold of some work on solar delineations and in their ignorance of the real science, presuppose that astrology merely consists of sun sign influence and nothing else. This sun sign affair is a purely modern one, and is not found in any of the old works on astrology, and in fact is one of the minor influences in the horoscope in the opinion of the writers referred to. It would appear that everyone born during a particular solar month has the same character, mentality, faculties and disposition etc., an idea which is entirely wrong and gives the outside public a wholly erroneous idea of Astrology ...directions

(?) are based purely on the progression of the sun through the twelve signs... a wholly fictitious and pernicious system of prediction. These of course are all ready made and sent out without regard to the birth time or anything else.

*(British Journal of Astrology*, February 1934, p.1)

The expression 'Sun sign astrology' had not yet been coined, and along with other writers, Naylor referred to 'periods' and 'birth months', just as his mentor Cheiro had done before him. Whatever people chose to call it, Sun sign astrology was becoming so popular that even Naylor became exasperated.

> The interested public must by this time be weary of reading about the twelve zodiacal types.

(Naylor, *Home Astrology*, p.222)

Naylor wasn't alone in holding the mantle for Sun sign astrology. Numerous other writers jumped on the bandwagon in the early 1930s, adding Sun sign astrology to the subjects included in the ever popular fortune telling books that already featured sections on tarot, palmistry, and lucky numbers. At last, astrology could be presented in a simple enough form for anyone to understand. Agnes Miall wrote in 1934 about what she called this "rough and ready" form of astrology:

> Now we come to another way of fortune telling – a very easy way based on astrology, the study of the stars. Astrology itself is very difficult and is rather beyond the average woman who is interested in telling the fortunes of herself and friends. But solar horoscopes, as they are called, are quite easy... They are based merely on the position of the Sun at birth not taking any notice of the other planets. As no doubt you know, the sun passes through one of the twelve signs of the zodiac every month...

(Miall)

The *Sunday Express'* rival *The People* wasted no time in following its lead and soon began featuring its own column written by Edward Lyndoe. Lyndoe copied Naylor's format, including monthly forecasts along with birthday and general political predictions but without actually using the names of zodiac signs. Born Thomas Edward Lyndoe Winter (Lyndoe was his mother's maiden name) 23 September 1901 in Strood, Kent, he was the son of a grocer and began his career as a newspaper astrologer for no more noble reason than he desperately needed the money. Having lost all of his savings in stock market crashes during the early 1930s, he was compelled to find a new way of making a living. Lyndoe was qualified for very little, but he had studied astrology for a number of years:

> Not so long ago there came a great tragedy into my life. All I had built crashed suddenly to the earth. The only sure thing left to me was my wife's loyalty and courage. I awakened one morning to discover I had lost every penny I possessed with the exception of a pound or two. That was a distressing moment I assure you... I am shy and not at all pushing. There were the facts and I had to face them as best I could. I sat down quietly and tried to think the whole matter over... I recalled my knowledge of astrology which I had studied for a number of years and I put it to some use. For some strange reason I had allowed it to drop out of my affairs... I began to wonder if, perhaps... I had not been that great fool who, holding the magic key to success in his hand, had forgotten to insert it into the lock and open the door.
>
> (Lyndoe, *Your Next Ten Years*, p.11)

Lyndoe couldn't afford to let this offer slip by. Fortunately, it seems that his astrological skills had already convinced him that an opportunity would arise and his fortunes change.

> The opportunity which I had been able to foresee was given to me by a great hearted man. I refer to the Editor of "The People" – Mr

> Ainsworth. Since then I have never looked back. I have not made a fortune – as still a poor man... I have had what I prize more than money, the friendship of thousands whom I have been able to help and the knowledge that I am putting my science to work in the interest of my fellow man.
>
> *(Lyndoe, Your Next Ten Years, p.13)*

His first column appeared 1 October 1933, entitled 'Plan with the Planets', and carried the disclaimer:

> If you believe that the planets exercise an influence on your destiny – well, here's all about it, by an astrologer. He may be able to help you. But don't forget that man is master of his fate. Whatever the planets may say, it is you yourself who control the course of your life, even if you do feel inclined to take a hint from the planets. In short, *"The People"* doesn't believe that planets or fate or anything of the sort can take the place of man's own power to work out his own salvation. But still, here's what the planets say.

Lyndoe's column appeared every Sunday and he soon became almost as popular as Naylor, receiving more than 100,000 letters a year from his readers – he once received 27,000 letters in a single week. He was careful to dissociate himself from any connection with psychism, saying that astrology was purely scientific. Until mid-1935, his column amounted to about an eighth of a page, gradually increasing in size until it reached half a page in 1939. Lyndoe was also the first astrologer for *Woman's Own* from 9 October 1937, a few months after it was launched. He moved to Wales where he married Norwegian-born Kristi Hauge in 1943 and he died in Brighton in 1982.

The *Sunday Dispatch* realised the potential of astrology for sales in 1936 and sought the services of William Joseph Tucker. Born 19 November 1896 in Hackney, London (at 8:19 a.m.), Tucker was employed in the fur trade until

1931. During his spare time, he took courses in civil engineering and chemistry. What Tucker wanted to be was a scientist, and astrology was his science.

Relatively new to the astrological world, Tucker first became interested in the subject in 1930 when writing his book *The How of the Human Mind*. He objected to the unscientific approach taken towards astrology in recent years, and in 1933 was responsible for forming the Scientific (Anti-Occult) Astrological Company. He employed canvassers to find clients which earned him a visit from the police – fortunately, Tucker managed to convince them of the sceintific nature of his work. In April 1935 he published the first issue of *Science and Astrology*; it came to an abrupt end in November 1936 when 30,000 of a total of 36,000 copies printed were returned by his American distributors as the covers began to come apart.

Tucker's connection with the *Dispatch* began on 23 September 1936 after he received a phone call from the editor. They met the following day, and he agreed to contribute a weekly feature article under the pseudonym 'Scorpio' entitled 'Your Future in the Stars'. (He wasn't the *Dispatch's* first astrologer – Mrs Cecil Campbell wrote psychic and astrological predictions from June 1931 – but he was to become the most famous.) The *Dispatch* wanted more than was already on offer in the *Express* and *People*. Readers were offered personal horoscopes at the price of 1s 6d, of which 6d was retained by the paper. The scheme was to be announced only three days later, so there was little time available to prepare. Tucker had to hire and train staff to process the coded horoscopes. The operation was a complete success. As far as Tucker was concerned, he was different to astrologers such as Naylor and Lyndoe. His astrology was serious and scientific. Even after undertaking work for the *Dispatch* he said of his Scientific Association of Astrologers:

> In the world's press we find hordes of others writing on the subject of astrology and dispensing 'forecasts' and opinions which have no astrological basis, and whose ability and knowledge are restricted to journalism. But this is not genuine astrology. This association together

with the International Association of Scientific Astrologers and the American Association of Scientific Astrologers have declared an implacable war against pretenders of that land who are casting grave discredit on astrology.

(*Psychic News*. London, 31 October 1936)

One by one, all the national press took up similar features. Some astrologers were to remain horoscope columnists for a very long time. Lyndoe was writing columns until at least 1973. The *Daily Express* featured 'Lord Luck' – Edward Whitman (1898-1968), an astrologer who managed to cross the divide by simultaneously writing horoscopes and being secretary of the Federation of British Astrologers. Constance Sharpe, a protégée of Tucker's, wrote for the *Sunday Pictorial* (taking over from Adrienne Arden) from 1938 to 1981.

A recent development in the newspaper world during the 1920s and 30s had been the practice of syndication to colonial and provincial newspapers. Astrology was a particular favourite commodity for the syndicating groups of Fleet Street, and astrological columns written in London appeared in the newspapers of India, Ceylon, Singapore, and Thailand. The British dominions – New Zealand, Australia, Canada, South Africa, and Rhodesia – soon all had their quota of astrological articles.

Many of the British columnists of the 1930s sound and look highly worthy. Photographs of Lyndoe and Naylor show them with serious expressions on their faces and their top collars tightly buttoned. But one of the most famous astrologers of this era was a little different.

According to his own account, Xavier or 'Gypsy' Petulengro was born in a tent near East Dereham in Yorkshire. He spent part of his childhood in Romania where his father traded Welsh ponies. Petulengro was the grandson of Ambrose Smith, known as Jasper Petulengro who was the semi-fictionalised subject of the books Lavengro (1851) and Romany Rye (1857) by George Borrow. Unusually among gypsies at the time, Petulengro had learned to read and write and later followed his father into the horse-trading business. Alternatively, he played violin for a number of Viennese bands, including the Gotleib Orchestra. He also served in the army, allegedly signing up after getting involved in a fight with a gamekeeper, and spent two years on an American plantation when young.

Almost none of this is true. Xavier Petulengro was the name used by Walter Leon Lloyd (1878-1957), a herbalist from Rochdale. In the early years of the twentieth century, Petulengro worked as a 'photographic artist' with his wife. In the 1920s Lloyd was invited to help re-establish a tradition of gypsy parties at Baildon in Yorkshire, an event that had died out in 1897. In 1929 the parties were revived and included 'real' gypsies alongside locals dressed in costume – it was a roaring success with over 100,000 people attending.

This was the era of the prophesising gypsy. Women's magazines in the 1920s and 1930s commonly featured fortune-telling columns headed by photos or drawings of a young woman wearing a headscarf and enormous earrings, shorthand for a gypsy heritage. 'Gypsies' interpreted dreams, read palms, peered into crystal balls and laid out cards at major events and on seaside promenades. Lloyd was a professional gypsy and toured the country with his Lady Hussars, playing in variety theatres.

On 17 March 1934, Lloyd was invited to speak on a BBC radio programme about the origin of British Romany. It was so popular he soon became a regular broadcaster and a household name. His radio success led to him writing for the *Bolton Evening News* and by 1937 he was writing 'Your Fate in the Stars' for in the *Sunday Chronicle*. He later wrote for the *Daily Sketch* and became the astrologer for *Woman's Own*. Lloyd was still involved in reviving gypsy carnivals and the 1937 Basildon event where he was crowned King of the Gypsies was widely reported. It was at this event that he officiated over the marriage of his son Leon Petulengro and Illeana Smith, cutting their hands to mingle their blood and binding their wrists with a silk cord. That same year he released a set of gramophone records describing the signs of the zodiac. (Other horoscope columnists released gramophone records about the signs, including R.H. Naylor.) When the *Weekly Horoscope* magazine was launched in September

1937, Petulengro was widely advertised as one of its main contributors. That didn't last long—he was replaced by R. H. Naylor a few months later.

Despite his popularity on the radio and in print, Lloyd didn't stopped touring, although now a big feature of his act was to offer horoscopes to audience members. Had he been born a little later, he would have become a TV astrologer. After his death, Lloyd's son, also named Walter Leon Lloyd, followed in his father's footsteps, legally changing his name to Leon Petulengro in 1937. He wrote the stars for *Woman's Own* for over twenty-five years.

By the early 1930s, astrology had begun to appear even more frequently in the American press. One reason for this may be that it was banned from the airwaves. Radio had grown hugely in the 1920s as stations popped up anywhere and everywhere. Evangeline Adams featured on CBS and her show *Your Stars* reached 44 stations. She offered free readings to anyone who sent in four Forhan's toothpaste coupons and after the first three months, she'd received fifteen thousand letters. Adams was only one of many astrologers broadcasting – Ethel Duncan in Los Angeles received eleven thousand letters a week and Zomar, in Birmingham, Alabama received twenty thousand letters during his first four weeks on the air. However, from 1933 the Radio Act included a ban on broadcasting 'lotteries'. In 1934 this prohibition was applied to fortune telling broadcasts – they were considered 'games of chance' because they contained private information for individuals and because many acted as advertising schemes. (Canada similarly, banned any radio programmes that featured horoscopes from 1937.)

Obviously, this didn't completely stop astrology from being broadcast. Many border stations simply moved into Mexican territory. However, it drastically reduced such content and there was a huge audience hungry for popular astrology who now needed to find it elsewhere.

Writers such as Belle Bart and Genevieve Kemble continued to supply columns to their syndicates, alongside new writers. The astrologer Sydney Bennett, writing under the name 'Wynn', was responsible for publishing *Wynn's Astrology Magazine* in the 1930s and 40s. He also wrote a column in the

*New York Daily News* from at least 1931. This was not a Sun sign column but focused on general and political predictions.

Another early Sun sign astrologer in the US was Ed Wagner (1906-1982). As a reporter for the *Cleveland Press,* in 1924 Wagner had collaborated with Harry Houdini on his exposé of spiritualist frauds. Houdini died in 1926, and Wagner decided to continue his work by preparing an exposé of astrology. As part of that process, he learned to cast charts and then studied astrology in earnest. Between 1928 and 1932 he was associated with the Rosicrucian Fellowship and he later took up astrology as his profession. From 1933-1935 he published his own *National Astrological Journal* and in 1936 Wagner started writing a syndicated column for the *New York Post* syndicate, later transferring it to *Consolidated News Features.* He was Editor in Chief for the Dell Publishing Company from 1946 to 1973.

Although he may not have been the earliest, the astrologer most often credited with writing the first Sun sign column in the USA, Dane Rudhyar (Daniel Chennevière; 1895–1985) was certainly the most prolific. (There probably isn't a word to describe just how prolific Rudhyar was.)

Originally a musician, Rudhyar had studied at the Sorbonne in Paris and at the Paris Conservatoire. He arrived in New York in 1916 and his orchestral arrangements and compositions were performed the following year by the New York Metropolitan Opera, and he later wrote extensively on music. Rudhyar was a theosophist and composed music for a production at the Society's headquarters in Los Angeles in 1920. In 1930 he married Marla Contento, secretary to theosophist Will Levington Comfort who introduced Rudhyar to Marc Edmund Jones, who taught him astrology. At this time, Rudhyar was also studying the works of Carl Jung and he sought to bring astrology and Jungian psychology together. His book *The Astrology of Personality* was published in 1936 and his astrological works were highly influential in the New Age movement of the 1960s and 1970s.

Along with Paul Clancy, the editor of *American Astrology,* Rudhyar is held by many to be responsible for popularising astrology in 1930s America.

Clancy's first magazine appeared on 20 May 1931. He was convinced that Sun sign astrology would prove popular and included it in *Popular Astrology* from the outset. This initial effort was a failure and in 1932, Clancy launched *American Astrology*. However, it wasn't until 1934, when a large distributor placed *American Astrology* on many newsstands, that the magazine achieved mass popularity.

Clancy published Rudhyar's writings from 1932, and after the two met at the end of that year, Rudhyar became a major contributor to the magazine. He wrote under a number of pseudonyms including Francis J. Ramsay and Daniel Morrison.

His detailed Sun sign predictions comprised predictions for each week as well as daily predictions.

> The Month of December for those Born December 22nd to January 19th
>
> November 29 to December 6
>
> Good influences from your ninth house make this a very progressive week; you will get support from your friends in the achievement of some advancement that you want; an intellectual associate helps you. Financial matters seem to be under some strain, but this is more a matter of seeming than actuality; a good deal of this matter is mainly in your mind; actually, your finances seem in pretty satisfactory shape, but you are concerned about them. Saturn is transitting your second house, and this means not necessarily that you are poor, but that you think you need more money than you have. Right now this seems especially true; but if you cut your pattern to your cloth, you will see that you really have enough. Your position in the world should advance this week, and you should be put in the way of achieving something that you want, through a very good and loyal friend who has some considerable private influence. An irritating domestic matter worries

you, but this is something that has been going on for some time, and is about over, so you will do well to forget it.

*(American Astrology,* December 1934, p.57)

Dec. 1— Commencing 1.39 a. m. ruler Moon. Write, travel; your fortunes advance through work; good social contacts are made.

*(American Astrology,* December 1934, p.58)

Rudhyar published several articles each month, not only in *American Astrology*, but also after 1939 in *Horoscope*, *World Astrology*, *Current Astrology*, *The Astrologer*, and others. In all, Rudhyar wrote over a thousand articles. And he was aware of the effect that his writing had:

The popularization of astrology had important implications. It meant that the magazines, the newspaper columns and even most textbooks had to emphasize the "Sun-sign" approach; that is, a type of astrology based on the birthday of individuals. As a result people began to say, "I am a Leo. What is your sign?" This meant that general yet definite psychological characteristics had to be given to the twelve signs of the zodiac and the Sun in a chart had to be considered as the most dominant or basic factor.

(Rudhyar, *The Astrology of Personality,* preface).

*American Astrology* gained a circulation of over 100,000 at its height. It was hugely popular and its Sun sign articles established the format for astrology columns in the USA just as Naylor's *Prediction* columns had done in the UK. The problems with wartime publication experienced in the UK did not apply to the USA. The interest in popular astrology there continued to rise unabated.

Mass-produced astrology reports also became popular, mainly relying on Sun sign forecasts. Few of these survive today. They tended to be used as a promotional device to sell more expensive, individualized horoscopes, as in one example from the *'Kastraka Observatories'*, written in the 1930s. This two and a half page typed report contained a delineation of the character of those born under Pisces, with paragraphs interspersed to sell the idea of a longer and more detailed report, at a cost of twenty shillings.

> On the day of your birth the life-giving Sun, King of our Solar System, was posited in that portion of the Zodiac known as Pisces... The Sun's rays passing through this sign tend to make you trustful, honest and humane... On examining your chart of the heavens, I am happy to state that you are about to pass into a period of great success and happiness. Jupiter and Venus, two beneficial planets of love and wealth are about to play an important part in your life. Success, a love affair and a journey are clearly indicated. The exact dates may be calculated but an extended investigation of your future life will be necessary... should you permit me to prepare for you a full life reading...
>
> *(Kastraka)*

Horoscope columns had whetted people's appetite for astrology and those of all classes happily spent money on reports outlining their future. Personal astrological analyses were previously expensive and relied on people knowing their time of birth – many people didn't. With Sun sign forecasts astrology was accessible to everyone – much to the distaste of serious astrologers.

> Their 'science' is not what I call astrology. A more fitting title would be 'empty quacker'. Birthday information is a device for fleecing the anxious poor out of their sixpences and ninepences, and the astrological bureaux that are springing up under the tutelage of 'savants' with self endowed 'degrees' are devices for fleecing the better classes of their guineas.
>
> (Holmes)

Astrological magazines, though forced to include Sun sign content, were careful to disassociate themselves from this type of astrology.

> There is no such thing as a ready-made horoscope. The printed or mimeographed forms which pass for such are NOT horoscopes, for a horoscope can only be calculated from the time of birth, and requires hours of careful work by one who has studied the principles of astrology and has considerable practice therein. The ready-made printed forms give nothing but a general delineation of anyone born between certain dates in a certain month and are Sun-sign readings and not a horoscope.
> (Franks, *Your Destiny*, April 1932, p.8)

Some Sun sign reports were more serious in intent than others. *American Astrology* produced one in the form of a bound booklet. As well as analysing the Sun sign, it also included the other planets in the individual's birth chart according to the solar house they fell in, as well as looking at the actual position of some of the planets during the year, compared to the positions of planets at birth. This was a compromise position, attracting those who wanted Sun sign forecasts while still including conventional astrological information, and presenting simple interpretations in a format similar to that used for a full birth chart.

Although there was a slight increase in the number of astrology books published during the 1930s, most Sun sign astrology appeared in general fortune telling books. Zodiastar's *Everybody's book of luck: A complete guide to fortune telling and GOOD LUCK* is a good example, containing alongside astrology information on palmistry, handwriting analysis, and reading bumps on the face.

After decades of trying to persuade people that astrology was worthy of attention, serious astrologers became almost petulant in their complaints about the lowering of standards now astrology was in vogue:

> We may rule out of the matter those people who use ready made readings, pigeon hole delineations based on the rising sign or the sun in the sign, as they cannot be recognized as astrologers in the true sense of the word. Their number is legion, and unfortunately they are

increasing daily in number, judging from the advertisements which appear in the papers.

(*British Journal of Astrology*, April 1933, p.121)

Astrology has nothing whatever to do with psychism or spiritualism.

(*British Journal of Astrology*, June 1933, p.162)

Unfortunately, astrologers from their camp were defecting to the Sun sign camp as fast as they could. Being at the centre of these discussions, Naylor felt that he had to justify the validity of Sun sign astrology:

> If the hour of birth be somewhere near dawn or somewhere near high noon the readings will be relatively more correct.
>
> (Naylor, *Year Book 1934*, p.9)

Sun sign astrology could be correct – but it was more correct some times than others. But whatever the views of the serious astrologers, Sun sign astrology was rapidly growing in popularity. Although a fortunate few managed to make more than a small income writing for the press, the myth began to circulate that astrologers were pulling in a fortune with their writing, selling out their beliefs and ideals to Mammon. In reality, this was no more true then than it is today, but the complaint persists.

> The teller of fortunes and writer of horoscopes is doing an excellent business. Hundreds of pounds are paid each week to professional fortune tellers in all walks of life, in order that they may have a peep into the future.
>
> (*Zodiastar*)

Sun sign astrology had become so pervasive that in 1933 the *Sunday Referee* opened its pages to a two month debate on the subject. The editor, Mark Goulden, was always eager for new material, and his tastes tended towards the unusual. He is mainly remembered today for having been unsuccessfully sued by the occultist Aleister Crowley when he rejected his articles and sacked him as a contributor.

The discussion in the *Referee* was prompted by the increased volume of astrological writings in the popular press. Early on in the discussion, astrologers emphasised that there was a vast difference between serious astrology and what most people now understood to be astrology.

> The cheap commercialisation of this vast and intriguing field of research on the part of certain papers is greatly to be deplored, but the pipings of 'Tin Pan Alley' did not shake the artistic truth of the 'Moonlight Sonata'.
>
> (*Sunday Referee*, 18 June 1933, p.8)

The twists and turns of the discussion included different approaches being suggested to test the validity of serious astrology, including statistical studies and comparing charts of those who held something in common, such as conscientious objectors. The arguments weren't original – they had been thrashed out on numerous occasions and still continue. However, for once they appeared in a major London newspaper, and not in an obscure astrological publication. Renowned astrologers such as Charles Carter and W.J. Tucker added their comments to those submitted by people who chose to operate under exotic sounding pseudonyms such as 'Preciosa'. The most telling comment was made by J.P. Larwood in the issue of 6 August 1933.

> For the most part astrology is virtually a new subject to the present generation.
>
> (*Referee*, 6 August 1933, p.14)

British women's magazines continued to carry astrological content as they had during the 1920s. One notable difference was that newly launched magazines chose titles that hinted at astrology – *Oracle*, *Miracle*, *Lucky Star* and *Silver Star* were all launched in the 1930s.

Sometimes, in what appeared to be a fit of contrariness, these columns became more technical in nature as Sun sign astrology began to increasingly appear in newspapers:

> Mercury the messenger is affected by Mars... tempers will be very touchy today and there will be many misunderstandings, think well before making any decisions from 7pm to 8pm... If you were born near the 26 February or August some deceit threatens, avoid going on the water today.
>
> (*Red Star Weekly*, 13 July 1932)

Astrological content appeared alongside clairvoyance and palmistry, and lucky gifts (usually cheap jewellery) were a selling point for numerous women's magazines. Nell St John Montague continued to write for any magazine who'd have her. For example, she had an ongoing column in *Woman's Friend* in 1931 and featured columns in *Peg's Paper* in 1932, 1935 and 1936.

Mystic Myrella was still checking out the future on behalf of readers of *Girls' Mirror* in 1931, describing in detail the astrological influences in the coming week:

> The new moon comes in on Wednesday this week, and you may be sure that this date will be favourable for your love affairs...
>
> (*Girl's Mirror*, 7 December 1931)

*Miracle* offered Madame Blanche who sometimes looked into her crystal and sometimes up at the stars to offer a generalised account of what you could expect for the next week. The *Oracle* offered daily forecasts accompanied by birthday readings. *Poppy's Paper* offered daily predictions from 1930. *Peg's Paper's* Woman of Mystery threw every lucky thing she could think of into the pot when making her Sun sign forecasts in the early 1930s – flowers, gems and lucky numbers were regularly featured. By 1935 the column had been re-titled 'Secrets of the Stars' and comprised daily predictions for a general audience. 'Fortilla' of *Woman's World* in 1933 offered birthday readings with comments on your general character, what to avoid, what to look for and your lucky gems and numbers.

What didn't yet exist was the twelve-sign format used in modern horoscope columns. It's unclear precisely when and where the first Sun sign column in this form first appeared, but a candidate must be the New York magazine entitled *Your Destiny* in January 1932. The column is unattributed but it seems likely it was the work of the magazine's editor, William Franks. *Your Destiny* was careful to outline the difference between an individual's horoscope and forecasts made using their Sun sign alone:

> *Your Destiny* requires of all Astrological advertisers that they furnish proof of their ability to calculate a birth chart accurately and to delineate such charts efficiently. The term horoscope cannot be used to apply to anything except an individual interpretation of a specific birth chart.
>
> (*Your Destiny*, January 1932)

In case any readers weren't totally clear, *Your Destiny* emphasised that the forecasts made related only to an individual's Sun sign:

> The following forecasts are arranged so that the reader will be able to ascertain at a glance what particular influence is affecting him or her during the month. These influences are based and judged from the position of the Sun at birth.

These forecasts are indistinguishable from what we read in a column today:

> This is a good period for the Sagittarians to make changes especially those born between December 6-9. This may take the form of business, financial readjustments or working conditions. Domestic matters are likely to be somewhat upset and those born between November 26-30 will need to be on their guard against deception and a scattering of energies.

*Your Destiny* hedged its bets by also including general forecasts based on planetary placements in the form that readers were more familiar with. Some of the best-known popular astrologers of the day ended up writing in *Your Destiny*. Sidney Bennett, known as 'Wynn', wrote an astrological column that gained him more than four million readers. He also edited his own astrological magazine and he began writing for *Your Destiny* in June 1932, his articles taking the form of what can only be described as astrological sermons. The following month Llewellyn George, founder of the astrological publishers Llewellyn, also became a contributor.

Twelve-sign columns began to appear here and there in newspapers and magazines (the Australian *Women's Weekly* carried twelve-sign columns from 1935), but they were still somewhat of a rarity and the text varied little in style to decades before.

> ARIES – For those born March 21 to April 19.
>
> Commencing 10:45 a.m. ruler Mars. Energetic but confused. Your position is good today, but you endanger it.
>
> (*Clinton Times-Tribune*, Oklahoma, 10 January 1935, p.3)

Dividing the horoscope column into twelve sections wasn't as obvious to early writers as it is to us. Indeed, some columnists experimented with other formats. For example, Adrienne Arden who wrote for the *News of the World* and the *Sunday Pictorial* (later renamed the *Sunday Mirror*) divided her columns into seven sections, according to the traditional ruling planet of the sign in question. This meant that the forecasts for Aries and Scorpio (both Mars ruled, Taurus and Libra (Venus ruled), Sagittarius and Pisces (Jupiter ruled) and Capricorn and Aquarius (Saturn ruled) were combined. The same approach was used by 'Asmodel' of the *Daily Mail* and 'Rama the Indian Seer' in *Silver Star* magazine in the late 1930s. (I haven't yet been able to identify either Asmodel or Rama, and it's possible these columns were also written by Arden.) Uranus and Neptune were sometimes mentioned as dual rulers of Aquarius and Pisces leading to Phyllis Naylor writing a nine-division column for the *Sketch* in 1940. She added Uranus and Neptune to the planetary rulers, giving Aquarius (Uranus ruled) and Pisces (Neptune ruled) their own heading. Aries and Scorpio and Taurus and Libra were still combined under the Mars and Venus headings.

### SATURN AND URANUS SUBJECTS

(All birthdays December 21-January 19 and January 20-February 18)

Your private affairs gain a definite ascendancy.

You find yourself directing great interest to domestic, friendship or family ties. It is a highly propitious time for both entertaining and visiting friends.

The outlook connected with your daily tasks is a stirring one. It looks as though you will be kept very busy to cope with the demands that are made on you.

(Adrienne Arden, *Sunday Pictorial*, 14 March 1937, p.34)

Sometimes the twelve-sign format simply took up too much space. Phyllis Naylor wrote for the *Daily Mirror* in the mid-1930s and her 'astro-telegrams' were only a few lines in length, squeezed into a box in the corner of a page.

ONE OF THOSE "NOT SO GOOD DAYS":

PARTNERS TRYING: EMPLOYEES TEMPERAMENTAL:

KEEP CHEERFUL AND SIMPLY JOG ALONG:

HEAVY MAIL, BUT LEAVE IMPORTANT MATTERS TILL TOMORROW:

(*Daily Mirror*, 22 August 1935, p.7)

Newspaper astrology columnists gradually began to experiment with the new twelve-sign format. Unlike some astrologers, Edward Lyndoe had no problems with the basic concepts of Sun sign astrology. He described how people tended to divide those they knew into types according to their political allegiances and similar, and saw no problem in therefore dividing humanity into twelve groups according to the position of the Sun in the zodiac. He believed that his predictions were made on a sound mathematical and scientific basis and maintained that his work was on a different level to "'hooey' crystal gazing or any of that tomfoolery." Lyndoe's first columns were divided between political forecasts, forecasts for those born on each day that week, and Sun sign forecasts, usually headed by date rather than zodiac sign. By 1939 he was regularly using the twelve sign format.

Naylor didn't use the twelve-sign format until he became the astrology writer for a new magazine edited by James Leigh, *Prediction*, launched in January 1936. Early issues included a number of writers renowned in their fields, for example, Nell St John Montague and Maurice Barbanell, the editor of *Psychic News*. Naylor was introduced with a fanfare. *Prediction* was clearly delighted to have gained the services of England's most renowned astrologer:

> Prediction presents R.H. Naylor, world famous astrologer, to write an exclusive monthly feature.
> 
> (*Prediction*, 1 January 1936, p.1)

Naylor's first article was entitled, 'What is astrology?' followed by a discussion of the horoscopes of those born in February. This set the ground for the twelve paragraph columns, which were headed 'the Aquarius type', 'the Pisces type' and so on, including the dates when the Sun was in that sign. Naylor described his analyses as 'broad outlines'.

The twelve-paragraph format was dropped in the March issue. When it was revived in August, the paragraphs were headed with the relevant dates having prominence and the zodiac signs as sub-headings. It seems that *Prediction* was uncertain about the best way of formatting Naylor's column, and it wasn't until the December issue that the column used bold headings for the signs accompanied by explanatory notes defining the dates that each sign covered.

As *Prediction*'s astrologer, Naylor's contributions went much further than his Sun sign columns. He wrote several pages of astrological articles for each issue. Although a number of these contained more detailed astrological content, including studies of individual's horoscopes, Naylor also wrote a number of articles about character analysis based on Sun signs. For example, in March 1936 he authored articles about the ideal partners for each sign and financial prospects by Sun sign.

Although some serious astrological journals had always carried Sun sign delineations (notably *Modern Astrology* and the *British Journal of Astrology*), they were now almost obligatory. A strange combination of conventional astrological predictions alongside Sun sign forecasts appeared, making astrological journals appear as if they couldn't make their minds up in which direction to turn. They didn't want to lose their potential new audience, but numerous serious astrologers would object if the more technical content were removed. For example, *Wynn's Astrology* in July 1936, carried the following:

> Wednesday July 15 1936 – Mercury-Neptune sextile favors endeavors that require inspiration from 11:15 am to 2 pm but warns against impractical arrangements with friends or in-laws. Avoid setbacks in personal and domestic activities during Moon-Saturn square, 9-10:30 pm.
>
> Aries opportunities in July 1936.
>
> For all those born in this sign March 21-April 19.
>
> How did you come out with last month's influences? The reason for asking is that you have still more of one of them this month – the square between Jupiter and Neptune, which continues till mid-way of the 26th. But that arms-wide-open-fists-unclenched-leading-with-the chin attitude that may or may not have characterized June (how wise were you?) will fold up somewhat this month, into the on-guard

position necessary for a meeting with your now old friends and sparring partners, Saturn-Neptune opposition...

By the late 1930s Sun sign astrology *was* astrology so far as most people were concerned. Although some columns helpfully gave the dates of Sun signs and explained what they were (as many still do today), they were no longer described as arcane knowledge. Most people knew their Sun signs and popular astrology had come home.

# 20

## The War and After

In the late 1930s, people craved reassurance that there'd be no war. Popular astrologers obliged. Later they sought assurance that the war would be short-lived, that the enemy was weak and it would soon be over and life could go back to normal. Again, horoscope writers obliged. One of the biggest blows to astrology's credibility was the failure to predict the Second World War.

Edward Lyndoe had no problem in making such predictions:

> I see absolutely no signs of a Great War during 1939.
> 
> (*People,* 1 January 1939, p.11)

> The Nazis attacking Britain? Don't make me laugh!
> 
> (*People*, 25 June 1939, p.6)

When it became obvious that he'd got it wrong, the only explanation that Lyndoe could offer was that Hitler had somehow defied astrology:

> A madman against the stars!
> 
> (*People*, 3 September 1939, p.10)

And on the day that Germany invaded Russia on 22 June 1941, R.H. Naylor predicted that there was no chance of Germany and Russia quarrelling in the near future. Xavier Petulengro later claimed he'd foreseen the fall of France but thought it better to keep it to himself.

By 1940, an astrology column appeared in every mass circulation Sunday newspaper, in most women's magazines and in many national and local daily newspapers. The *Daily Mail* carried a 'Fortune Forecasts' column, 'Gypsy' Petulengro wrote 'Your Fate in the Stars' for the *Sunday Chronicle,* Lyndoe wrote for the *Daily Express* and Adrienne Arden headed 'Your Stars and You' in the *News of the World.* A paper shortage prevented astrology from growing further during the war years, and many newspapers dropped their astrology columns. The *Daily Express,* for example, was reduced in size from thirty pages to only ten and its astrology column didn't return until 1 January 1954.

In 1941 Mass Observation, the government social research organisation formed in 1937, added astrology to the significant social trends it was analysing, and found that about forty percent of the population had some belief in astrology.

> The DEPTH of belief ranges all the way from occasional humorous interest to fanaticism. But after studying hundreds of comments and conversations, it is impossible to doubt that astrology is now a very considerable influence in determining the minor decisions of many private lives, and is an appreciable contributory factor in influencing attitudes to wider, international events.
> 
> (*New Statesman*, 16 August 1941, p.153)

Mass Observation also noted:

> Women who believe in astrology tend to be appreciably more cheerful, confident and calm than those who do not.
> 
> (*New Statesman*, 16 August 1941, p.153)

That was nice, as astrology still filled many pages of popular women's magazines. Paper rationing made huge changes to the magazine industry. Reduced pages meant a loss of profits from advertising and many titles disappeared while others amalgamated. As magazines became a scarce commodity, readership of individual issues increased drastically. The shortage of consumer goods after the War meant it took some time for advertising to return, and magazine editors were free to focus on content without paying too much attention to commercial considerations. Gradually, the focus shifted from escapist stories to real-life drama, and what better to support a focus on real life than a prediction or two? The audiences for women's magazines in the post-war years was huge. For example, *Woman* went from 750,000 readers in 1938 to over a million in 1946 and over three million in the mid-1950s.

*Peg's Paper* was one of the titles that didn't survive – it merged with *Glamour* in 1940. Madame Sunya was there to solve your problems with astrology to the end. She not only offered daily predictions (generalised, not by sign) but also answered letters and offered astrological solutions:

> I know you are shy because your date reveals a very sensitive, perplexed creature. But you'll gain self-confidence once you have been about more. That always happens to early March girls...
>
> (*Peg's Paper*, 20 May 1939)

Also in 1941, a temporary dent in astrology's popularity took place when *Picture Post* tested the accuracy of the top five newspaper astrologers – Lyndoe, Naylor, Old Moore, Arden, Petulengro – against nine outstanding events during 1939 to 1941. The predictions were rated from 0, representing totally wrong, to 5, totally correct. The low ratings of the astrologers caused a furore in the press and astrology columns were temporarily suspended in a number of publications. But only temporarily.

As the War went on it became more and more difficult to distinguish between propaganda and traditional forecasts. Astrological predictions were used as a propaganda weapon by both sides. The British dropped leaflets predicting a ghastly future for the Germans, and Goebbels retaliated by scattering prophecies (supposedly from Nostradamus) among Allied personnel. He also issued encouraging horoscopes, which described an inevitable bright future. Many readers became bored with the whole business. They had become saturated with Sun sign astrology to such a point that now almost everyone knew their Sun sign. With Sun sign columns in almost every newspaper and numerous magazines there seemed to be no further for Sun sign astrology to go.

The continued popularity of astrology meant that Professor C.E.M. Joad felt obliged to debunk astrology on the radio. Joad was head of the philosophy department at Birkbeck College, London, and a regular on the BBC radio programme *The Brains Trust*, which went out twice a week to twenty million listeners. He thought astrology was 'bunk' and described it as:

> Chief of the aspirins—invented for cure of the world's headache.
> (*Belfast Telegraph*, 22 August 1942, p. 2)

After the War, horoscope columns gradually returned to the British press. They'd never ceased in the USA and had hung on determinedly in women's magazines.

In 1951 G.H. (George) Bratley wrote a horoscope column for *Red Star Weekly*. (Author of a book on gems in 1907 – *The Power of Gems and Charms* – he also wrote for *Prediction* magazine in 1936.) Although the names of the signs didn't appear, it used the twelve-division format and entries were headed by the relevant dates. 'Pierre Vidal' who wrote for *Glamour* in the early 1950s did use the signs to head his column:

> SAGITTARIUS (*November 20th – December 20th*)
>
> You are more settled this week but there may be further important decisions to make. Lucky colour, gold. Day, Wednesday.
> (*Glamour,* 27 November 1951*)*

Newspapers took longer to catch on than magazines, but by the mid-1950s, the twelve-sign format had become standard. For example, John Naylor's (son of R.H. Naylor) column in the *Daily Mirror* used this format from May 1954. He'd replaced Ann Maritza who'd also used the twelve-division, although without the names of the signs in the early 1940s.

In 1955, the *People* invited readers to fill in a lengthy questionnaire. Over fourteen thousand of these were returned, and about a third analysed. The *People* found that half of those who responded read Lyndoe's column regularly and only one tenth of respondents claimed never to read it. This didn't mean that Lyndoe's column was taken seriously. Almost half of those who responded didn't think there was anything to horoscope columns. It appeared that astrology had ground to a halt. However, a new generation was due to discover astrology and take in a direction that would have made any nineteenth-century theosophist proud.

# 21

# 1960s and 70s

> When the Moon is in the seventh house
> And Jupiter aligns with Mars
> Then peace will guide the planets
> And love will steer the stars
> This is the dawning of the Age of Aquarius
> The Age of Aquarius
> Aquarius! Aquarius!
>
> 'Aquarius', *Hair*

It's much easier to find someone who can sing the above, than it is to find someone who can explain what it means. It probably means that the Moon is in the seventh sign – Libra – while Jupiter and Mars occupy the same degree of the zodiac. (It's unlikely to mean when the Moon is where astrologers normally describe as the seventh house, as this relies on a location, and here we're talking about a global phenomenon). Jupiter aligns with Mars about every twenty-seven months and the Moon changes signs every two and a half days. Strangely, the one sign that the Moon doesn't appear in when Mars and Jupiter are conjunct from 1960 to 2004 is Libra. It's debatable whether the song was written by astrological illiterates, as has been claimed, lifting jargon from tabloid horoscopes. Or whether the writers were smarter than we realise and deliberately chose a combination that simply wasn't going to happen in the foreseeable future. No Age of Aquarius for this generation.

What is clear is that this is the first astrological age that comes with a theme tune.

The above are, of course, the lyrics of a song from the hugely controversial hippy musical *Hair*, first performed in 1967. The song was a hit single for the Fifth Dimension in 1969. It went platinum and has since been covered by multiple artists.

*Hair* was a collaboration between the Canadian composer Galt McDermot and dramatists Gerome Ragni and James Rado. It was an instant success when launched on 17 October 1967. *Hair* comprised a series of clichéd cameos from hippy life, and gained a number of column inches because of the full cast appearing nude in the final scene. The show was also charged with the desecration of the American flag and the use of obscene language. The case eventually went to the US Supreme Court. It also effectively marked the end of stage censorship in the United Kingdom. The original production included a company astrologer (Marie Elise Crummaire) who was consulted on casting. *Hair* went on to be performed all over the world and a film version was made in 1979. It continues to be revived at regular intervals.

Astrology's popularity increased vastly in the 1960s, partially because of the counterculture movement. Interest had grown in all forms of mysticism, the occult, and unconventional forms of religion – unconventional to Westerners at least. Instead of being a form of ancient knowledge, requiring long and arduous study, astrology began to be associated with the dawn of the new age – the Age of Aquarius. Not only was astrology simple enough to be understood by everyone through Sun sign astrology, it was also modern.

The Age of Aquarius was by no means a new idea. Since the early twentieth century, the terms 'New Age' and 'Age of Aquarius' have often been used as synonyms.

The Age of Aquarius is based on the astronomical phenomenon of the precession of the equinoxes. A slight wobble in the Earth's axis means that the zodiac as viewed from Earth is gradually slipping backwards in the heavens. Each year, when the Sun reaches the spring equinox (when the ecliptic and equator meet) the zodiacal background to this event has slipped backwards – one degree every seventy-two years. Over 25,868 years, this point slips right around the zodiac to complete a revolution known as the Great Year. This year can be divided into twelve Great Months, giving each zodiac sign its own age of 2,155 years.

Precession was known about from ancient times, certainly by the ancient Greeks if not earlier. However, the concept of astrological ages appears to be relatively recent. In modern astrological theory, the Age of Aquarius heralds a major shift in human consciousness and civilisation, the previous Age of Pisces having heralded the age of Christianity.

> The use of the precession of the equinoxes as a means of dividing historical epochs has no basis in astrological tradition prior to the late nineteenth-century. It emerged out of late eighteenth-century radicalism and the attempt to establish sun-worship as the original form of all religion...
>
> (Campion. *Prophecy*)

Theosophy was influential in establishing the idea of an astrological new age. Although Blavatsky didn't identify her newly arriving spiritually enlightened era as the Age of Aquarius, theosophically inclined astrologers were happy to take on that task.

Astrologers in general were slow to incorporate the concept into their work, and the earliest known reference to the precessional ages occurred in the astrologer Zadkiel's *Textbook of Astrology* in 1879. Some astrologers, including Sepharial, incorporated the idea of astrological ages along with their interest in pyramidology. Sepharial offered the date of 1881, being the length of the Great Gallery of the Great Pyramid of Giza. But it was a non-astrologer, Gerald Massey (whose work Blavatsky cites) who in 1883 produced the first substantial argument that different precessional eras were expressed through the world's religions.

By the beginning of the twentieth century, the concept of a current or imminent shift into a new precessional age was central to the work of many, including that of Rudolf Steiner and Max Heindel. By the 1960s, it was accepted almost without question. The fact that historical ages bear only the most flimsy of relationships to the real history of the period has done nothing to reduce the idea's popularity. Eminent thinkers, such as Carl Jung, were as capable of jumping on astrology's new bandwagon as much as any newspaper columnist.

The big problem for astrologers, and it's a seriously large problem, is that there's no consensus as to when the Age of Aquarius actually begins. Numerous dates have been offered for its beginning, ranging from Cheiro's suggestion of 1762 through to Rupert Gleadow's suggestion of 3000 CE, with 1881 being one of the most popular dates. However, a popular contender was 1962, when all seven of the traditional planets appeared in the sign of Aquarius on 5 February accompanied by a solar eclipse.

As if this combination alone weren't enough, American clairvoyant and astrologer Jeanne Dixon announced that she had experienced a dream in which she saw a baby born in the Middle East who was to become the anti-Christ. This was a year of dissent and cultural upheaval, a time when the hippy utopia began to appear achievable.

The height of the newly discovered interest in the Age of Aquarius could be regarded as taking place on 14 January 1967. A quarter of a million people gathered at the Polo field in Golden Gate Park, San Francisco for the first human be-in. Thousands of hippies were joined by the Grateful Dead, Jefferson Airplane, Timothy Leary – the writer and psychologist who campaigned for psychedelic drug research and use – and the poet Allen Ginsberg. The only reason to be there was to be there. This was the year of the summer of love, where hundreds of thousands of people, not only astrologers were gathering to welcome the new age. Everyone had their face turned to the stars – it was the era where man would land on the Moon for the first time – so far the only time.

Hippies tended to be under thirty, wore long hair and scruffy clothes, took drugs, and sought peace, love and understanding. Although generally against organised religion, they became enchanted with a range of mystical thought systems, often linked to drug-induced hallucinations. Astrology, tarot, and I Ching were all thrown into the pot. The hippy's day had little structure, and it was fashionable to disdain appointments and schedules. Few hippies wore a watch. The mechanics and techniques of astrology excited little interest. What appealed was an accessible astrology – one that looked at the inner person. Sun sign astrology could fulfil the role of simultaneously being an ancient mystical system of knowledge, provide a means to understanding the self and tie in with the emerging popular psychology, and at the same time required no more expertise than remembering your birth date.

Astrology had at the same time grown smaller and larger. It was smaller in that for many people astrology was confined to Sun sign columns and brief analyses of character through Sun signs. It was larger in that astrology was the key to a new age, a new way of being and a time for a new start for humanity. Serious astrology began to decline, and the door was left open for 'astrologers' who were really clairvoyants. Few technical astrological texts were available as Sun sign books began to corner the market.

But popular was still around and can be found in some unexpected places. One of the most influential books of the 1960s was Robert Heinlein's *Stranger in a Strange Land* published in 1961. The best-selling Hugo award-winning novel was so successful that Heinlein and his wife were forced to live behind a barbed wire fence to protect themselves from eager pilgrims to their door.

The story tells of an expedition to Mars where everyone died except for a baby brought up by Martians. That baby, now the adult Valentine Michael Smith, is back on Earth and the centre of political intrigue. A journalist and a nurse try to rescue him while he struggles to understand what's going on around him. Mike wanders about the US looking at things and then starting a Martian-influenced 'Church of all Worlds' where everybody gets to have lots of sex with no jealousy and learns to speak Martian. Finally, he is killed as a martyr and his friends eat his body.

*Stranger* hasn't aged well, primarily for its representation of women and of homosexuality. But it's notable here as it features an astrologer as one of its characters. Becky Vesey, who works under the name of Madame Alexandra Vesant, uses her ability to subtly direct people's actions in what she views as beneficial ways. In the book it's stated that she's not really using astrology but 'senses' the truth and then makes up the astrology to fit.

Sometimes astrology appeared in TV shows as an entertaining aside. In Britain, one of the earliest TV shows to include astrology was *The Avengers*. Starting as an espionage series in 1961, as time went on the stories became increasingly characterised by a futuristic, science-fiction bent. In February 1963, in the episode 'White Dwarf' a leading astronomer predicted that the earth was about to be destroyed, forcing the main characters Steed and Cathy to investigate a conspiracy to silence him. At the end of the episode, Cathy inspected a consignment of books Steed had received and discovered they were about astrology rather than astronomy. Steed opened one and asked Cathy for her birth date (5 October) and then read Cathy her horoscope for the coming week, which told her it was time to break out of her rut and live dangerously.

During the 1960s, a space in which astrology could be featured was on children's TV. In January 1967, ABC broadcast a three-part episode of *Batman* where the hero dealt with the Joker committing crimes based on zodiac signs. And when creating *Thunderbirds* (first broadcast in 1964), Sylvia Anderson, wife of Gerry Anderson and the show's co-creator, assigned birthdays to characters based on their personality characteristics to bring them in line with their Sun signs. For example, Lady Penelope was born on 24 December, making her a Capricorn.

Less glamourous than Lady Penelope was the character of Leonard Swindley played by Arthur Lowe in *Coronation Street* (1962-1965), the manager of a clothing shop and a lay preacher who had frequent run-ins with Ena Sharples. After being sacked in 1966, Swindley and his friend Wally Hunt travelled the country as professional speakers on astrology and paranormal subjects and investigated supernatural mysteries in the spin-off *Turn Out the Lights*. In one episode, they had to solve the mystery of a missing astrologer – Mr. Merlin. The story came to a climax when the astrologer's receptionist drew a knife on Swindley.

By the end of the 1960s astrology had found a home in popular music. Diana Ross gamely advised us in 'No Matter What Sign You Are' in 1969 that you can disregard all warnings of sign compatibilities. She knew that a special individual would be hers no matter what his rising sign. Similarly, Curtis Mayfield in 'Readings In Astrology' asserted a disregard for astrological signs, a view not shared by the object of his affections. As we moved into the 1970s, Cilla Black warbled that she'd 'read in the papers that Gemini people will make it tonight' in the song 'Something Tells Me'. And in 1972 Shel Silverstein's 'The Man Who Got No Sign' on his album *Freakin' At The Freakers Ball* made sure to give all the signs a mention. In many people's minds, astrology was related to dating – 'What's your sign?' making a good question to open a conversation. In 1977 the Floaters had their only hit with 'Float On' in which the lyrics spotlighted each member of the band, who introduced themselves with their name and sign:

Aquarius and my name is Ralph

Now I like a woman who loves her freedom..

It didn't matter what sign you were - someone would have written a song about it. For example, 'Capricorn', Miles Davis (1967); 'Gemini Childe', Mamas and Papas; 'Gemini', Eric Burdon and the Animals (1968); 'Aquarian', Van Der Graaf Generator (1969); 'Virgo Clowns', Van Morrison (1970); 'Aries', Supertramp (1971); 'Maybe I'm A Leo', Deep Purple; (1972) 'Son of Sagittarius', Eddie Kendricks (1973) and 'Leo', John Coltrane (1974).

Some people regarded astrology as rather silly. Certainly, the Monty Python team did. Their 1973 sketch 'What the Stars Foretell' featured a discussion between Mrs. Trepidatious (Terry Jones) and Mrs. O (Eric Idle) in which they read their horoscopes to ascertain:

> The zodiacal signs, the horoscopic fates, the astrological portents, the omens, the genethliac prognostications, the mantalogical harbingers, the vaticinal utterances, the fatidical premonitory uttering of the mantalogical omens ...
>
> (*Monty Python*, BBC, 4 January 1973)

And the prediction for Aquarius, which was:

> A wonderful day ahead. You will be surrounded by family and friends. Roger Moore will drop in for lunch, bringing Tony Curtis with him. In the afternoon a substantial cash sum will come your way. In the evening Petula Clark will visit your home accompanied by the Mike Sammes singers. She will sing for you in your own living room. Before you go to bed, Peter Wyngarde will come and declare his undying love for you.
>
> (*Monty Python*, BBC, 4 January 1973)

It was about this time that one of the most revered of British horoscope columnists made his name. Patric Walker (1931-1995) was rumoured to have one billion readers at the height of his fame. His interest in astrology began when he met American astrologer Helene Hoskins at a dinner party in 1960. Hoskins taught him astrology and when the glossy magazine *Nova* wanted an astrologer on its launch in 1965, Hoskins suggested Walker. He began writing under the name of Celeste, the pseudonym Helene Hoskins had used, for *Queen* (later *Harpers & Queen*) in 1974. Walker then worked for the *Mirror* magazine before moving on in 1976 to *Associated Newspapers*, where he wrote for the *Evening Standard* and the *Mail on Sunday*. Walker's column first appeared in the *Standard* in 1980, and it was later syndicated in North and South America as well as the Middle and Far East. By the end of his life Walker was extremely rich. He owned several homes despite his extravagant lifestyle and a passion for jewellery. Credited with a higher literary standard than many horoscope columnists, Walker even received (often grudging) acceptance from serious astrologers.

In the 1970s Walker was active in the London social scene, hanging out with stars such as Elton John and the Beatles. He tired of partying and moved to Lindos on the Greek island of Rhodes in 1982 after falling in love with the village during a visit in 1979. While he was planning his move, Monty Python's *Life of Brian* was released. In this film, the titular character is introduced as being born under the sign of Capricorn.

> Mandy: So, you're astrologers, are you? Well, what is he then?
>
> Wise man #2: Hmm?
>
> Mandy: What star sign is he?
>
> Wise man #2: Uh, Capricorn.
>
> Mandy: Uh, Capricorn, eh? What are they like?
>
> Wise man #2: Ooh, but ... he is the son of God, our Messiah.
>
> Wise man #1: King of the Jews.
>
> Mandy: And that's Capricorn, is it?
>
> Wise man #2: No, no, no. That's just him.
>
> Mandy: Oh, I was going to say, 'Otherwise, there'd be a lot of them.'
>
> (*Life of Brian*, 1979)

But things were about to change. No-one knew the effect it would have on the world at the time, but the internet was coming into being in the US with the first message sent across the network in 1969. Soon, popular astrology would have a much bigger audience than anyone would have thought possible.

# 22

# Linda Goodman

The story of Sun sign astrology would be sadly incomplete without a look at the work of Linda Goodman (Mary Alice Kenery – usually given as Kemery). Sun sign astrology was well established by the 1960s, with columns syndicated in most of the daily and weekly press. More technical astrology books appeared at intervals, along with a number of mass-market fortune-telling books.

The public perception of astrology had changed little. There were few astrological teachers, and most fledgling astrologers obtained their knowledge from books. Serious astrological literature still comprised books written in the late Victorian period, or were works drawn from that material. Newer works produced by the likes of Dane Rudhyar and Marc Edmond Jones were too difficult for most astrologers to easily understand. The vast majority of people sought the same type of Sun sign astrology as had been popular in the last few decades.

This changed in 1968 when Goodman's book *Sun Signs* appeared. A runaway success, it soon made the New York Times best-seller list, selling over five million copies. *Sun Signs* was to spawn two sequels, *Love Signs* and *Star Signs*, and bring Sun sign astrology into the fore of public consciousness.

*Sun Signs* was often the first book read by those who later became astrologers. Straightforwardly written and instantly accessible to a wide audience, it describes the character of those born under each of the twelve zodiac signs, with sections classifying each as man, woman, child, employer and employee.

There were no attempts at prediction. Instead, the entire five hundred and forty-nine page book was devoted to detailed analyses of personality and behaviour, set out in a way for readers to use the information in their everyday lives. It is now slightly dated – women are much less likely nowadays to aim at marriage as their greatest achievement and leave their jobs when they land their man. However, *Sun Signs* remains in print and continues to sell in large volumes. Sun sign astrology had finally reached adulthood.

Born in Parkersburg, West Virginia, Goodman began her career as a journalist and radio announcer. First married to the writer William Snyder, she adopted the name Linda and married her second husband, Sam Goodman, in 1955.

Her interest in astrology began in 1963, when she was living in New York City and she read books bought from the supermarket. At this time, Goodman would spend up to twenty hours a day studying books and casting charts. The writing of *Sun Signs* was an obsessive labour of love. Goodman would sit at her table writing until she fell asleep and then awaken to simply begin typing again

Goodman soon found herself placed firmly amongst society members. She dined with the Kennedys and spent time with Howard Hughes. Celebrities including Steve McQueen, Princess Grace, and Sonny and Cher sought her counsel. However, Goodman's personal life was problematic. Three of her five children died in infancy and in 1970 she separated from Sam Goodman and moved to the remote mining town of Cripple Creek, Colorado, to write. She soon met twenty-four year old marine biologist Robert Brewer and began a two-year relationship with him.

In 1973, Goodman's twenty-one year old daughter, Sarah (known as Sally) disappeared. Before Sally's disappearance, the two of them had been conducting research into unethical medical experiments in hospitals. They had already received threats for their work. Sally was later found to have committed suicide by taking an overdose. Her stepfather Sam Goodman identified her body and arranged her cremation. Linda refused to believe that her daughter was dead.

Goodman flew to New York to search for her missing child and argued that the autopsy photos she saw showed the dead woman's skin (brown from days of decaying in a warm apartment) was darker than Sally's and that an astrological analysis showed that Sally was still alive. She spent ten days sleeping outside St. Patrick's Cathedral in Manhattan to call attention to what she believed was an official cover-up of her daughter's fate and contacted the FBI and CIA, believing the whole incident to be a government plot.

Goodman's financial fortunes continued to increase. The paperback rights for her second book, *Love Signs*, were sold in 1978 for a then-record $2.25 million. Still believing her daughter to be alive, Goodman spent $400,000 on private detectives to keep up the search. As time went on, Goodman began to claim that celebrity figures such as Elvis Presley, Marilyn Monroe and Howard Hughes were still alive and in hiding. Her beliefs became more bizarre as she became convinced that she was a descendant of Abraham Lincoln.

In the mid-1980s Goodman became a virtual recluse after having the lower part of her leg amputated. Her extravagance finally led her into bankruptcy. She continued to write until her death on 21 October 1995 from complications brought on by diabetes.

A true child of the 60s, Goodman's innovation wasn't a change in astrological technique, but a public acknowledgment of the role that Sun sign astrology now had, and an ability to analyse Sun signs in an almost bewildering amount of detail. As a follower of Rudolf Steiner's thinking, Goodman took the theosophical tradition firmly into the mainstream. It wasn't until after her death that Goodman's own birth data was discovered – nine days later than the 1 April 1925 date she often claimed – and that her original surname was Kenery, rather than Kemery. A whole number of myths have developed around her, leading some of her more obsessive followers to plead confusion as to why she wasn't immortal.

Astrologers aren't renowned for attaining immortality. However, Sun Signs still remains a basic text for beginner astrologers, and has ensured

Goodman the type of literary immortality that many writers only achieve in their dreams.

# 23

# Attacks on Popular Astrology

Throughout the 1970s and 80s, the readership of horoscope columns in the press was rising and continued to do so. An American survey showed horoscope columns to be the fifth most popular feature in newspapers amongst fourteen to twenty-five year olds. Almost half of those surveyed read horoscope columns a few times a week or more, with two thirds of readers being female. The number of daily newspapers carrying horoscope columns or astrological features at least once a week rose steadily.

The same story applied in Britain, and to a lesser extent, continental Europe. By the mid 1970s, almost everyone in the English-speaking world knew something about astrology. Even those with no interest in it tended to know what sign they were born under, and the basic meanings of that sign. That's why stories abound of "What's your sign?" being used as a pick-up line at parties, often invoking the 'witty' responses of 'exit' or 'stop'. No doubt you had to be there.

Popular astrology had become so pervasive in the 1970s that, in the American *Humanist* magazine of September 1975, a statement appeared signed by 186 leading scientists objecting to astrology under the name of 'Objections to Astrology'.

It certainly wasn't the first time that modern scientists had made public objections to popular astrology. In 1938 Dr Harold Spencer Jones, (Astronomer at the Royal Observatory, Greenwich, UK) wrote 'The Queen of Humbug', which was published in *News Review* on 5 August 1939.

Spencer Jones was to go down in history for his response to a journalist in 1957 when asked about the possibility of space travel. He said, "Space travel is bunk." Two weeks later the first Sputnik was launched.

Since the 1930s, articles damning popular astrology had appeared in the press from time to time. Many of them took the form of examining predictions against what actually happened, and compared astrology with other forms of divination. Yet, none of these had the force of the 1975 statement – after all, this was backed by REAL scientists.

> Scientists in a variety of fields have become concerned about the increased acceptance of astrology in many parts of the world. We, the undersigned-astronomers, astrophysicists, and scientists in other fields – wish to caution the public against the unquestioning acceptance of the predictions and advice given privately and publicly by astrologers. Those who wish to believe in astrology should realize that there is no scientific foundation for its tenets. It is simply a mistake to imagine that the forces exerted by stars and planets at the moment of birth can in any way shape our futures... In these uncertain times many long for the comfort of having guidance in making decisions... We are especially disturbed by the continued and uncritical dissemination of astrological charts, forecasts, and horoscopes by the media and by otherwise reputable newspapers, magazines, and book publishers. This can only contribute to the growth of irrationalism and obscurantism.
>
> (*The Humanist*, September 1976, p.4)

The man responsible for 'Objections' was Paul Kurtz, editor of *The Humanist*. Kurtz was Professor Emeritus of Philosophy at the University at Buffalo (SUNY), but has become better known for his prominent role in the American sceptical community. Asteroid 6629 (Kurtz) is named in his honour. He is largely responsible for the secularisation of humanism, which before the 1980s, was widely perceived as a religion that excluded the supernatural.

Kurtz's concern about the revival of astrology in the US led him to circulate a letter to leading scientists and academics. He was able to collect 186 signatures of support from astronomers, astrophysicists, and other scientists, including those of eighteen Nobel Prize winners.

The statement itself was the work of Professor Bart Jan Bok. A Dutch-American astronomer, Bok had urged the Council of the American Astronomical Society to issue a statement telling the world that they believed that there was no scientific basis for a belief in astrology. He was turned down twice.

'Objections' was sent to every newspaper in the United States and Canada. It gained plenty of attention and was discussed on the front page of the *New York Times*. Other newspapers picked up the article, many of them responding negatively. Before long the statement gained worldwide attention.

Not everyone who received 'Objections' signed it. The physicist and mathematician Freeman Dyson and astronomer Carl Sagan both refused.

> I find myself unable to endorse the objections to the astrological statement, not because I feel that astrology has any validity whatever, but because I feel the tone is authoritarian. That we can think of no mechanism for astrology is relevant, but unconvincing... those who object [to astrology] on grounds of unavailable mechanism are merely confirming the impression that scientists are rigid and closed minded.
>
> (Sagan)

After its publication in *The Humanist*, the statement was published by Kurtz's publishing house, Prometheus Books, along with an article attacking the research claims of the prominent French astrologers and statisticians Michel and Françoise Gauquelin by Lawrence Jerome. (The Gauquelins analysed astrology statistically by studying various correlations using very large samples of birth data and Michel Gauquelin's book *The Scientific Basis for Astrology* was published in 1970). Jerome's thesis was that astrology was a form of magic and since we know magic is bogus, astrology must be also bogus. Bok's book made it clear that his major objections were to Sun sign astrology.

> During the past ten years, we have witnessed an alarming increase in the spread of astrology. This pseudoscience seems to hold fascination especially for people of college age who are looking for firm guideposts in the confused world of the present. It is not surprising that people believe in astrology when most of our daily newspapers regularly carry columns about it and when some of our universities and junior colleges actually offer astrology courses.
>
> (Bok, p.2)

> I have learned that many people who take astrology seriously were first attracted to the field by their reading of the regular columns in the newspapers. It is deplorable that so many newspapers now print this daily nonsense. At the start the regular reading is sort of a fun game, but it often ends up as a business. The steady and ready availability of astrological predictions can over many years have insidious influences on a person's personal judgment.
>
> (Bok, p.29)

Not everyone approved of the attack against astrology. A *Washington Star* editorial thought it futile and hoped it made the scientists feel better.

A number of scientists had been worried about the upsurge in interest in the occult for some time. One group with an interest in the matter was Resources for the Scientific Evaluation of the Paranormal (RSEP). Its members included Martin Gardner, Ray Hyman, James Randi, and Marcello Truzzi, all of them magicians.

Martin Gardner (1914-2010) was a mathematician with an interest in religious belief. His book *Fads and Fallacies in the Name of Science* is known as a classic amongst sceptics. Gardner also has an asteroid (2587) named in his honour. Ray Hyman (1928 -) was Professor Emeritus of Psychology at the University of Oregon.

James Randi (Randall James Hamilton Zwinge; 1928-2020) had worked as a professional stage magician and escapologist since 1946 and appeared as

'The Amazing Randi' on the television show *Wonderama* from 1967 to 1972. He entered the international spotlight in 1972 when he challenged the public claims of Uri Geller, accusing him of being a charlatan and using magic tricks. He was most well-known for the One Million Dollar Challenge in which the James Randi Educational Foundation said it would award a prize of one million dollars to anyone able to show evidence of paranormal, supernatural, or occult power or event. The challenge started in 1964 when Randi put up $1,000 of his own money. In 2015, the Foundation announced that the Challenge was terminated due to Randi's retirement. Randi had asteroid 3163 named for him.

Marcello Truzzi (1935-2003), Professor of Sociology at Eastern Michigan University, was also a member of the Parapsychological Association. Unfortunately, Truzzi and Hayman were short-changed on the asteroid front, and so far have no planetary bodies named after them. However, at least Truzzi's name was placed on the Stardust spacecraft launched in 1999.

RSEP was to form the heart of a new organisation, the Committee for the Scientific Investigation of Claims of the Paranormal. (CSICOP) which was established as an outgrowth of 'Objections' at the April 1976 annual conference of the American Humanist Association in Buffalo, New York. CSICOP took on for itself the task of examining:

> Openly, completely, objectively, and carefully... questionable claims concerning the paranormal and related phenomena, and to publish results of such research.

CSICOP's early membership was drawn from the RSEP, and a number of individuals associated with Kurtz and *The Humanist* including the debunker of UFOs Philip J. Klass, novelist L. Sprague de Camp, philosopher Ernest Nagel and Bermuda triangle expert Larry Kusche as well as the aforementioned. Although a co-founder, Truzzi left CSICOP shortly after it formed saying that many of those involved:

tend to block honest inquiry, in my opinion. Most of them are not agnostic toward claims of the paranormal; they are out to knock them. [...] When an experiment of the paranormal meets their requirements, then they move the goal posts.

(Caldwell)

CSICOP knew how to play the media. Kurtz held a press conference in New York to announce a campaign to purge the media of occultist leanings. Worldwide syndicated stories announced CSICOP's formation. They received front-page coverage in the *New York Times* and *Washington Post*. CSICOP began a new campaign against Sun sign astrology in 1984, when it urged US newspapers and magazines to label their columns with a disclaimer saying they were for entertainment purposes only, and had no factual basis. A small number did so, although some editors refused to print a disclaimer on the grounds that no educated person would take Sun signs seriously.

CSICOP's charter states that it exists to pursue six major goals:

1. Maintain a network of people interested in critically examining paranormal, fringe science, and other claims, and in contributing to consumer education.
2. Prepare bibliographies of published materials that carefully examine such claims.
3. Encourage research by objective and impartial inquiry in areas where it is needed.
4. Convene conferences and meetings.
5. Publish articles that examine claims of the paranormal.
6. Do not reject claims on a priori grounds, antecedent to inquiry, but examine them objectively and carefully.

Over the years, CSICOP has conducted investigations into many paranormal claims. Notable members of CSICOP have included TV science program host

Bill Nye, Carl Sagan, illusionist Milbourne Christopher and science fiction author Isaac Asimov. Interestingly, Asimov, in speaking out against astrology, has noted that (like John Sladek below) he can't have a horoscope prepared being unsure of his birth date.

CSICOP's examinations of claims of paranormal phenomena apply accepted scientific and academic methodologies to topics that most scientific organizations ignore as fringe science or pseudoscience. CSICOP continues today, although Randi left in 1995 when he was in the process of being sued by Uri Geller, the case being resolved through private settlement.

In November 2006, CSICOP changed its name to CSI (Committee for Skeptical Inquiry), stating that this was due to the prominence of the word 'paranormal' leading to misunderstandings.

CSI Chairman Paul Kurtz, founder of the Center for Inquiry, emphasised that, although CSI will remain true to its early CSICOP mission, the organisation has never confined itself exclusively to the investigation of paranormal claims. CSI will continue to deal with a wider range of topics emerging in the contemporary world, such as unfounded ethical opposition to stem cell research.

> "Today there are new challenges to science," Kurtz writes in Skeptical Inquirer. "Yet powerful moral, theological, and political forces have opposed scientific research on a whole number of issues."
>
> (CSICOP – CSICOP Becomes CSI)

The decision to change their name was made after more than ten years of discussion on the subject. In case you're wondering, one thing that there was no doubt about was that the letters CSI would be used; what they stood for was the subject under discussion.

And yes, we know there is a popular science oriented television program (actually three of them) with CSI in the title but thought, frankly, that that was as much an advantage for us as a disadvantage.

(CSCOP – It's CSI Now)

So now we know.

Did the scientists and sceptics succeed in their mission? Not in the slightest. After 1975, interest in astrology actually grew and the number of Sun sign columns in newspapers increased. Apart from those interested in astrology's history, professional skeptics and paranormal debunkers, hardly anyone remembers the 1975 manifesto.

Attacks on popular astrology continue to this day, notably in Britain by Richard Dawkins, an eminent British ethologist, evolutionary theorist, and popular science writer who held the Charles Simonyi Chair in the Public Understanding of Science at Oxford University from 1995-2008. He first came to prominence with his 1976 book *The Selfish Gene*, which popularised the gene-centric view of evolution and has written several best-selling popular books on evolution as well as appearing in a number of television programmes.

Dawkins wrote an article entited "The Real Romance in the Stars" in the *Independent on Sunday* newspaper on 31 December 1995. Although a tirade against astrology in general, the article was mainly focused against Sun sign columnists.

> It is, of course, sun sign astrology's well-heeled practitioners in newspapers and on television that I am attacking as exploitative charlatans.
>
> (*Independent on Sunday*, 31 December 1995)

This footnote didn't appear in the original piece. In fact, Dawkins added it when asked by the Astrological Association of Great Britain if his article could be reprinted in their *Journal*. He appears to have been less willing to attack serious astrology or astrologers – at least in their own environment.

Dawkins continued to rail against astrology. In his Channel 4 documentary *The Enemies of Reason* in 2007, he claimed that astrology was invented by Ptolemy in the second century CE and hasn't changed since.

Every so often an eminent scientist makes a vitriolic statement against astrology. Some astrologers get indignant, some people offer rejoicing support – and the vast majority of people continue to read their horoscope columns as if absolutely nothing has happened.

# 24

# Thirteen Signs

One thing that astrologers, scientists, and people who like to read their horoscopes over a nice cup of coffee agree on is that there are twelve zodiac signs. Although very ancient Babylonians greedily used eighteen, for the last couple of millennia we've been more than satisfied with twelve. So where *did* we get the idea that there may be thirteen signs in the zodiac?

The zodiac signs have a long and rich history. Their early naming and meaning is usually attributed to ancient Babylon. Babylonian boundary stones dating from the twelfth century BCE host instantly recognisable pictorial representations of the signs. Over the centuries, different interpretations of the meanings of the pictures have been given. And it's notable that a thirteenth symbol is occasionally included – that of the raven. So it's tempting to think that there was a time when Babylonians used thirteen zodiac signs.

Tempting – but wrong. The Babylonian calendar had twelve lunar months meaning that their year lasted 354 days. That gave them the problem of tying their calendar in with the solar year, which lasts about 365 days. Our present calendar gets round this issue by removing the tie between the lunar phase and the calendar month. The Babylonians came up with a simple, yet elegant solution. They added leap months to their calendar. The raven was simply a symbol of a leap month.

So far as we know, the zodiac consists of twelve signs, and has done so since astrology reached a form we'd recognise. Its antiquity is why Virgil, the Latin poet, could write in his *Georgics* in 29 BCE a joke about the stars withdrawing to make space for Caesar as a thirteenth sign of the zodiac.

As any astrologer will tell you, although the zodiac signs and constellations share the same names, they aren't actually the same. The zodiac signs have only ever approximately coincided with the constellations. For example, Cancer is a small constellation, and Pisces is huge, but both are accorded one twelfth of the Sun's annual path. The constellation Cancer has never coincided exactly with the sign of Cancer. In the West, we use the tropical zodiac. This is based on a division of the Sun's apparent path across the sky into twelve equal segments of thirty degrees each. In India, the sidereal zodiac is used, which reflects the actual position of the constellations, rather than their past position as in the West. There are differences between the two systems. But no-one argues that there are more than twelve signs.

Contrary to the belief of some scientists, astrologers don't fall over backwards in shock when it's pointed out that the zodiac signs don't match the constellations. They already know this, and they know why. While the earth spins once in twenty-four hours, it also has other movements. Like a spinning top, the earth has a slow wobble as it spins, taking 26,000 years to do one wobble. This causes the zodiac constellations to drift through the sky, in the process known as precession.

Ancient astrologers chose signs that matched the constellations. Because of precession, the moving constellations left the signs behind. Today the tropical zodiac is out of step by about one sign. Astrologers are also aware that planets aren't actually 'in' constellations, they pass in front of them. This is an optical illusion. If you were on a different planet, they would appear to be in front of different constellations as compared to a view from earth. And it doesn't change the fact that there are twelve zodiac signs.

There is a small number of astrologers who believe that there should be thirteen signs. They often justify this by saying that there are thirteen lunar months in the year, and therefore there should be thirteen signs. An odd rationalisation considering that the zodiac is based on the Sun's passage through the heavens and not the Moon's. The thirteen sign issue is not a tale lost in the mists of history. We actually know why some people believe there to be thirteen zodiac signs and who was responsible. It was the science fiction writer John Sladek.

Sladek was an American science fiction author who became known for his satirical and surrealistic novels. He spent the 1960s in London and was part of the New Wave which began in 1964 when Michael Moorcock took over as editor of the science fiction magazine *New Worlds*. Moorcock had a policy of publishing unusually literary stories, and *New Worlds* sought to distance itself from traditional science fiction. The content of *New Worlds* focused on taboo breaking and a more people focused approach. New Wave writers saw themselves as part of a general literary tradition and openly mocked the traditions of pulp science fiction. The New Wave also had a political subtext with many of its writers coming from Marxist and socialist political traditions.

Sladek's most famous novel, *The Müller-Fokker Effect*, was published in 1971 and was the story of how an attempt to preserve human personality on tape goes awry – although many readers were simply entranced by its title. Sladek was also known for his parodies of other science fiction writers.

While science fiction was redefining itself as literature, a new type of writing was becoming popular in the mass market - pseudo-science as scientific fact. And no-one was more adept at producing such work, or to be more renowned for it than the Swiss author, Erick von Däniken. Von Däniken produced a number of books about extra-terrestrial influence on human culture since prehistoric times. He is one of the key figures responsible for popularising ancient astronaut theories. In 1967, while von Däniken was spending time in prison on charges of embezzlement, forgery, and tax evasion, his first book *Chariots of the Gods* was published. He wrote his second book, *Gods from Outer Space* while still in prison.

Sladek wrote a scathing attack on von Däniken and his work in 1969. By this time, Moorcock had published Sladek's work in *New Worlds* magazine, and was planning to write a book on irrational beliefs. When Moorcock realised he was never likely to write that book, he turned the title and some of his sources over to Sladek. In no time at all Sladek was hooked. He became a born again sceptic and wrote *The New Apocrypha: A Guide to Strange Sciences and Occult Beliefs* (1973).

Initially, Sladek had hoped to find something in parapsychology, but all he found was badly conducted experiments and outright fraud. He couldn't resist poking fun at every topic he covered. The tone of the book can be gleaned from the chapter title on flying saucer cults – 'Will U kindly FO?' *Apocrypha* covered a huge range of material, from Nostradamus to psychic detectives, taking in eternal motion machines, the secret codes that prove that Bacon wrote Shakespeare, Noah's Ark, and Erich von Däniken. Sympathy for Däniken was in short supply and Sladek continued to parody him, for example in his 1974 short story *Space Shoes of the Gods*.

> A ruined edifice in Peru bears a weird inscription: two horizontal lines crossed by two vertical lines. In other words, the figure for tic-tac-toe, a game played by the latest giant computers. Likewise the Ankara Museum displays clay tablets pierced with holes – the same holes used in modern IBM cards.

Despite the humorous tone, Sladek's expositions were impressively researched, and he let his subjects speak for, and demolish, themselves. *Apocrypha* attacked many who Sladek saw as false gurus, including Immanuel Velikovsky and L. Ron Hubbard, the founder of scientology. The Church of Scientology threatened legal action as Sladek quoted an article from *Queen* magazine without knowing they'd already successfully sued for libel over it. In lieu of damages, they had the section on scientology altered in the British paperback edition of Sladek's book.

Responses to *Apocrypha* mixed approval and anguish, agreeing that most targets were junk science, with one exception, an exception that varied each time. Sladek had developed a fascination with unorthodoxy and the occult, as well as its adherents. The year following *Apocrypha*'s publication was filled with stories of Uri Geller's spoon bending antics, Koestler's coincidence theories, and the Berlitz triangle. The 1975 Manifesto meant that astrology was pushed to the forefront of the news and made a prime target. Or was there was a more personal reason for Sladek's astrological spoof? After all, owing to a discrepancy between hospital and state records, Sladek didn't know whether he was born in October 1937 (as suggested by hospital records) or on 15 December 1937 (as according to Iowa State records). He chose to celebrate his birthday on the latter date.

Whatever the precise reason, two years after the Manifesto Sladek published *Arachne Rising: The Thirteenth Sign of the Zodiac* under the name of James Vogh.

The idea of additional zodiac signs wasn't new. Indeed, in 1970 Stephen Schmidt had suggested a fourteen-sign zodiac including Ophiuchus and Cetus as signs in his book *Astrology 14*. However, Sladek's book reached a much larger audience.

The temptation for Sladek to devise his own occult system had been irresistible, and his detailed research allowed him to convince his readers. *Arachne Rising* claimed to be an account of a thirteenth sign of the zodiac being suppressed by the scientific establishment. Sladek offered historical, mythical, literary, and numerological evidence for the suppressed sign of Arachne the spider.

To fit Arachne into the zodiac, Sladek divided it into thirteen and inserted Arachne between 25° 23' Taurus and 23° 5' Gemini. He included statistics that showed that people born under Arachne (13 May to 9 June) were usually psychics, leading to enthusiastic mail from Arachnoid readers who claimed they'd known this all along. The symbol of Arachne is a circle with a cross at the centre, a common symbol for the earth.

Alert readers noticed that alongside interpretations of charts of people such as Uri Geller, Sladek included astrological case histories for Cassandra Knye, the name under which Sladek and the writer Thomas Disch had published spoof Gothic novels, and James Colvin, a *New Worlds* house pseudonym often used by Michael Moorcock.

Sladek's thirteenth sign was identified roughly with the constellation Auriga, and supposedly took more account of the influence of the Moon. He argued that Auriga was the thirteenth sign in the lunar zodiac used by the Druids amongst others. According to Sladek, Auriga was widely known as a zodiac sign in ancient times but deliberately suppressed after the Middle Ages because of its psychic lunar connections. The Church apparently opposed the use of Arachne due to its Celtic ancestry. (The idea of an ancient Celtic zodiac reappeared in 1992 with Helen Patterson's book *The Celtic Lunar Zodiac*.)

Auriga was known as Ariadne by the Minoans and so was connected to the labyrinth and the magic thread that guided Theseus. From the magic thread of Ariadne we take but a short step to the weaver goddess Arachne. Or a short step to Arianrhod the Celtic Goddess of the Moon and Stars, and of the silver wheel of the heavens. Sladek described how Arianrhod drives her chariot around the heavens, leading us and connecting us to the source, like Theseus in the labyrinth, and like the spider goddess weaving her web of fate.

The book read like, and quoted, serious astrological and historical sources. Presumably because not enough astrologers read science fiction, it was accepted as a serious astrological text – if a little peculiar. But any astrologer knows that there is no shortage of peculiar astrological texts. The book was republished in 1979 under the new title of *The Thirteenth Zodiac: The Sign of Arachne*.

Sladek later announced that the whole thing had been a hoax. Unfortunately, that did little to stem the enthusiasm of some astrologers, who continued to use the 'new sign'. He claimed to have been surprised that people took the book so seriously. Perhaps it was his surprise that persuaded him to write a follow-up volume *The Cosmic Factor* in 1978 and, under the name of Richard A. Tilms, *Judgment of Jupiter* in 1980.

In the greater scheme of things, Sladek's books had caused hardly a ripple. Although the concept of a thirteenth zodiac sign was firmly planted in many people's heads, it would take another twenty years before an astronomer came into the picture to introduce the idea of a missing zodiac sign.

In 1995, Dr Jacqueline Mitton (Public Relations Officer of the Royal Astronomical Society) acted as a consultant to the BBC and appeared in the third episode of their television series about astronomy, entitled *Heavenly Bodies*. While filming, she mentioned that the zodiac contained a thirteenth constellation, and pointed out that there was a difference between her astrological Sun sign as usually given and the true position of the Sun on her birthday.

The first episode of *Heavenly Bodies* was scheduled for broadcast on Sunday 22 January 1995. The BBC sent out their publicity material, and it landed on the desk of Roger Highfield, the science editor of the *Daily Telegraph*.

Stories about astrology make good copy, so Highfield contacted Mitton to talk to her about her views on astrology and the astronomy behind them. These were reported in an article that included a diagram illustrating the difference between the traditional zodiac divided into twelve equal signs, and an "astronomically correct" zodiac based on the true path of the Sun through the sky.

The following day the rest of the press followed suit with their own stories and the Royal Astronomical Society began to field calls from all over the world about the new zodiac sign.

> Between 2,000 and 3,000 years ago the dates on which the sun appeared in the different constellations were worked out by apportioning one twelfth of the sky to each constellation. Those dates are still used by astrologers for their predictions. Because the stars are only visible during the night most people have to take the astrologers' word for it when they talk about being 'in' a particular star sign: that is when the sun is in front of a particular constellation. Unfortunately for astrologers, the constellations cover different sized areas of the sky, according to the International Astronomical Union. 'Some constellations cover much

bigger areas than others,' said Dr. Mitton. This means that each zodiac sign should, in reality, cover a different number of days. Worse still, in the intervening years the direction of the earth's axis has been slowly changing. This causes the seasons, and thus our calendar, to shift with respect to the star's positions.

(*Daily Telegraph,* 20 January 1995)

Mitton was referring to the International Astronomical Union redrawing the boundaries of the constellations in 1930 and including a thirteenth constellation along the ecliptic. According to the official modern constellation boundaries that astronomers use, the sun now passes through thirteen constellations, and not twelve. This thirteenth constellation is Ophiuchus the Serpent Bearer, and the Sun is in front of its stars during approximately 30 November to 17 December.

A thirteenth sign would destroy the principle of the twelve-fold division of the zodiac if astrologers accepted it. And Mitton was perfectly correct in her assertion that the equally sized zodiac signs don't correspond to the constellations. They never have. (Alert thirteenth sign hunters remembered that Sladek had in fact pointed out the position of Ophiuchus on the zodiac belt in Arachne).

Ophiuchus is an ancient constellation, one of the original Ptolemaic constellations, and appears in the *Almagest.* In his *Tetrabiblos,* Ptolemy treats Ophiuchus as a non-zodiacal constellation. Ophiuchus also appears on the *Farnese Globe,* a Roman copy of a second century BCE depiction of Atlas holding the celestial sphere. The Moon and planets can be seen against the stars of Ophiuchus.

Astrologers had no choice but to respond to the idea that their zodiac had changed. Articles appeared in astrological publications, and for a short time, there was excited discussion. Most astrologers rubbished the idea saying that the zodiac and the constellations aren't and had never been the same so there was no reason for any changes. A few astrologers were tempted by the new sign because of the association with the thirteen lunar months.

A small minority looked to the myth of Ophiuchus so that they could incorporate its meaning into their work. Ophiuchus was better known in classical times as Asclepius, the God of Medicine. He learnt his art from Chiron, the Centaur. On either side of Ophiuchus in the heavens lie the two parts of the sign of the serpent he holds, Serpens Caput, the serpent's head and Serpens Cauda, the serpent's tail. The serpent staff is the badge of the medical profession to this day in the form of the caduceus. It is from the serpent that Ophiuchus learnt the secret of the elixir of life.

Plato drew a correspondence between Ophiuchus and the god of the underworld, Pluto. Medieval Christians used an image of Saint Paul holding a viper to represent Ophiuchus before dropping it altogether. (Not the viper.)

Ophiuchus is always shown with his foot resting on Scorpius. In ancient Greek legend, the earth Goddess Gaia sends Scorpius to kill Orion, the Hunter, who has threatened to hunt down all the animals of the earth. Scorpius stings Orion, who would have died had it not been for the intervention of Ophiuchus. Ophiuchus gives Orion a sip of the divine elixir and restores him to health.

The older Babylonian version is a little different. Here the serpent is Tiamat, the Monster of the Bitter Ocean. Holding Tiamat is Marduk, the Sun God of the Babylonians. They are doing battle together in the eternal fight of good against evil.

To please those of you who want to become Ophiucheans, the Sun sign dates incorporating Ophiuchus are as below.

|  |  |
| --- | --- |
| Aries | April 19 - May 13 |
| Taurus | May 14 - June 20 |
| Gemini | June 21 - July 19 |
| Cancer | July 20 - August 9 |
| Leo | August 10 - September 15 |

| | |
|---|---|
| Virgo | September 16 – October 30 |
| Libra | October 31 – November 22 |
| Scorpio | November 23 – November 29 |
| Ophiuchus | November 30 – December 17 |
| Sagittarius | December 18 – January 18 |
| Capricorn | January 19 – February 15 |
| Aquarius | February 16 – March 11 |
| Pisces | March 12 – April 18 |

With almost unseemly haste, Walter Berg's *The Thirteen Signs of the Zodiac* was published on 22 May 1995. And then the idea sank into astrological history – temporarily.

On 14 January 2011 the *Los Angeles Times* reported a 'new astrological sign':

> The astrological calendar is all wrong. That public comment from a Minnesota astronomy professor set the Internet aflame this week.

The story described how Parke Kunkle had pointed out the thirteenth sign of Ophiuchus, and being born under it meant you were a seeker of wisdom. (He did acknowledge he wasn't the first person to mention this.) The resulting media frenzy may have been related to the post that appeared on NASA's website a short time later pointed out that the Babylonians had excluded Ophiuchus from the zodiac. The text appeared on an educational site for children called 'The Space Place'. This was barely noticed until in 2016 when *Cosmopolitan* magazine (the UK edition) ran a story about the thirteenth sign that went viral. It stated that NASA had researched zodiac signs and re-drafted the zodiac to include Ophiuchus, NASA was forced to release a press statement denying they'd done any such thing. It didn't matter—the zodiac had changed.

NASA has just gone and dropped the mother of all bombshells to announce there's another zodiac sign and we've basically been living our lives under false pretenses this whole time. Way to go NASA, ruin our lives why don't you?

(Elle, 18 September 2016)

In 2020 the story had again circulated so widely that NASA tweeted a link to their 2016 statement.

The story about the zodiac being 'wrong' and how we need to take notice of a thirteenth sign appears every summer. (Why has never been satisfactorily explained.) And every year astrologers get indignant all over Facebook.

# 25

## 1980s and 1990s

In 1986 Prince sang 'ain't no particular sign I'm more compatible with' in 'Kiss'.

This was the decade when fantasy went mainstream. Terry Pratchett's first Discworld book *The Light Fantastic* appeared in 1988. As the series went on, with astrology and astrological references were sprinkled throughout. For example, in *The Light Fantastic*, the wizard Trymon obtains Rincewind's (the main character) place and time of birth from university records so an astrologer can cast a horoscope. And in Terry Pratchett's and Neil Gaiman's *Good Omens*, published in 1990, the local newspaper has a surprisingly specific horoscope for Libra, on the day the apocalypse begins. This is just after a discussion of medieval Bishop Usher's contribution to Creationism, in which he worked out from the Bible that God created Earth in October, 4004 BCE 9.00 am making the Earth Libra. The time was apparently incorrect by about a quarter of an hour.

That same year, Douglas Adams in *The Long Dark Teatime Of The Soul* described how the Great Gazanga was an astrologer and friend of the protagonist Dirk Gently and aimed his horoscopes at Dirk to wind him up. The Great Gazanga produced what might be the best astrological prediction ever in the thrid book of the series:

> Today you will meet a three-ton rhinoceros called Desmond.
> (Adams, *The Salmon of Doubt,* p.248)

When it comes to astrology in popular fiction during this period, the example that will leap to most people's minds is J. K. Rowling's Harry Potter. The first novel of the series, *Harry Potter and the Philosopher's Stone*, was published 26 June 1997. By February 2018, the books had sold more than 500 million copies worldwide, making them the best-selling book series in history, and had been translated into eighty languages.

Astrology appears throughout the series. In *Harry Potter and the Order of the Phoenix,* the centaurs are described as practising astrology only to predict major, world-changing events while humans also used it to predict mundane, day-to-day occurrences and better understand themselves. Centaurs viewed these things as too trivial to be affected by the movement of the planets.

Coinciding with the Discworld series was the first new-style computer game – *Final Fantasy*. First published in 1987, *Final Fantasy* was created by Hironobu Sakaguchi and conceived as his last-ditch effort in the game industry. It took game design onto a whole new level. A huge success, *Final Fantasy* spawned sequels and other genres such as tactical role-playing, action role-playing, multiplayer online role-playing, CGI films, anime, manga and novels. The series has sold more than 144 million units, making it one of the best-selling video game franchises of all time.

*Final Fantasy* provides birthdates for the main cast in its supplementary material and the relationships between the signs were integrated into the strategy. *Trines* caused the two units to be more effective against each other; *squares* resulted in the units being less effective against each other; oppositions had effects dependent on characters' genders (if of the opposite gender, they would be most effective against each other because opposites attract). Each game has different astrological elements.

Astrology continued to feature in the design of computer games such as in *The Sims,* which has sold nearly 200 million copies worldwide and is one of the best-selling video games series of all time. In *The Sims 2*, zodiac signs represent specific combinations of personality points, and are unrelated to when a character is born as there are no dates, as such, although modifications are available. When the chemistry feature was introduced, compatible signs contributed towards higher chemistry, which made it easier to unlock new social interactions.

And it also featured in tabletop and card games. In 1993, in the collectible card game *Magic: The Gathering,* the zodiac signs were used to define creatures. A year later the RPG *The Elder Scrolls* had thirteen birth signs that the player could choose during character creation.

Throughout the 1990s there were scattered references to astrology on TV and in music. For example, the 1992 BBC TV series *Moon and Son* starred Millicent Martin as a clairvoyant (Gladys Moon) and John Michie as her psychic son (Trevor Moon). The two of them travelled between Kent and France, doing readings and selling occult and astrological goods from their caravan, getting involved in various adventures along the way. And in the 27 June 1996 episode of *Men Behaving Badly,* Tony (played by Neil Morrissey) makes crude attempts to win over Deborah (played by Leslie Ash) who is into astrology by drawing his birth chart and claiming that sex with him is in the stars: "I must lie down here in conjunction with you."

The Australian-American science fiction series *Farscape,* which premiered in 1999, featured a character called 'Scorpius' who embodied the symbolism associated with the zodiac sign of Scorpio. Born as a result of an inter-species rape, Scorpius escaped at the age of twelve and turned himself over to the Peacekeepers (law-keeping force), offering them inside information about the Scarrans (the non-'human' race he was descended from). Dressed usually in black leather, Scorpius had the ability to see other being's energy signatures, allowing him insight others didn't have. He was also depicted as lying, cheating, stealing and abandoning allies or enemies alike. One of his main opponents, and one of the main characters in the series, was Aeryn *Sun.*

Astrology plays a much greater role in *Battlestar Galactica.* Beginning with a TV series in 1978, the franchise consists of book adaptations, original novels, comic books, a board game and video games.

But by far the biggest boost to popular astrology in the West came from an unexpected direction in the late 1980s – from Japan.

Japanese girls had embraced Western astrology along with numerous other divination methods during the divination boom. Although older forms of divination (such as palmistry and Chinese astrology) still had plenty of adherents, multiple new genres were adopted, invented and mashed with existing forms. Tarot reading became hugely popular both on mobile phones via websites and in divination booths in shopping centres. Western astrology soon appeared in most monthly women's magazines, TV shows, and was displayed on LCD screens hanging down in subway trains. It became common to add zodiac signs to selfies.

Astrology also appeared in manga and anime which became highly popular in the West from the mid-1990s. And none was more influental, or responsible for producing a new generation of astrology fams, than Naoko Takeuchi's *Sailor Moon*.

The original *shōjo* (for teenage girls) manga series was serialised in *Nakayoshi* from 1991 to 1997 in eighteen volumes. It was licensed for an English release by Mixx (later Tokyopop) in North America and published as a serial in *MixxZine* from in 1997 and later made into a separate monthly comic. The anime series was broadcast in Japan from 1992 to 1997. A live-action television adaptation, *Pretty Guardian Sailor Moon*, aired from 2003 to 2004, and a second anime series, 'Sailor Moon Crystal', began simulcasting in 2014. Three animated theatrical feature films based on *Sailor Moon* have been released in Japan and a TV special was aired on in Japan in 1995. There have been numerous companion books and novel adaptations. In 1993, the first musical theatre production premiered. At least thirty musicals have been produced as well as a live-action television series, and the franchise has spawned several video games and table top games. A *Sailor Moon* attraction exists at Universal Studios Japan. *Sailor Moon* has been broadcast all over the world.

*Sailor Moon* is about a fourteen year old girl named Usagi (*Usagi* is a Japanese term from *Tsuki no Usagi*, the rabbit that lives on the Moon in folklore;

she's called Serena in the English translation) who meets Luna, a talking cat, who tells her that she is Sailor Moon. When evil strikes, she turns into a super-hero called Sailor Moon. In this form, Usagi must fight evil and enforce justice in the name of the Moon. She meets other people destined to be *senshi* (soldiers) and together, they fight the forces of evil.

Astrological references provide the basis for the sailor soldiers' backgrounds and attacks as well as defining their personalities. For example, Sailor Mercury (Ami) speaks many different languages and spends her free time studying and reading. And Sailor Venus routinely refers to herself as a soldier of 'love and justice'. Sailor Saturn has a number of titles, including 'Soldier of Silence', 'Soldier of Destruction' and 'Soldier of Ruin and Birth'.

It's impossible to overstate the popularity of *Sailor Moon*. For example, in 2004 there were 3,335,000 websites about Sailor Moon. In 2012, 35 million copies of the manga had been sold worldwide as well as $5 billion worth of merchandising. It's also been credited with being integral to the rise of popularity of manga in the US, and it was also popular amongst adults in the US, which made up 22-38% of its viewers.

Other manga and anime featuring astrology have also become popular in the West. For example, from 2001 *Zodiac PI* featured a detective who used spirits of the zodiac signs of murder victims to help solve her cases.

*Saint Seiya* (also known as *Knights of the Zodiac*) was written and illustrated by Masami Kurumada. It first appeared in *Weekly Shōnen Jump* from 1986 to 1990.The story follows five warriors (the Saints) who fight wearing sacred sets of armour the design of which is based on the constellations the characters have adopted as their guardian symbols, and empowered by a mystical energy called 'Cosmo'. The Saints have sworn to defend the reincarnation of the Greek goddess Athena in her battle against other Olympian gods who want to dominate Earth. Over 35 million copies of the manga had been sold by 2017. It became popular in France in 1988, but wasn't translated into English until 2003.

*Fairy Tail,* written and illustrated by Hiro Mashima tells the story of Natsu Dragneel, a teenage wizard who is a member of the wizard guild Fairy Tail, as he searches for the dragon Igneel. The manga was adapted into an anime series which began broadcasting in Japan in 2009. By February 2017, *Fairy Tail* had 60 million copies in print. In *Fairy Tail,* celestial spirit mages can summon celestial spirits, which are based on constellations, through magical keys. The golden keys summon the twelve zodiac signs while the silver keys summon other constellations. However, the spirits don't always match the meanings of signs, for example, Aries is shy and non-combative.

Some featured Chinese astrology references such as *Fruits Basket* which tells the story of Tohru Honda, an orphan girl who has to battle twelve enemies that are possessed by the animals of the Chinese zodiac and turn into their animal forms when they are weak, stressed, or when they are embraced by anyone of the opposite sex that is not possessed by a spirit of the zodiac.

While popular astrology was meeting fantasy in one world, it was dealing with new technology in another. The rates paid to horoscope columnists had already started to plummet when in 1988 astrology phone lines were launched. What had been a paid feature suddenly became a huge income stream.

In 1984 Gordon Robson had just joined the recently privatised British Telecom. He was responsible for setting up premium rate chat and entertainment services. Their first venture was Talkabout, a service that allowed up to nine people to chat. You called a premium rate number and ended up in a chatroom with other users, much like an early internet chat room. This was followed by Dial a Disc, where you could dial up to hear your favourite song. Robson then set up a meeting with Kelvin Mackenzie, the editor of the *Sun* newspaper, to discuss the idea of the *Sun* running telephone entertainment and information services. This led to the birth of numerous phone products – including the astrological phone line. And no-one made more of a success of these phone lines than Jonathan Cainer (1957-2016).

Cainer had become interested in astrology in the early 1980s and enrolled at the Faculty of Astrological Studies, gaining their certificate in 1984. Around that time, Cainer had a humorous vegetarian recipe book published. When these publishers heard he was studying astrology, they asked him to write a Sun sign book. The book led to his being approached by magazines to write for them. He accepted an offer from the new *Today* newspaper and his first column appeared on 4 March 1986.

In 1992 he moved to the *Daily Mail* after a huge promotional campaign. In 1999 Cainer announced he was moving to the paper's rival, the *Express*. One of the arguments between Cainer and the *Mail* was the split of profits from the premium rate phone lines. The *Mail* offered him £1 million to stay and threatened him with a lawsuit when he refused. Cainer left.

Along with these and media appearances, Cainer had an income of about £1 million a year, of which £80,000 was the basic fee for his column and a growing staff of about fifteen. The deal with the *Express* was no fee for his column, but all the takings from his phone lines. In January 2001 Cainer moved to the *Daily Mirror*. In 2004 he decided to return to the *Mail*, only able to do so after a lengthy legal battle with the *Mirror*. He was Britain's highest paid astrologer.

It didn't take long until every horoscope columnist was expected to do a phone line, although most didn't receive much for their work. After BT, the hosting company and the publication had taken their cut, there was only a small percentage left for the astrologer. Then workplaces began to block calls and interest dwindled. Phone line revenue began dipped in the 1990s and became negligible for regional publications. Cainer was an exception.

There was no way the phone lines could compete with what was on offer on the internet and they soon became redundant.

There was, of course, still television. Russell Grant (5 February 1951 –), best known as a camp, plump, woolly-jumpered, media astrologer, had learned his astrology in his teens after visiting a clairvoyant. He became a spiritualist and worked as a platform medium in spiritualist churches in Middlesex. In 1976 he set up the British Astrological and Psychic Society, later taking on an astrology column in *Tatler* and then another in *TV Times*. In 1978, he got his big break, when the Queen Mother visited a stand at the Ideal Home Exhibition, entitled *The Stars In Your Life*, for a personal astrological consultation with him. Grant was dubbed 'Astrologer Royal' by the media and offers came flooding in. Following some regional TV work, the BBC snatched him for the launch of *Breakfast Time* in 1983. He became an instant hit as a television astrologer, and within a few years defected to ITV's TV AM.

And from 1994 to 2000 Mystic Meg appeared weekly on the National Lottery Live in 'Mystic Meg Predicts' – a short spot in which she predicted facts about the future winner.

Born Margaret Anne Lake, later Markova (1942 –), Meg was easily recognisable by her shiny black hair, bright red lips, intense stare and high-collared red cloak. A former *News of the World* sub-editor and deputy editor of its colour magazine, Meg claimed to have learned astrology from her Romany grandmother. By the mid-1980s she'd become the paper's regular astrologer. She currently has an astrology column in the *Sun* and hosts Mystic Meg's Wheel of Destiny for Sun Bingo.

Plenty of pop stars were still sprinkling astrological references throughout their songs. In 1993 Kurt Cobain sang in 'Heart-Shaped Box': 'She eyes me like a Pisces when I am weak' and Suede sang 'You're a water sign, I'm an air sign' in 'Sleeping Pills'. And in 2003, Rufus Wainright sang 'Everything's a sign of my astrology' in 'Pretty Things' and Beyoncé sang 'I was in love with a Sagittarius he blew my mind' in 'Signs' (thoroughly checking out her chances with all the zodiac signs).

But if there is one instance that sold astrological ideas to a generation in the 80s and 90s (to echo its theme song), it's the one named *Sailor Moon*.

# 26

# Astrology Online

Taylor Swift changed the face of modern popular astrology when on 21 October 2014 she tweeted:

> #mercuryGETOUTOFRETROGRADE

Swift explained what she meant in an MTV interview on 22 January 2015:

> When Mercury is in retrograde, basically that means that everything is going to be completely wrong and messed up and miscommunicated.

After decades of popular astrology focusing on the twelve zodiac signs alone, another factor had been brought into play.

Astrologers were perfectly aware of what Mercury retrograde meant. And in the past they didn't find it particularly exciting. Late nineteenth-century publications like the *Astrologer's Magazine* connected Mercury retrograde with heavy rainfall. Characterisations of it as an ill omen appeared in a handful of articles, but its association with personal disaster is relatively recent.

In the 1970s, Mercury retrograde began to appear in horoscope columns. But it took the internet to bring the concept to a mass audience. Mercury retrograde featured widely on Instagram memes throughout the late noughties and was soon familiar to millennials.

The birth of the internet meant that astrology was available to a bigger audience than ever before – in all its forms. By 2019 over half the world's population had access to the internet. In the developed world, 87% of people were internet users. Every day billions of people connect to read the news or weather, shop, find out the latest sports scores and follow their personal interests, no matter how obscure (or rude – pornography has never been so widely available).

Internet use isn't entirely passive – social media sites make it easy to chat, see what your friends are up to or make new contacts. Or you can learn new skills or promote your business. The possibilities are endless. But does it offer good astrology?

Many astrologers worry that it doesn't. They see the offerings on websites as superficial, even inaccurate. They view it as trivialising their art, and this makes them very cross. In fact, they make exactly the same complaints as astrologers did in the 1930s when horoscope columns became ubiquitous. This isn't 'real' astrology. On the plus side, the internet makes it easier for astrologers all over the world to connect with each other – and moan about the bad quality of what they see on the internet. Alongside them are self-proclaimed scientists who regard it as their mission to persuade the deluded to throw off their superstitions and embrace a more rational worldview.

There are thousands of places online where you can learn astrology, find a consultant astrologer, discuss the subject with like-minded people and attend seminars. Or you can read your horoscope every day, just like generations before you. Despite what astrologers would like, most people browsing the internet are more likely to listen to Taylor Swift than them. And more people access Sun sign horoscopes than serious astrology content.

What is different nowadays is the sheer number of people you can reach quickly with a horoscope column. Astrology accounts on platforms like Twitter amass hundreds of thousands of followers, checking their weekly horoscopes.

In the 2010s huge shifts in technology led to smartphones being widely adopted. Now you could access the internet while on the train to work, in the bath... anywhere, really. It's no coincidence that this increased easier access to the online world coincided with the popularity of memes. And many of these memes were astrological in nature. Instagram (and to a lesser extent Tumblr) were full of them. By 2018 newspapers like the *Guardian* in the UK and the *New York Times* in the US reported a millennial obsession with astrology.

It's debatable whether millennials really have become obsessed with astrology – as we've seen earlier, newspapers report astrology being a new fad every few years. However, Google Trends report that searches for 'birth chart' and 'astrology' hit five-year peaks in 2020. And TikTok, 2020s fastest-growing app in terms of monthly active users, has introduced popular astrology to a new generation. Emerging from it are dozens of freshly-formed internet astrology celebrities.

Of course, being under lockdown during the COVID19 crisis is likely to have skewed search results – perhaps they are due to people worrying about their mental health or feeling isolated as many suggest, or perhaps it's simply boredom. Millennials might be mildly interested and at a loose end rather than 'obsessed'.

The new astrologers born on the internet include Canadian Chani Nicholas (1975–). She built her following through posting memes to her Instagram account and turned her interest into a business in 2014. By 2017, 12,000 people had paid to study her classes and that year her blog attracted about a million regular visitors. When Nicholas' book *You Were Born for This* appeared in January 2020, it sold over 14,000 copies in its first week.

Nicholas also launched her own app – Chani. Apps have abounded during the last few years. Co-Star, for example, had more than five million users in 2019. With the apps you can calculate your full horoscope on your phone and read about what it means. And the apps beep notifications at you with constant updates. You could be sipping a nice cup of tea when an app tells you imperiously it's about time you got your act together and went out. Of course, if your own future looks a little dodgy, you can put in a friend's details and keep an eye on their life. They might appreciate that, depending on what sort of friends you have.

Although there may have been heightened interest in 'real' astrology recently, that doesn't change the fact that Sun sign astrology is still highly popular and is the form of astrology most people recognise.

Today, you can open your newspaper and read your horoscope column as countless people do every morning. You can buy a book or browse the web to find out how you're likely to get along with people of other signs. Like thousands of people before you, you may choose to look deeper into astrology, and learn how to calculate your birth chart. Or you may choose to pay an astrologer to interpret it for you. But if you're like the vast majority of people in the West today, horoscope columns will be as much a part of your life as the weather forecast. You might not take much notice of them while they're there, but you'd miss them if they were gone.

Whenever you read your horoscope column, you're using a form of divination that has existed for unknown centuries and shows no sign of disappearing. The world has changed much less than we'd like to believe.

We are still living the story.

# Bibliography

## Books

Adams, Douglas. *The Salmon of Doubt* (New York: Harmony Books, 2002).

Adams, Evangeline. *Astrology: Your Place Among the Stars*. (London: GP Putnam and Sons, 1930).

*Astrology: Your Place in the Sun*. (New York: Dodd, Mead and Co. 1928).

*Bowl of Heaven*. (New York: Dodd, Mead & Co, 1970).

*Evangeline Adams' Own Book of Astrology, This Book Contains your Solar Horoscope if you Were Born Between Feb. 20$^{th}$ and March 21$^{st}$*. (New York: Tower Books, 1931).

Adamson, Ian. *The Old Fox: A Biography of Gilbert Hugh Beyfus*. (London: Frederick Muller, 1963). Reprinting.

Berg, Walter. *The Thirteen Signs of the Zodiac*. (London: Harper Collins, 1995).

Blavatsky, Helena Petrovna. "Stars and Numbers", *The Theosophist*. (Madras: Theosophical Publishing Company, June 1881*)*.

*Isis Unveiled*. (Pasadena: Theosophical University Press, 1988. (Originally published 1877).

Bok, Bart Jan. *Objections to Astrology*. (Buffalo, New York: Prometheus Books, 1975).

Braithwaite, Brian. *Women's Magazines: the First 300 years*. (London: Peter Owen, 1995).

Broughton, Luke. *Elements of Astrology* (New York: 1898).

Butler, Hiram Erastus. *Creative Principles*.(Boston: Esoteric Publishing Co., Boston, 1887).

*Mind Control*. (Boston: Esoteric Publishing, Boston, 1893).

*Practical Methods to Ensure Success.* (Boston: Esoteric Publishing Co., Boston, 1893).

*Solar Biology: a scientific method of delineating character.* (Boston: Esoteric Publishing Co., 1887).

*The Revised Esoteric.* (Boston: Esoteric Publishing Co., Boston, 1895).

Capp, Bernard. *Astrology and the Popular Press: English Almanacs 1500 1800* (London: Faber, 1979).

Cheiro. *The Cheiro Book of Fate and Fortune: Palmistry, Numerology, Astrology.* (London: Barrie and Jenkins, 1971).

*Confessions: Memoirs of a Modern Seer.* (London: Jarrold, 1932).

*"Madame Blavatsky, Founder of the Theosophical Society", Reminiscences of a Society Palmist.* (London: W. Rider and Son, 1912).

*When were you Born? Your Future, Marriage, Character, Tendencies, Clearly Shown and Described by Cheiro.* (London: Herbert Jenkins, 1913).

*You and Your Stars.* (London: Herbert Jenkins, undated).

Christiansen, Arthur. *Headlines All My Life.* (London: Heinemann, 1961).

Christino, Karen. *Foreseeing the Future: Evangeline Adams and Astrology in America.* (Stella Mira, 2019).

*Compost et kalendrier des bergiers.* The Kalendar of Shepherds: Being Devices for the Twelve Months. [With an introduction by AHDiplock.] (London: Sidgwick & Jackson, 1908).

*Compost et kalendrier des bergiers.* The Kalendar of Shepherds. Sommer, H.O. The edition of Paris, 1503, in photographic facsimile. A faithful reprint of R. Pynson's edition of London, 1506. (London: Kegan Paul and Co, 1892).

*Le grand Kalendrier Compost des Bergers, compose par le Berger de la grand tables, etc.* Montaigne, G.L. (Paris, 1569).

*Compost et kalendrier des bergiers.* Here beginneth the Kalendar of Shepherds, newly augmented. Translated from the French by R. Copland. (T. Este for J. Wally: London, 1570?)

*Compost et kalendrier des bergiers.* Hesletine, GC (ed). The Kalendar and Compost of Shepherds, from the original edition published in Paris. 1493, and translated into English c.1518. (London: Peter Davies, 1930).

Crawford, SJ. *Byrhtferth's Manual.* (London: Early English Text Society, 1929).

Crowley, Aleister. *The Confessions of Aleister Crowley.* (London: Arkana, 1989).

Curry, Patrick. *A Confusion of Prophets.* (London: Collins and Brown Ltd, 1992).

Davies, Owen. *Cunning-folk: Popular Magic in English History.* (London: Hambledon and London, 2003).

*Witchcraft, Magic and Culture, 1736-1951.* (Manchester: Manchester University Press, 1999).

Dean, Geoffrey and Mather, Arthur. *Recent Advances in Natal Astrology.* (Australia: Subiaco, 1977).

Dee, Gabriel. *The Complete Fortune Teller.* (London: John Long Limited, 1933).

*The Propitious Moment.* (London, 1928).

Farnell, Kim. *The Astral Tramp: A Biography of Sepharial.* (Nottingham: Ascella Publications, 1998).

*Cheiro the Wonderful* (forthcoming).

*Modern Astrologers: The Story of Alan and Bessie Leo.* (Self-published, 2019),

Gettings, Fred. *The Book of the Hand.* (London: Paul Hamlyn, 1965).

Giuntini, Francesco. *Speculum Astrologiæ.* (Cologne, 1583).

Godwin, Joscelyn; Chanel, Christian and Deveney, John P. *The Hermetic Brotherhood of Luxor.* (New York: Weiser, 1995).

Greenfield, A.H. *The Roots of Modern Magick: An Anthology* (Lulu, 2004).

Hall, Manly Palmer. *The Story of Astrology.* (London: Peter Owen, 1959).

Hind, Arthur M. *An Introduction to a History of Woodcut, with a Detailed Survey of Work Done in the Fifteenth Century. Volume: 2.* (New York: Dover Publications, 1963).

Howe, Ellic. *Urania's Children, The Strange World of the Astrologers.* (London: William Kimber, 1967).

Hyland, M.E.F. *Birthday Readings.* (Chesterfield: Derbyshire Courier, 1910).

Indagine, John. *A Compendious Description of Natural Astrology Never so Briefly Handled Before.* (1523).

King, Teri. *Astrological Horoscopes, Gemini 2005.* (London: Element, 2004).

Leo, Alan. *The Key to Your Own Nativity*, 'Astrology for All' Series. (London: Modern Astrology, 1904).

*Everybody's Astrology*. (London: Modern Astrology, undated 10th edition).

*Everybody's Astrology*. (London: Modern Astrology, 1909).

*How to Judge a Nativity*. (London: Modern Astrology, 1922).

*The Progressed Horoscope*, 'Astrology for All' Series, (London: Modern Astrology, 1906).

Leo, Bessie. *The Life and Work of Alan Leo*. (London: Modern Astrology, 1919).

Lyndoe, Edward. *Everybody's Book of Fate and Fortune*. (London: Odhams Press, 1935).

*Plan with the Planets*. (London: Herbert Jenkins, 1949).

*Your Next Ten Years and After*. (St. Albans: Lyndoe Publications, 1935).

Matheson, Lister M. *Popular and Practical Science of Medieval England*. (East Lansing, Michigan: Colleagues Press, 1994).

McCaffery, Ellen. *Astrology: Its History and Influence in the Western World*. (New York: C Scribner's Sons, 1942).

Miall, Agnes. *Complete Fortune Telling*. (London: Arthur Pearson Ltd, 1934).

Montague, Nell St John. *Revelations of a Society Clairvoyante*. (London: Thornton Butterworth Limited, 1929).

Naylor, P.I.H. *Astrology: An Historical Examination*. (London: Robert Maxwell, 1967).

Naylor, R.H. *Home Astrology. A Non-Technical Outline of Popular Astrological Tradition*. (London: Hutchinson and Co., 1934).

*Naylor's Year Book. A Delineation of What the Stars Foretell for 1934*. (London: Hutchinson and Co., 1934).

Neugebauer, O. *The Exact Sciences in Antiquity*. (New York: Dover Publications, 1969).

Omar, Lela. *Your Future: The Zodiac's Guide to Success*. (Philadelphia: Penn Publishing Co, 1904).

Oppenheim, Janet. *The Other World: Spiritualism and Psychical Research in England, 1850-1914*. (Cambridge: Cambridge University Press, 1985).

Parr, Johnstone. *Tamburlaine's Malady: And Other Essays on Astrology in Elizabethan Drama.* (Tuscaloosa, Alabama: University of Alabama Press, 1953).

Petulengro, Gipsy (or Gypsy or Xavier). *A Romany Life.* (New York: Dutton, 1936).

Petulengro, Leon (Leon Lloyd). *Romany Boy.* (London: Hale, 1979).

Randi, James. *Flim Flam: The Truth About Unicorns, Parapsychology and Other Delusions.* (London: Prometheus Books, 1994).

Ransom, Josephine. *A Short History of the Theosophical Society.* (Madras: Theosophical Publishing House, 1938).

Raphael, (Cross Smith, Robert) *The Familiar Astrologer.* (London, 1831).

Raphael. (Cross, Robert Thomas) *Raphael's Almanac and Prophetic Messenger.* (London: Foulsham, 1851).

*Raphael's Almanac and Prophetic Messenger.* (London: Foulsham, 1922; 1923; 1930; 1932).

Richards, Jeffrey (Ed). *The Unknown 1930s: An Alternative History of the British Cinema 1929-39.* (London: I.B .Tauris, 1998).

Rogers, Clement Francis. *Astrology in the Light of Science and Religion.* (London: Student Christian Movement Press, 1941).

Rudhyar, Dane. *The Astrology of Personality.* (NewYork: Doubleday, 1970).

Russell, Eric. *Astrology and Prediction.* (London: B.T. Batsford, 1972).

Sladek, John. *The New Apocrypha. A Guide to Strange Science and Occult Beliefs.* (London: Hart-Davis, MacGibbon, 1973).

*Solar Biology Birthday Calendar.* (London: Nichols and Co., 1897).

Soutar, Andrew. *The Veiled Doorway: Experiences of Modern Fortune Telling.* (London: John Long Limited, 1935).

Spencer, Neil. *True as the Stars Above.* (London: Gollancz, 2000).

Taavitsainen, Irma. *Middle English Lunaries: A Study of the Genre.* (Helsinki: Societe Neophilologique, 1988).

Tilms, Richard. (Sladek, John). *Judgement of Jupiter.* (London: New English Library, 1980).

Vogh, James. (Sladek, John.) *Arachne Rising.* (London: Hart-Davis MacGibbon, 1977).

*The Cosmic Factor.* (London: Hart-Davis MacGibbon, 1978).

Waite, Arthur Edward. *Shadows of Life and Thought. A Retrospective Review in the Form of Memoirs*. (London: Selwyn and Blount, 1938).

Walter, Charlotte Abell. *Under a Lucky Star*. (London: William Heineman, 1901).

Ward, J. *This Instructing Gypsy or the True Fortune Teller*. (London: T Hughes, 1804).

West, John Anthony. *The Case for Astrology*. (London: Arkana, 1991).

White, Cynthia. *Women's Magazines 1693–1968* (Michael Joseph, 1971).

Wohl, Louis de. *I Follow my Stars*. (London: George G. Garrap and Co. Ltd., 1937).

Wright, Edward J. *The Early History of Heaven*. (New York: Oxford University Press, 2000).

Zadkiel. (Morrison, Richard James). *The Grammar of Astrology*. (London, 1849).

Zodiastar. *Everybody's Book of Luck: A Complete Guide to Fortune Telling and GOOD LUCK*. (London: Success Publishing Co, 1933).

Zolar. (King, Bruce). *The History of Astrology*. (London: Foulsham, 1974).

*Zolar's Fortune Teller*. (New York: Street and Smith, 1980).

## Periodicals

*American Astrology,* December 1934.

Bock, Barbara. 'An Esoteric Babylonian Commentary: Revisited'. *The Journal of the American Oriental Society*. Volume: 120. Issue: 4. 2000.

Butler, Hiram Erastus (Ed). *The Occult and Biological Journal,* Boston: Esoteric Publishing, Boston, 1910.

Butler, Hiram Erastus, MacKay, C.H. Latham J. and Severy M.L. (Eds.) *The Esoteric. A magazine of advanced and practical esoteric thought,* Boston, Massachusetts: Applegate Esoteric Publishing Co, August 1887 - September 1889.

Dean, Geoffrey and Mather, Arthur. 'Sun Sign Columns: An Armchair Invitation', *Astrological Association Journal*, Frome: Astrological Association, Volume 38, No.3 pp.143-155, 1996.

*Destiny: the magazine of Astrology,* Lincoln, Hadleigh, Thornton Heath, June 1904 - October 1905.

Eccles, Bernard. *Astrological Association Journal,* Frome: Astrological Association, Volume 38, pp.306-10, 1996.

Hague, Thomas, *The Horoscope,* 1840.

Hansen, George P. *The Trickster and the Paranormal: Magicians Who Endorsed Psychic Phenomena.* The

Linking Ring *[monthly magazine of the International Brotherhood of Magicians],* August 1990, Volume 70, No. 8, pp.52-54.

Sagan, Carl "Objections to Astrology" (letter to the editor), *The Humanist,* vol.36, no 1 (January/February 1976) p.2 reprinted in *The Demon-Haunted World* pp.302-303 (1995)

# Web References

Blavatsky, HP. *Esoteric Section of the Theosophical Society.*
http://www.katinkahesselink.net/esinstr3.htm
1889. *On Pseudo Theosophy.*
http://www.blavatsky.net/blavatsky/arts/OnPseudo Theosophy.htm
*Stars and Numbers*
http://www.wisdomworld.org/additional/ScienceAndTheSecret Doctrine/SeriesNumber92-of-103.html

Caldwell, Daniel H. "Parapsychology, Anomalies, Science, Skepticism, and CSICOP", https://blavatskyarchives.com/zeteticism.htm.

Chambers, Robert. 1869. *Chambers Book of Days.*
http://www.thebookofdays.com/misc/primitive_almanacs.htm

Coues, Elliot. *Blavatsky Unveiled!*
http://www.blavatskyarchives.com/coues.htm

CSICOP http://www.csicop.org/si/2001-05/editor.html

Dean, Geoffrey. 1996, *Sun Sign Challenge.*
http://groups.google.com/groups?q=astrology+1930&start=20&hl=en&lr=&ie=UTF-8&selm=34851F22.E43%40pacbell.net& rnum=24

Dean, Geoffrey and Mather, Arthur. 2000, *Sun Sign Columns: Response to an Invitation.* http://www.findarticles.com/p/articles/mi_m2843/is_5_24/ai_ 67691838

Escobar-Vargas, Carolina and Lawrence-Mathers, Anne. 'Report of astrological fears and predictions in 1186' in *Magic and Medieval Society* (Routledge, 2014).

*Feuilletez les plus belles pages des trésors de la Médiathèque.*

https://web.archive.org/web/20051018151847/http://www.mediatheque-agglo-troyes.fr/bmtroyes/_/feuilletoir/index.html

I-Village. *All about You, Your Sun sign, Aries.*

http://www.astrology.com/allaboutyou/sunsigns/aries.html

James, Jonathan. 2002. *Natal and Predictive Astrology.*

http://www.windandsky.com/

Judge, William Q. 1889. *Occultism for Barter: Esoteric Colleges and False Prophets.* http://www.blavatsky.net/theosophy/judge/articles/occultism-for-barter.htm

Law Reform Commission, *Report on Vagrancy and Related Offences,* http://www.lawreform.ie/publications/data/volume4/lrc_30.html

*Newgate Calenda*r. Ex-classics website, https://www.exclassics.com/newgate/ngintro.htm.

Orwell, George. 'Boy's Weeklies', *The Orwell Foundation,* https://www.orwellfoundation.com/the-orwell-foundation/orwell/essays-and-other-works/boys-weeklies/.

Parker, Derek and Julia. 1983. *History of Astrology.*

http://www.meta-religion.com/Esoterism/Astrology/history_of_astrology.htm

*Particulars of claim in the High Court of Justice Chancery Division between Ordo Templi Orientis (incorporated in California USA), Claimant and (1) John Symonds, (2) Anthony Naylor, (3) Mandrake Press Ltd Defendants.* http://user.cyberlink.ch/-koenig/dplanet/or/particul.htm

Petronius (Titus Petronius or Gaius Petronius Arbiter), *Satyricon.* Project Gutenberg http://www.gutenberg.org/

Philipson, Garry. 2006. *An Interview With Dennis Elwell.*

http://www.skyscript.co.uk/elwell.html.

Wykle, Stacey.S. 'The public will vs. the public trust: Early American radio as a public information resource', *Proceedings of the Association for Information Science and Technology* 53: 1-10. https://doi.org/10.1002/pra2.2016.14505301080

## Other sources

Mass Observation: Report 813.

Statute of James I, Witchcraft Act, 1604.

Campion, Nicholas. *The Extent and Nature of Contemporary Belief in Astrology*. (PhD thesis submitted Bath Spa University College: 2004).

Carpenter, Garth. *Chaucer's Solar Pageant: an Astrological Reading of the Canterbury Tales.* (PhD Dissertation, Victoria University of Wellington, 1997.)

Trial horoscope for Miss R. Taylor, born 27 February 1912. *The Kastraka Observatories.*

# Index

Abano, Peter of, 56
Abu Ma'shar, 32
Academy of Astrologians, 116, 120
Adams, Douglas, 220
Adams, Evangeline, 86, 92, 93, 112, 118, 135, 167
*Against Heresies*, Hippolytus, 8
*Age of Aquarius*, 187, 188, 189, 190
Agorel *see* Leo, Alan
Agrippa, Heinrich Cornelius, 37, 56
Al Kindi, 32
Alfred the Great, 11
Allen, Elsa, 116
*Almagest*, 216
Almanacs, 5, 26, 38, 39, 42
*American Astrology*, 168, 169, 170, 172
American Humanist Association, 204
Anderson, Sylvia, 192
*Anglo-Saxon Chronicles*, 11
Aphorel see Lacey, Frederick
Aquarius characteristics, 21, 40, 59, 129
*Arcandam*, see Roussat Richard 36, 43
Arden, Adrienne, 165, 177, 183, 194
Aries characteristics, 23, 29, 35, 37, 57, 67, 69, 89, 91, 193

Arthur, King, 15
Ashmole, Elias, 47
*Astrologer* magazine, 87
*Astrologer's Magazine*, Alan Leo, 88, 228
*Astrologer's Magazine*, Ebenezer Sibly, 56
Astrological Association, 89, 207
Astrological Congress of 1927, 123
Astrological Lodge of the Theosophical Society, 89
Astrological Society, The, 89
*Astrology for All*, Alan Leo, 89
*Astrology of Personality*, Dane Rudhyar, 168
*Astrology, Your Place Among The Stars*, Evangeline Adams, 94
*Astrology, Your Place In The Sun*, Evangeline Adams, 94
*Astronomical Calendar of 1448*, 40
Augustus, Emperor, 6
Aurelian, Emperor, 8
Auriga, constellation, 214
*Avengers*, 192

Babylonian numbers, 6

Bailey, E. H., 77, 88
Barbanell, Maurice, 152, 153, 179
Barley, Annie, 88
Barrett, Francis, 56
Bart, Belle, 118, 167
*Batman*, 192
*Battlestar Galactica*, 222
Bayeaux tapestry, 12
Bayley, Kingsley, 109
Bennett, Sidney, 167, 177
Berg, Walter, 218
Bernhardt, Sarah, 135
Besant, Annie, 109, 134
*Betty's Paper*, 126, 132
Beyfus, Gilbert, 154
Beyoncé, 227
Bickerstaff, Isaac, 49
*Birthday Book of Fate*, 69
Black, Cilla, 193
Blake, Doris *see* Donnelly, Antoinette
Blake, Mary, 116
Blavatsky, Helena, 73, 76, 77, 78, 79, 85, 88, 134, 189
Block books, 20
Bok, Bart Jan, 202
*Boston Globe*, 85, 93
*Boston Post*, 65
*Boston Record*, 65
*Bowl of Heaven*, Evangeline Adams, 94
Bradshawe, James, 106
Brahe, Tycho, 36
*Brains Trust*, 185
Bratley, George, 185

British Association for the Advancement of Astral Science, 106
British Astrological and Psychic Society, 226
*British Journal of Astrology*, 77, 88, 180
*British Movietone News*, 147
British National Association of Spiritualists, 74
Brotherhood of Eulis, 83
Broughton, Luke, 63, 93, 120
Buchanan, Robert, 78
*Buffalo Courier*, 116
Burghley, Lord, 42
Butler, Hiram Erastus, 78, 79, 80, 84, 91
*Byrhtferth's Manual*, 13

Cables, Josephine, 80
Cainer, Jonathan, 225
Camerarius, Joachim, 38
Campbell, Mrs Cecil, 164
Cancer characteristics, 37
*Canterbury Tales*, Geoffrey Chaucer, 24
Carter, Charles, 174
Celestial Brotherhood, 87
*Celestial Intelligencer*, 105
*Celtic Lunar Zodiac*, Helena Patterson, 214
Chaldean order, 34
*Chariots of the Gods*, Erich von Daniken, 211
Charles I King, 46
Charles, I King, 47
Charubel *see* Thomas, John, 87
Chaucer, Geoffrey, 24

Cheiro, 98, 114, 133, 134, 141, 142, 145, 161, 190
Cheiro's *Book of the Hand*, 135
*Christian Astrology*, William Lilly, 46, 48
Christian festivals and astrology, 8, 39
Christianity and astrology, 8, 11, 12, 14, 28
Christiansen, Arthur, 145
Cinematograph Films Act, 1927, 147
*Circus Shadows*, 149
Clancy, Paul, 168, 169
Clarendon, Earl of, 42
Claudius, Emperor, 7
Cobain, Kurt, 227
Coltrane, John, 193
Colvin, James, 214
Comet, Halley's, 12
Comet, Negra, 19
Comets, 11
Company of Stationers, 42, 48, 53
Complete Illustration of the Celestial Art of Astrology, 55
*Concerning the causes of the properties of the elements*, Albertus Magnus, 19
*Conjurer's Magazine*, Ebenezer Sibly, 56
Constantine, Emperor, 8
Constellation, names, 3
Constellations, number, 3
Cooke, Christopher, 106
Copestick, Francis, 106
Copland, Robert, 28
Corfield, John, 56
*Coronation Street*, 192
Corumphiza, 15

*Cosmic Factor, The*, John Sladek, 214
*Cosmopolitan*, 218
Coues, Elliot, 73
Council of the American Astronomical Society, 202
Craig, Katherine Taylor, 97
Crowley, Aleister, 94, 174
Crummaire, Marie Elise, 188
CSICOP, 204, 205, 206
Culpeper, Nicholas, 48
Cunning folk, 43, 59
Cusp of a sign, 69, 136

*Daily Mail*, 64, 122, 157, 183
*Daily Mirror*, 64, 121, 185
*Daily Telegraph*, 215
Darwin, Charles, 62
Davis, Andrew Jackson, 62
Davis, Miles, 193
Dawkins, Richard, 207
*De Occulta Philosophia*, Heinrich Cornelius Agrippa, 37
Dead Sea Scrolls, 5
Dee, Gabriel, 148
Dee, John, 36
Deep Purple, 193
Destinaries, 21
Diocletian, Emperor, 8
Disch, Thomas, 213
*Discworld*, Terry Pratchett, 220, 221
*Divine Pymander of Hermes Mercurius Trismegistus*, 79
Dixon, Jeanne, 190
Do Dacia, Petrus, 41
Dodson, Joseph, 107
Donnelly, Antoinette, 117

Doyle, Arthur Conan, 114
Druids, 10, 214
Duncan, Ethel, 167
Duncan, Helen, 153, 157
Dyson, Freeman, 202

Eclipses, 11, 14, 15, 16, 19, 40, 41, 190
*Elder Scrolls*, 222
Elements, 3
Elizabeth I, Queen, 36, 42
*Enuma Anu Enlil*, 2
*Epic of Gilgamesh*, 4
Equinox, autumn, 9
Eric Burdon and the Animals, 193
Esoteric Fraternity, 86
*Esoteric, The*, Hiram Butler, 81, 82
Essex, the Parliamentary General, 42
Evans, Rhys, 45
*Evening News*, 63, 166
Everybody's Astrology, Alan Leo, 90

Faculty of Astrological Studies, 89, 225
*Fairy Tail*, 225
*Familiar Astrologer, The*, Raphael (Robert Cross Smith), 37
Farnese globe, 216
*Farscape*, 222
Fifth Dimension, 188
*Final Fantasy*, 221
First astrology column, American, 65
*Float On*, 193
Floaters, 193
Folk astrology, 10
Fortune telling machine, 70
Fox family, 63
Franks, William, 176

Freakin' At The Freakers Ball, 193
Freemasonry, 55
*Fruits Basket*, 225

Gaiman, Neil, 220
Galilei, Galileo, 36
Gardner, Martin, 203
Gauquelin, Michel and Francoise, 202
Geller, Uri, 204, 206, 213
Gemini characteristics, 43, 67, 193
Geoffrey of Monmouth, 15
George, Llewellyn, 177
*Georgics*, Virgil, 210
Gettings, Fred, 137
Ginsberg, Allen, 190
*Girls' Mirror*, 128, 175
Giuntini, Francesco, 38
*Glamour*, 131, 184, 185
Glastonbury abbey, 12
Gleadow, Rupert, 190
Gods from Outer Space, Erich von Daniken, 211
Golden number, 39
*Good Omens*, Neil Gaiman and Terry Pratchett, 220
Goodman, Linda, 196
Gordon, John, 153, 154
Graham, George W., 58
Grand conjunction, 1186, 15
Grand conjunction, 19, 32
Grant, Russell, 226
Great Fire of London, 47
*Great Jasper, The*, 149
Gregorian calendar, 35
Gregory of Tours, 11

*Guild-Book of the Barber Surgeons of York*, 22
Gutenberg, Johannes, 40

**Hague, Thomas**, 60
*Hair*, 188
Harries, John, 58
*Harry Potter*, 221
Harvard University, 55
Hazelrigg, John, 120, 121
*Heavenly Bodies*, 215
Heber Smith, J., 93
Heindel, Max, 190
Heinlein, Robert, 191
*Heptameron*, Peter of Abano, 56
Hermes Trismegistus, 5
Hermetic beliefs, 55
Hermetic Brotherhood of Luxor, 79, 80, 83, 88
Heron-Allen, Edward, 135
Highfield, Roger, 215
Hippolytus, 8
*Historia Regum Britanniae* (History of the Kings of Britain), 15
Hll, Manley P., 150
*Home Chat*, 125, 127
*Home Companion*, 126
Horoscope as a word, 70
*Horoscope, The*, Thomas Hague, 60
Houdini, Harry, 168
Hubbard, L. Ron, 212
Humphries, Christmas, 154
Hyman, Ray, 203

*I'm No Angel*, 148, 149
Idle, Eric, 194

Indagine, John ab, 33, 35, 36, 38
Index of Prohibited Books, 33
International Astronomical Union, 215
Internet, 195, 225, 226, 228
Irish astrology, 12
*Isis Unveiled*, Helena Blavatsky, 75

Jerome, Lawrence, 202
Joad, C. E. M., 185
Jones, Marc Edmonds, 196
Jones, Terry, 194
Judge, William Quan, 73
*Judgment of Jupiter*, John Sladek, 214
Junctinus *see* Giuntini, Francesco
Jung, Carl, 190

*Kalendarium Novocum*, 40
Keiro, 107
Kemble, Edward Winsor, 120
Kemble, Genevieve, 120, 167
Kendricks, Eddie, 193
Kenery, Mary Alice *see* Goodman, Linda
Kepler, Johannes, 36
*Key to Scientific Prediction*, Joseph Simmonite, 140
Klass, Philip, J., 204
*Knights of the Zodiac*, 224
Knye, Cassandra *see* John Sladek
Koestler, Arthur, 213
Kunkle, Parke, 218
Kurtz Paul, 201, 202, 204, 206
Kurumada, Masami, 224
Kusche, Larry, 204

Lacey, Frederick, 87, 88

*Ladies' Mercury*, 131
*Ladies' Diary*, 54
Larwood, J. P., 174
Law and astrology, 94, 99, 123, 151
Le Rouge, Nicolas, 27
Leary, Timothy, 190
Leigh, James, 179
Leo characteristics, 30
Leo, Alan, 77, 86, 87, 96, 107, 108, 114, 135
*Life of Brian*, 195
*Light Fantastic*, Terry Pratchett, 220
Lilly, William, 41, 45
*Lives of the Caesars*, 6
Lloyd, Walter Leon *see* Petulengro, Xavier
Lodge, Oliver, 114
London Astrological Research Society, 141
*London Correspondent*, 57
*Long Dark Teatime Of The Soul, The*, Douglas Adams, 220
*Love Signs*, Linda Goodman, 196, 198
Lowe, Arthur, 192
*Lucifer*, 78
Lucky and unlucky days, 10, 27, 69
*Lucky Star*, 130, 131, 174
Lunaries, 21, 22, 38
Lyndoe, Edward, 148, 162, 164, 165, 178, 182, 183, 184, 186

Mackenzie, Kelvin, 225
Magia naturalis, Porta, Giambattista, 56
*Magic: The Gathering*, 222
Magnus, Albertus, 19
Mamas and Papas, 193
*Magus, The*, Francis Barrett, 56
Marchant, Guy, 27
Margaret, Princess, 138, 141
Mashallah, 32
Mashima, Hiro, 225
Massey, Charles Carlton, 74, 107
Massey, Gerald, 189
Mayfield, Curtis, 193
McClure syndicate, 66
McLean, Hugh, 108, 109
Medicine and astrology, 11, 17, 20, 23, 41, 42, 48
Memphis Occult Products, 141
*Men Behaving Badly*, 222
Mercury retrograde, 228
*Merlinus Anglicus Junior*, William Lilly, 41
Mesmer Harmonic Philosophical Society, 55
Mesmer, Franz Anton, 55, 62
Miall, Agnes, 161
*Miami News*, 116
Middlesex Lodge of the Theosophical Society, 89
*Mind Control*, Hiram Butler, 86
*Miracle*, 174, 175
Mitchell, C. E., 122
Mithraism, 3, 8
Mitton, Jacqueline, 215
*Modern Astrology*, 88, 90, 108, 110, 180
Montague, Nell St John, 124, 130, 175, 179
*Monty Python*, 193, 195

*Moon and Son*, 222
Moon lore, 21, 60
Moorcock, Michael, 211, 214
Moore, Francis, 43
Morrison, Richard James *see* Zadkiel I
Morrison, Van, 193
Muller, Johann, 40
Müller, Max, 76
*Müller-Fokker Effect*, John Sladek, 211
Mystic Meg, 227

Nagel, Ernest, 204
NASA, 218
*National Astrological Journal*, 168
Natural astrology, 10, 11, 33, 38, 55, 60
Naylor, John, 157, 185
Naylor, Phyllis, 145, 157, 178
Naylor, R. H. 138, 140-146, 150, 152-157, 159-161, 166, 167, 170, 173, 179, 180, 182, 184, 185
Nechepso, Pharaoh, 5
*New Abelard, The*, Robert Buchanan, 78
*New Apocrypha, The*, John Sladek, 212
*New Worlds*, 211, 214
Newsreels, 147
Nicholas, Chani, 230
Nye, Bill, 206

Objections to Astrology, 200
*Occult and Biological Journal*, 86
*Occultist, The*, 88
Occultist's Defence League, 107
Ohmart, Eli, 82, 84
Olcott, Henry Steel, 73
Old, Walter *see* Sepharial

Ophiuchus, constellation, 213, 216-219
Opposition to Sun sign astrology by astrologers, 123, 150, 160, 172-174
Opposition to Sun sign astrology by scientists, 200
*Oracle*, 174, 175
*Origin of Species*, Charles Darwin, 62
Orwell, George, 125

*Pam's Paper*, 127
Paris Consilium, 19
Partridge, John, 49, 50
Pathé, 147, 148
Patterson, Helena, 214
Pearce, A. J. *see* Zadkiel II
*Pearson's Weekly*, 63
*Peg's Paper*, 129, 131, 175, 184
Penny, Richard Henry, 63, 106
*People, The*, 162
Pepys, Samuel, 47
*Personal Secretary*, 150
Petosiris, 5
Petronius, 7
Petulengro, Leon, 166, 167
Petulengro, Xavier, 165, 182, 183, 184
Philip VI, King, 19
Phone lines, 225
*Picture Post*, 145, 184
Pisces characteristics, 31
Planet, personal, 20
Planets, activities and occupations, 20
Planets, days of the week, 21
Planets, souls of the zodiac, 21
Plato, 217
Pliny, 10
*Poor Robin*, 42

*Poppy's Paper*, 127, 128, 130, 175
Porta, Giambattista, 56
Poulton, Phyllis *see* Phyllis Naylor
Powell, Robert, 101
*Practical Methods to Ensure Success*, 86
Pratchett, Terry, 220
Precession, 188, 210
*Prediction*, 130, 170, 179, 185
*Predictions for the Year 1708*, 49
Priess, Adele, 112
Prince, 220
*Principles of Nature (The), Her Divine Revelations*, Andrew Jackson Davis, 62
*Prophecies of Merlin*, 15
*Prophetic Messenger*, 57, 58
*Psychic News*, 152, 179
Ptolemy, Claudius, 3, 5, 30, 38, 216
Publius Nigidius Figulus, 6
Pynson, Richard, 28

*Queen*, 194

Radio Act, 167
Ramsay, David, 45
Ramsay, William, 45
Randi, James, 203
Randolph, Paschal Beverly, 83
Raphael, 25, 37, 38, 57, 77
*Red Letter*, 128
*Red Star Weekly*, 128, 185
Regiomontanus, Muller Johannes, 40
Resources for the Scientific Evaluation of the Paranormal, 203
*Revised Esoteric*, 86
Robson, Gordon, 225

Rosicrucian Fellowship, 168
Ross, Diana, 193
Roussat, Richard, 36
*Rover, The*, 125
Rowling, J. K., 221
Royal Astronomical Society, 215
Rudhyar, Dane, 168, 169, 196

Sagan, Carl, 202, 206
Sagittarius characteristics, 43
*Sailor Moon*, 223, 227
Sakaguchi, Hironobu, 221
*Salt Lake Tribune*, 116
*San Francisco Examiner*, 116, 117
*Satyricon*, Petronius, 7
Schmidt, Stephen, 213
Scientific Association of Astrologers, 164
*Scientific Basis for Astrology, The*, Michel Gauquelin, 202
Scientology, 212
Scorpio characteristics, 3, 43, 65, 67, 117, 148
Scott, John, 46
Season, Henry, 54
*Secret Doctrine, The*, Helena Blavatsky, 75
*Selfish Gene, The*, Richard Dawkins, 207
Sepharial, 63, 77, 88, 90, 96, 189
*Seven Creative Principles*, 86
Seven division horoscope column, 177
Sharpe, Constance, 165
Sharpe, Maud, 111
*Shepherd's Calendar*, 26, 29, 40
Sibly, Ebenezeer, 55

*Silver Star*, 174
Silverstein, Shel, 193
Silvester, Bernard, 14
*Sims, The*, 221
Sinnett, Alfred Percy, 74, 77, 109, 111
Sladek, John, 211, 206, 211, 212, 213, 214, 216
Smith, Robert Cross *see* Raphael
Society for Esoteric Culture, 81, 84
Society for Psychical Research, 153
Society for the Suppression of Vice, 102
Society of Astrologers, 48
Sol Invictus, 8
Solar biology, 4, 71, 78, 80-82, 85-86, 90, 91, 92, 94, 95, 138
Solar horoscope, 4, 95
Solstice, winter, 8
Soutar, Andrew, 151
*Space Shoes of the Gods*, John Sladek, 212
Spencer Jones, Harold, 200
Spiritualism, 63, 72
Sprague de Camp, L., 204
*Squire Bickerstaff detected*, 51
*Star Signs*, Linda Goodman, 196
*Star, The*, 63
Steiner, Rudolf, 190, 198
Stephenson, Charles and Martha, 107
*Stepping Sisters*, 149
Stonehouse versus Masson, 155
Story, Joseph, 141
*Straggling Astrologer*, Raphael I, Robert Cross Smith, 58

Stranger in a Strange Land, Robert Heinlein, 191
Suede, 227
Suetonius, 6
Sun sign astrology as an expression, 161
Sun sign astrology, different names for, 4
*Sun Signs*, Linda Goodman, 196, 198
*Sunday Chronicle*, 166
*Sunday Dispatch*, 163
*Sunday Express*, 138, 141, 146, 153, 154, 157, 162
*Sunday Pictorial*, 151, 165, 178
*Sunday Referee*, 173
Supertramp, 193
Swedenborg, Emmanuel, 62
Swift, Jonathan, 49, 52
Swift, Taylor, 228

Taisnier, Jean, 38
Takeuchi, Naoko, 223
Taurus characteristics, 5, 43, 69, 140
Temple of the People, 120
*Tetrabiblos*, Ptolemy, 6, 38, 216
Theosophical Society, 73, 74, 79, 83, 85, 88, 89, 90, 134
*Thirteen Signs of the Zodiac, The*, Walter Berg, 218
*Thirteen Women*, 149
Thirteenth sign, 209
*This Instructing Gypsy or the True Fortune Teller*, 59
Thomas à Becket, 24
Thomas, John, 87
Thompson, Catherine, 93

Thunderbirds, 192
Tiberius, Emperor, 6
Tilms, Richard A. *see* Sladek, John
*Times* (London), 63, 196, 202
*Times* (Louisiana), 116
Trithemius, Johannes, 37
Truzzi, Marcello, 203, 204
Tucker, W. J., 163, 165, 174
*Turn Out the Lights*, 193
Twelve-sign horoscope column, 176

*Urania, The*, John Corfield, 56
Usher, Bishop, 220

Vagrancy Act, 99, 100, 105, 151, 152, 153, 154, 156, 157, 158
Van Der Graaf Generator, 193
Van der Noot, Thomas, 27
Velikovsky, Immanuel, 212
Vérard, Antoine, 27, 28
Vidal, Pierre, 185
Virgil, 209
Vogh, James *see* Sladek, John
Volvelle, 22
von Däniken, Erick, 211, 212
*Vox Stellarum*, 42, 43

Wagner, Ed, 168
Wainright, Rufus, 227
Walker, Patric, 194
Warde, William, 36
*Weekly Horoscope*, 146, 166
Welsh astrology, 12, 15, 59
Wharton, George, 46, 47
*When were you Born?* Cheiro, 136
*When Were You Born?* Gabriel Dee, 150
*When's Your Birthday?* 149
White, Thomas, 105
Whitelock, Bulstrode, 46
Whitman, Edward, 165
Wilde, George, 141
Wilde, Oscar, 135
William, clerk to the constable of Chester, 16
Williams, Grace Ellery, 116
Witchcraft Act, 100, 153, 157, 158
Withers, Fabian Withers, 36
*Woman*, 184
*Woman's Friend*, 130, 131, 175
*Woman's Life*, 128
*Woman's Own*, 157, 163, 166, 167
*Woman's Weekly*, 125, 128
*Woman's World*, 175
Wren of Norwich, Bishop, 42
Wright, Gilbert, 45
Wynkyn de Worde, 28
Wynn *see* Sydney Bennett

Yalden, Thomas, 51, 52
Yale University, 55
*Your Destiny*, 176

Zadkiel I 57, 106
Zadkiel II, 77, 189
Zodiac man, 5, 17, 41
*Zodiac PI*, 224
Zodiac sign symbols, 3, 4, 7, 128
Zodiac sign, born under, 23
Zodiac signs, as standards, 6
Zodiac signs, characteristics, 3
Zodiac signs, first use, 5
Zodiac signs, names standardised, 6

Zodiac symbol, Capricorn, 6
Zodiac symbol, Scorpio, 3
Zodiac, 86, 161, 170, 213, 215
Zodiac, Babylonian, 3
Zodiac, definition, 2
Zodiac, Egyptian, 3
Zodiac, eighteen-sign, 3
Zodiac, start of, 2, 3
Zodiac, time measuring, 2
Zodiac, twelve-sign, origin, 3
Zodiology, 4, 5, 59, 71
*Zolar's Fortune Teller*, 69
Zomar, 167

www.ingramcontent.com/pod-product-compliance
Lightning Source LLC
Chambersburg PA
CBHW050344230426
43663CB00010B/1981